HOW TO KILL A PANTHER TANK

UNPUBLISHED SCIENTIFIC REPORTS FROM THE SECOND WORLD WAR

CRAIG MOORE

FONTHILL

Fonthill Media Language Policy

Fonthill Media publishes in the international English language market. One language edition is published worldwide. As there are minor differences in spelling and presentation, especially with regard to American English and British English, a policy is necessary to define which form of English to use. The Fonthill Policy is to use the form of English native to the author. Craig Moore was born and educated in London, England; therefore, British English has been adopted in this publication.

Fonthill Media Limited
Fonthill Media LLC
www.fonthillmedia.com
office@fonthillmedia.com

First published in the United Kingdom and the United States of America 2020

British Library Cataloguing in Publication Data:
A catalogue record for this book is available from the British Library

ISBN 978-1-78155-796-9

Typeset in Minion Pro 10pt on 13pt
Printed and bound in England

CONTENTS

ACKNOWLEDGEMENTS

Thanks to Herbert Ackermans, Jason Belgrave, Pierre-Oliver Buan, Adrian Barrell, Lauren Child, Rob Cogan, Hilary Louis Doyle, Brigadier General (rtd) Rudi Ehninger, Daniel Enriquez, Massimo Foti, Marcus Hock, Jonathan Holt, Richard Langdon, Sue Moore, Steve Osfield, John Osselaer, John Pearson, Steve Tatham, Ed Webster, Alex Wheatcroft. Bovington Tank Museum, Kubinka Tank Museum, Overloon Museum, The Wheatcroft Collection, and US Army Armor and Cavalry Collection at Fort Benning.

GLOSSARY

Annulus:	the region between.
AP:	armour-piercing shell.
APC:	armour-piercing capped shell.
APCBC:	armour-piercing capped ballistic cap shell.
APCBCHE:	armour-piercing capped ballistic cap high-explosive shell.
APDS:	armour-piercing discarding sabot shell.
AT:	anti-tank (some sources use 'A/T').
Azimuth:	an angular measurement in a spherical coordinate system. The vector from an observer to a point of interest is projected perpendicularly onto a reference plane; the angle between the projected vector and a reference vector on the reference plane is called the azimuth. An example of azimuth is the angular direction of a star in the sky. The star is the point of interest, the reference plane is the local horizontal area, and the reference vector points north. The azimuth is the angle.
Brinell Hardness Test	a widely used and standardised hardness test in engineering and metallurgy.
Broadside:	length-wise, full length exposed.
Burster Boards:	sheets of wood suspended in the air at set heights that when hit by a shell explode it to simulate an airburst.
Butt:	a protected pit with three raised sides used in test firing weapons: a part of a gun that rests against a soldier's shoulder.
cwt:	hundredweight.
DS:	discarded sabot.
DTD:	Department of Tank Design.
Dunkelgelb:	dark sandy yellow.
Dunkelgrau:	dark grey.
Elfenbein:	ivory white.
ft/s:	feet per second (though some sources use 'f.s.').
FVPE:	fighting vehicle proving establishment.
Fahrgestell-Nummer Serie:	hull number.
Flammenvernichter:	flame-suppressor exhaust mufflers.
Glacis plate:	The sloped armoured plate at the front of the tank hull.
HC:	high capacity.
HE:	high-explosive shell.
Hispano:	a 20-mm cannon and armour-penetrating ammunition.
inch:	= 2.54 cm and 12 inches makes one foot = 30.48 cm

Kampfwagenkanone:	tank gun.
Kugelblende:	ball mount for a machine gun.
lb:	pound (1 lb = 0.45 kg).
Louvre:	a set of angled slats fixed at regular intervals.
Mantlet:	bulletproof screen around a gun.
Mk:	Mark or version.
Nahverteidgungswaffe:	smoke grenade, signal flare, and fragmentation grenade launcher.
Nearside:	left-hand side.
Normal:	head-on attack at a right angle.
Offside:	right-hand side.
Olivegrün:	olive-green.
Pannier:	British Armour term for the part of the hull along the side that projected over the tracks. It could sometimes be used for stowage.
Panzer:	abbreviation for tank (literally 'armour').
Panzerkampfwagen:	tank (literally 'armoured battle vehicle').
Panzerschürzen:	skirt armour.
pdr:	pounder (the weight of a shell also used as a gun designation).
PIAT:	projector, infantry, anti-tank handheld weapon.
Poldi Hardness tester:	This is a piece of equipment that measures the hardness of Armour and produces Brinell Hardness scale figures.
PzKpfw:	abbreviation for *Panzerkampfwagen*.
PzKw:	British version of the abbreviation *Panzerkampfwagen*.
Rohrausblasevorrichtung:	gun gas extractor fan.
Rotbraun:	reddy-brown.
Round:	one piece of ammunition, a shell or bullet.
Schnelllauffähige Kette für Kraftfahrzeuge:	fast-running track for motor vehicles.
Schürzen:	skirt (armour).
schwimmende Bolzen:	swimming/rotating bolt.
Splash:	fragments of ammunition.
Stahlguß aller Legierungen:	steel castings of all alloys.
Tarnlampe:	headlights.
Tenon:	tenon joint used in carpentry to interlock two pieces of wood. Also used on the panther tank armour plate.
Trockenbolzen-Scharnierkette:	dry single-pin track.
Turmzielfernrohr:	Turret binocular gunsight.
Witness card:	paper or card used to detect weapon penetration inside a tank.
Yard:	3 feet (91.44 cm).
Zahnradfabrik:	gear factory.

INTRODUCTION

An original Panzer V Ausf. A Panther tank, cosmetically restored and on display at the War and Peace show, Kent, England, before it was fully restored to a working condition by Bruce Compton's Axis Track Services Ltd for the new owners, the Australian Armour and Artillery Museum in Cairns, Northern Queensland, Australia.

Using only original official period documents from the Second World War, this book tries to provide the reader with the same information that was available to British and Commonwealth senior officers and tank crews. As soon as intelligence reports confirmed the existence of the Panther tank, the hunt was on to find reliable information on how to knock out this new German tank.

The first four chapters briefly cover the development and production of the Panzer V Panther tank from the first version (the Ausf. D) to the second version (the Ausf. A) and to the final production version (the Ausf. G).

The Soviets captured the first Panther tanks. One of these captured tanks had the turret number 521 and hull number 210055. Chapter 5 contains the details of the examination of this Panther tank by the Canadian military *attaché* in Moscow and the report sent back to Canada, America, and London in October 1943.

After analysis of the technical data in the Moscow report, the British Army worked on how to best educate tank crews on how to knock out this new tank. Chapters 6 and 7 reproduce the British military advice 'Panther Armour Thickness' poster and the 'Pamphlet on Attack on Panther PzKw V and Tiger PzKw VI'. At this stage, no live-firing trials on captured Panther tanks had been conducted in Britain. It is worth noting that the British did not use the same abbreviations for the German word *Panzerkampfwagen* (armoured combat vehicle) as the German Army, who used the abbreviation Pz.Kpfw.

By March 1944, the first captured Panther tank arrived in Britain. Its performance was compared against a selection of Allied tanks. The staff of the Fighting Equipment Division and the Department of Tank Design (DTD) conducted an initial examination and assessment of this tank. Its turret number was 433, and its hull number was 213101. Their findings were set out in a number of reports dated May 1944. No live firing trials had taken place at this stage in Great Britain. These reports have been reproduced in Chapters 9, 10, 11, and 12.

Chapter 13 reproduces the British scientific report on the live firing trials against Panther tank armour using British anti-tank weapons. Three captured Panzer V Ausf. G Panther tanks were used as targets at the British Government testing facilities at Shoeburyness, on the south-east coast of Essex in England. 'Witness Cards', pieces of paper or the larger 'Burster Boards', pieces of thin wood, were used to register penetration of the Panther tank's armour by different types of ammunition fired at it. The scientist used the term fired 'at Normal'; this means a head-on attack, at 90 degrees to the target. They mainly use imperial measurements rather than metric. Velocity is recorded in feet per second (ft/s, though some sources use the abbreviation 'f.s.'). Weights are in pounds and ounces (lb oz) and imperial tons (ton) except when the information is obtained from a German document, then the notation for a metric ton is used (tonne).

Most people believe that the only way to stop a Panther was to penetrate its armour with an armour-piercing round. This report shows that the British were looking for how to knock them out by using high explosive artillery rounds or 20-mm air attack aircraft cannon rounds to penetrate and damage the tank's rear engine deck and puncture the vehicle's radiators. Loss of water would cause the engine to overheat and stop working. Tank radiators were large, and spares were not carried on the tank. If the Panther could not be recovered back to a maintenance depot, the crew would have to abandon the tank and disable it by setting off internal explosive charges.

The second set of trials were conducted to determine the general battle worthiness of the hull and turret of a Model G. Panther against 6-pdr and 17-pdr armour-piercing capped ballistic cap (APCBC) and discarded sabot (DS) shots, 75-mm APCBC and high-explosive (HE) shells, and 25-pdr HE shells. Consecutive hits on the same piece of armour can reduce its strength. This was taken into consideration by the scientists when producing their final reports. The information in those reports were used to produce instruction manuals for tank crews.

Tests were also conducted using a 3-lb projector, infantry, anti-tank handheld weapon (PIAT) on stowed ammunition. Trials took place to determine what minimum combination of grenades anti-tank (AT) No. 75 or of AT mines (British Mk V HC) were required to break the Panther tank's track.

The Germans were aware of the vulnerability of the Panther tank's rear engine deck to attack. They printed a pamphlet explaining how to fabricate the authorised structural modifications designed to protect the Panther's air intake and exhaust louvres on the rear engine deck. This increased ballistic protection was to be made from spare side skirt armour plate. This is covered in Chapter 14.

During and immediately after the Second World War, many German tanks were claimed to have been knocked out by an air attack. The large numbers claimed has since been proved to wildly exaggerated. Chapter 15 covers the wartime air-attack trials on a Panther tank that was painted white with a large black cross on it to make it easier to see in the middle of a green field. The results of this controlled experiment are surprising.

Chapter 16 has photographs and information on the Allied weapons used in the live firing trials. Chapter 17 contains extracts from operational Second World War battle reports on Allied engagements with German Panther tanks.

Throughout the live firing reports covered in this book, the scientists used abbreviations to report on damage seen on the panther tanks after they had been hit by a weapon. These abbreviations were set down in an official booklet called *The Armour Code*. It is reproduced in Chapter 18.

Chapters 19 and 20 use official German wartime documents to explain the German tank track classification system and why each German tank has a bucket attached to the rear of the tank.

Chapter 21 has been included to provide a list of the surviving Panther tanks and their location to help you plan a visit to go and inspect a Panther tank close up. Always phone the museum or local town hall to see if the tank is still there before driving to the location. Tanks move. That may seem a silly statement, but tanks change locations. Some are sold or temporarily transferred to other museums. Some are withdrawn from public view to enable them to be restored or undergo maintenance.

1

THE PANTHER TANK PROTOTYPES

The last surviving Panzer V Ausf. D Panther tank in Breda, Holland.

Panther tanks first saw action on the Eastern fronts. They were also used in Italy, France, Belgium, and Holland. They took part in the Ardennes offensive (the Battle of the Bulge), plus the defence of Germany. It had better cross-country mobility than the Tiger tank and had the same if not more hitting power, with its 7.5-cm KwK 42 L/70 long-barrelled, high-velocity anti-tank gun. Around 6,000 were produced.

The use of sloped armour kept the weight of the tank down but maintained its protection level. The angled front 80-mm armour glacis plate gave more protection than the Tiger tank's 100-mm vertical armour plate. This fact is not often mentioned. An enemy's standard armour-piercing round fired from directly in front of the tank hitting the glacis plate in a straight line had to penetrate 139 mm (5.4 inches) of armour due to the angle of the armour. If the enemy tank was firing at the front of a Panther tank, but at a 45-degree angle to it, the shell would have to pass through 197 mm (7.7 inches) of armour.

Enemy tank crews always tried to outflank Panther tanks to fire at its more vulnerable side or rear armour. German Panther tank crew's tactics involved presenting their frontal armour towards enemy tanks as much as possible.

EARLY DESIGNS

Work on a replacement tank for the Panzer III and IV began in the early stages of the Second World War. In 1940, the design department of the German company MAN (*Maschinenfabrik Augsburg-Nürnberg*: Machine Works of Augsburg and Nürnberg) was working on plans for the hull of a new 20-tonne class medium tank. The project was given a code VK.20.01 (M). The letter 'M' was an abbreviation for the company MAN. The letters 'VK' are an abbreviation '*Vollketten*' (fully tracked) followed by the weight class and the sub-variant. The later VK.30.01 identifies a fully tracked vehicle in the 30- tonne class variant 1 and the Panther prototype code VK.30.02 was the fully tracked variant 2 of the 30- tonne class design.

During Operation Barbarossa (the invasion of the Soviet Union), which started on Sunday, 22 June 1941, German forces encountered Soviet T–34 tanks for the first time. Battlefield reports were sent back to Berlin. They praised the Soviet tank's wide tracks, sloping armour, and powerful anti-tank gun. A panel of experts was sent to examine knocked out T-34 tanks and speak with German tank crews. In early 1942, the German High Command issued new specifications for a 30- tonne class tank that included many of the same design features used on the T-34 tank. The Daimler-Benz design team worked on plans for the next German medium tank that met these specifications, in competition with MAN.

THE DAIMLER–BENZ PANTHER TANK DESIGN

The Daimler-Benz design team tank used the design codename VK.30.02 (DB). They decided to use a traditional leaf spring suspension system, large doubled roadwheels, no track return rollers, and a track drive sprocket at the rear. MAN used a similar suspension system as used on Henschel's Tiger design—its pairs of large, interleaved wheels provided their design with lower ground pressure as well as better traction and mobility.

The front glacis plates were sloped, and so were the side panniers that covered the top of the wide tracks as well as the rear of the tank. The hull was narrower than the MAN design to keep the weight down, but this limited the size of the turret ring diameter and the size of the turret. It was 50 mm smaller than the MAN design. The internal space inside the hull and three-man turret was cramped. Daimler-Benz decided to use a new diesel engine where MAN used the same Maybach HL 210 P30 petrol V12 water-cooled 650-hp engine that was currently in production and would be used in Henschel's Tiger tank design, thus reducing maintenance and logistics problems.

The Daimler-Benz design had their turret in a forward position, very much like the Soviet T-34 tank. The MAN tank design had their turret more in the centre of the hull. As there was no space above the heads of the driver and radio operator in the Daimler-Benz tank design for escape hatches, two large circular hatches were inserted into the side armour, one on each side.

The Daimler-Benz designs used interlocking tenon wedge joints to make the junction between the glacis plate armour and the side pannier armour stronger. It was also used on the front of their turret. The MAN prototype design did not use this method. This would be a feature that would appear on the production Panther tank hull.

THE MAN PANTHER TANK DESIGN

The design team at MAN incorporated sloping armour on the sides of the tank hull to cover wider tracks and steeper angled armour at the front of the vehicle hull as per the German Army design requirements. These features can be seen on drawing dated 2 May 1942, with the codename VK.30.02 (M). These plans also incorporated the proposed turret designed by the German company Rheinmetall-Borsig, that was armed with a 7.5-cm Kw K 42 L/70 anti-tank gun.

The German words for experimental trial series are 'Versuchs-Serie'. This is why the two MAN Panther tank hull proto-types were given the designation V1 and V2. At first, a large metal weighted box was fitted on top of the V1 hull in place of the turret while it underwent cross country trials. Later, the Rheinmetall-Borsig turret was fitted to both V1 and V2 tanks; both were ready for trials by September 1942.

THE FINAL DECISION

German High Command wanted the new Panther tank in production by December 1942 so that there would be enough numbers available for the spring and summer offensives of 1943. In May 1942, the Daimler-Benz VK.30.02 (DB) and the MAN VK.30.02 (M) paper designs were submitted.

The MAN design eventually won the contract because of several issues with the Daimler-Benz design. The major ones were that its turret was not ready for production. Its hull was too small to mount the approved larger Rheinmetall-Borsig turret. It did not use an engine that was already being produced and fitted in other tanks. This would have caused a logistics problem as well as manufacturing delays. The suspension system and wider tracks of the MAN design gave a lower ground pressure reading.

It should be noted that the MAN tank hull prototype design did not use the strong interlocking tenon joint design on its armour plate junctions. This Daimler-Benz feature was added to the final production design. Both the V1 and V2 prototypes displayed numerous minor design aspects that were not used in the production Panther. The two prototype vehicles were used to test different features prior to starting a production run.

2

PANZER V AUSF. D PANTHER TANK
(Sd.Kfz.171)

The turret on this surviving Panther Ausf. D in Breda, Holland, has two binocular gunsight apertures on the gun mantlet to the left of the 75-mm gun. The factory-fitted *Nebelwurfgerät* (smoke grenade launchers) are missing from the side of the turret following instructions to remove them in June 1943. The driver's rectangular armoured vision port cover can just be seen to the left of the sign on the front hull glacis plate. The hull machine gunner's vertical 'letterbox' armoured cover can be seen to the right of the sign painted green.

The first production Panther tank was the Ausf. D, not the Ausf. A. This confuses many people. In the past, German tank versions started with the letter 'A' and then went on to 'B', 'C', 'D', etc. However, in January 1943, MAN produced the first production series Panther Ausf. D tank. 'Ausf' is an abbreviation for the German word '*Ausführung*', which means version. The Panzer V Ausf. D Panther tank *Fahrgestell-Nummer Serie* hull numbers range from 210001 to 210254 and 211001 to 213220.

The Panther Ausf. D had a curved gun mantlet. On the left of the gun were two holes for the *Turmzielfernrohr* 12 binocular gunsight. To stop water obscuring the gunner's view, later versions of the gun mantlet had a semi-circular rain guard over the two holes. (*John Osselaer*)

THE MAIN GUN

The Panther Tank was armed with a long-barrelled, high-velocity 7.5-cm *Kampfwagenkanone* (KwK) 42 L/70 tank gun that could knock out most Allied and Soviet medium tanks at long distances. It had an effective direct fire range of 1.1–1.3 km. With a good, experienced crew, it could fire six rounds a minute. The barrel length, including the muzzle brake, was 5,535 mm (5,225 mm without the muzzle brake). It had an elevation range of -8 to +20 degrees. It was fitted with a *Turmzielfernrohr* 12 binocular gunsight. Seventy-nine rounds of 75-mm ammunition could be stored inside the tank. There was a coaxial 7.92-mm MG 34 machine gun next to it.

Straight-cut, interlocking tenon joints were used to join the front upper and lower glacis plates before welding on the Panzer V Ausf. D Panther tank. This made for a stronger joint. The driver had two covered fixed-position periscopes fitted to the hull roof above his seat: one facing forward and the other at a 45-degree angle from the front. (*John Osselaer*)

ARMOUR

To defeat uncapped armour-piercing shells, the front, side, and rear hull armour plates were face-hardened. The external armour plate used an interlocking tenon joint arrangement. It was found this gave the welds added strength.

The bottom of the Ausf. D hull was made from a single sheet of 16-mm thick armour plating. This would change on later versions of the Ausf. D—some were constructed of two 16-mm plates and others of three 16-mm plates. The thickness of these belly plates would be increased in the later Panther Ausf. A to help the tank cope with anti-tank mine explosions.

Most tanks of this period in time had vertical armoured sides and thin metal track guards that came out at a right angle from the hull side. They were used to store tools and stowage boxes. Using sloping armour on the upper sides of the Panther tank hull, which covered the top of the tracks, was a clever idea. It formed an internal triangular 'pannier' stowage area over the tracks and gave more room inside the tank. Angled armour means that there is more metal for incoming enemy armour-piercing rounds to penetrate and there is a higher chance of the shot ricocheting.

A wedge-shaped interlocking armoured plate was welded to the bottom of the pannier at the rear of the tank and to the rear armoured plate. It provided additional protection to the engine compartment. This was not fitted on the later Panther Ausf. G tank. (*John Osselaer*)

The hull front glacis plate was 80 mm thick and fitted at 55 degrees. If an armour-piercing shell hit the side armour straight on, at normal, that shell would have to penetrate 139.48 mm of armour. If it hit at an angle of 45 degrees, that shell would have to penetrate 138 mm of armour. However, this does not take into account the effect of normalising and overmatching of different ammunition and weapons. The lower front plate was 60 mm thick and at an angle of 55 degrees. Both the lower and upper glacis plates had a Brinell hardness rating of 265-309.

The armour used on the lower hull side was 40 mm thick and vertical. It was often targeted by Allied anti-tank guns as it was a lot easier to penetrate than the frontal armour. If an armour-piercing shell hit the side armour at 45 degrees, that shell would have to penetrate 56.57 mm of armour.

The sloped upper side armour was also 40 mm thick but at an angle of 40 degrees. If an armour-piercing shell hit the side armour straight on, at normal, that shell would have to penetrate 56.57 mm of armour. If it hit at an angle of 45 degrees, that shell would have to penetrate 80 mm of armour. They had a Brinell Hardness rating of 278-324.

The top deck of the Panther hull and the belly armour were both 16 mm thick. The top of the turret was also 16 mm thick. They had a Brinell Hardness rating of 309-353.

The sides and rear armour of the Panther tank's turret was 45 mm thick fitted at an angle of 25 degrees. It had a Brinell Hardness rating of 278-324.

The turret front and rounded gun mantlet were made of armour 100 mm thick. The turret front armour was mounted at an angle of 12 degrees. It had a Brinell Hardness rating of 235-276.

As was discovered in the British firing trials, the bottom section of the rounded gun mantlet acted as a 'shot trap' that deflected incoming armour-piercing shells downwards into the thin 16-mm-thick hull decking, killing the driver or bow machine gunner. This is why on the late production turret of the King Tiger tank, the front of the turret and the gun mantlet are nearly vertical to overcome this problem. The King Tiger's early production turret had the same design defect as the Panther. On the Ausf. G Panther tank, a revised gun mantlet design was introduced that had a 'chin' guard to stop the ricochet problem.

To maintain the strength of the face-hardened armour plate, components were not welded onto its surface. Instead, metal strips were used to hold and attach fastenings for tools, stowage boxes, and spare parts. They were welded to the underneath of the side panniers and onto the top of the hull roof at the front near the driver and radio operator's positions.

The only exception to this was the cylindrical tube that contained the main gun-cleaning rods. It was not part of the original design—it was an oversight, so it was welded onto the outside of the pannier just under the turret. Spare track hangers were bolted onto the rear-deck, but the spare track hung over the sides of the pannier at the rear of the tank.

◄ Straight-cut, interlocking tenon joints were also used to join the side turret armour to the front armour plate on the Panzer V Ausf. D Panther tank. They were also used to join the side pannier sloping armour to the top of the upper glacis plate. This made for a stronger joint. The co-driver/hull machine gunner had two covered fixed-position periscopes fitted to the hull roof above his seat: one facing forward and the other at a 45-degree angle from the front.

➤ The Panther's armoured glacis plate interlocked with the side superstructure plate and they were welded together. This was stronger than earlier tank design welds. The angled front glacis plate was 80 mm thick. An enemy shell fired at the front of the Panther at the normal angle had to penetrate 138 mm of armour because of the slope of the plate. (*John Osselaer*)

PANZERSCHÜRZEN: SKIRT ARMOUR

The German designers added protective skirt armour made from 4-mm soft steel to protect the visible 40-mm hull side armour that could be seen between the top of the track and below the pannier. It was believed this area would be vulnerable to penetration at close range by Soviet anti-tank rifles. The *Schürzen* protective skirt armour was added starting in April 1943.

ZIMMERIT: ANTI-MAGNETIC MINE PASTE

The Germans had developed magnetic anti-tank mines for use by their infantry. They believed the Soviets would soon equip all their infantry units with a similar device. Starting in late August and into early September 1943, the factories started to apply *Zimmerit* anti-magnetic mine paste on all upright surfaces of the Panther tanks on the production line. The paste was rippled to increase the distance to the tank's surface.

HEADLIGHTS

Two Bosch *Tarnlampe* headlights with blackout covers were fixed onto the armour of the front glacis plate, one above each track guard. Starting in July 1943, only one was installed on the left side of the glacis plate.

THE DRIVER'S VISION PORT

On the early Panzer V Ausf. D tanks, a rectangular hole was cut out of the front armour on the left side of the tank and covered with an armoured vision port. The driver could open this hinged port when not in a combat zone. This was perceived as a weak spot and was also a feature that took time to fabricate. To streamline production and enable more tanks to be built quickly, the driver's vision port was not fitted on later models. He could only see where he was driving by looking through two fixed armoured periscopes and later only one swivelling periscope that projected out of the hull roof.

◀ When the Panther Ausf. D tank was in a combat situation, the driver had to rely on his two armoured periscopes that protruded out of the hull roof to see where he was going. Away from the battlefield, he could open his large rectangular vision hatch. This hatch was removed on later designs as it took too long to construct and was a weak point. (*John Osselaer*)

▶ The driver's two armoured periscopes, which protruded out of the hull roof, were fixed into position: one looked forward and the other looked left. These were later replaced with a single swivelling periscope. (*John Osselaer*)

THE CO-DRIVER/HULL MACHINE GUNNER'S PORT

The early Panzer V Panther tanks were not fitted with an armoured ball mount for the 7.92-mm MG 34 machine gun. A rectangular 'letterbox' slit was cut into the front sloping glacis plate to enable the radio operator to fire his machine gun when necessary. A small armoured door covered this opening. He had two periscopes fixed to the roof of the hull: one faced forward and the other to the right side of the tank.

A rectangular 'letterbox' slit was cut into the front sloping glacis plate of the Panther Ausf. D and covered with an armoured hatch. The radio operator could fire his 7.92-mm MG 34 machine gun out of the opening. On later versions of the Panther, this was replaced with an armoured ball mount. (*John Osselaer*)

SUSPENSION

The tank's suspension system consisted of a front-drive sprocket wheel that powered the track, a rear idler wheel, and eight large double-interleaved rubber-rimmed steel road-wheels on either side of the hull.

Many tanks during the Second World War had suspension units bolted onto the outside of the tank hull. When they were damaged by mines, they were easily replaced with a new one. The Panther's suspension system was not as easy to repair. When the torsion bars were damaged, it sometimes needed a welder's torch to cut them out.

The large, interleaved road-wheels caused problems for the crew when they had to replace a damaged internal wheel. They had to unbolt several wheels to get at the broken one, which was time-consuming. Ice, mud, and rocks could clog the interleaved wheels. In the severe winter weather on the Eastern Front, they could freeze solid overnight.

These problems were considered acceptable because the dual torsion bar system allowed for relatively high-speed travel for such a heavy vehicle over undulating terrain. The extra wheels did provide better flotation and stability by allowing wider tracks to be fitted, and they also provided more armour protection for the tank's hull sides. Each road-wheel had sixteen bolts around the rim. This was increased to twenty-four rim bolt road-wheels in later production models of the Ausf. D.

The road wheels fitted on the Panzer V Ausf. D Panther tank had sixteen bolts around the outer rim. On later versions, this was increased to twenty-four. The front-drive sprocket wheel that powered the track was at the front of the tank.

TRACKS

Its wide tracks and large, interleaved road-wheels resulted in lower ground pressure. This helped it traverse waterlogged or deep-snow covered rough terrain, providing better traction and mobility.

The Panther Tank's track was a *Trockenbolzen-Scharnierkette* (dry single-pin track). There were eighty-seven track links per side that were kept together with a dry, ungreased metal rod. It had a cap on the inside section and a split ring in a groove on the outside. The track was in contact with the ground for a length of 3.92 m. The tracks gave the tank a ground pressure reading of 0.88 kp/cm² on the Panther Ausf. D and Ausf. A and 0.89 kp/cm² on the Panther Ausf. G, which was good for such a large heavy vehicle. A complete length of track weighed 2,050 kg.

◄ This is the tank track fitted to the Panzer V Ausf. D Panther tank at Breda, Holland. (*John Osselaer*)

► Starting from August 1943, the track mould was changed so that six chevrons were part of the design on the face of each track link to decrease slipping. It looks like the Breda Panther Ausf. D tank track was repaired using some of these new track links. These links can be seen at the rear of the tank. (*John Osselaer*)

The track was called Kgs 64/660/150. The number 660 means the width of the tracks (660 mm). The number 150 is the 'chain pitch' (150 mm). The chain pitch was the distance between one drive sprocket tooth to the next. The letter 'K' was an abbreviation for '*Schnelllauffähige Kette für Kraftfahrzeuge*' (fast-running track for motor vehicles, unlike agricultural tractors). The letter 'g' was the code for '*Stahlguß aller Legierungen*' (steel castings of all alloys) and the letter 's' was short for '*schwimmende Bolzen*' (swimming/rotating bolt). Due to reported problems of tanks slipping, the track link was redesigned. Starting in July 1943, new track links were cast with six chevrons on each track face.

ENGINE

A Maybach HL 210 P30 petrol V12 water-cooled 650-hp engine was installed in the first 250 Ausf. D tanks. This was later replaced with the more powerful Maybach HL 230 P30 petrol V12 water-cooled 700-hp engine.

The HL 230 engine's crankcase and block were made of aluminium. The HL 230 engine's crankcase and block were made of grey cast iron and the cylinder heads from cast iron. The engine deck armour was 16 mm thick. The four engine-cooling air intake vents were protected by four rectangular armoured louvres and a mesh screen. The two large circular engine-cooling air exhaust fans were protected by two circular armoured louvres and a mesh screen. When the tank had to ford a deep river, the normal engine air intake pipes could be locked in the closed position and a telescopic snorkel pipe fitted to the back of the engine deck. When this was not in use, the hole in the rear deck was covered with a metal circular blank flange as seen on the back of the engine deck of the Panther Ausf. D in Breda, Holland.

◀ Left-side armoured circular casing over the engine-cooling exhaust fans on the rear engine deck next to the armour base for the 2-m antenna. (*John Osselaer*)

▶ Right-side armoured circular casing over the engine-cooling exhaust fans on the rear engine deck. (*John Osselaer*)

 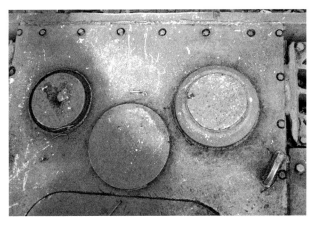

◀ Rear right-side rectangular armour casing over the engine-cooling air-intake vents on the engine deck. There were four of these vents built into the engine deck. (*John Osselaer*)

▶ At the rear of the engine deck, there are three circular caps: from left to right, they are the rain guard for the fuel-filler cap, blank flanged cover for the air-intake hole (where a deep-water fording snorkel tube could be fitted), and the coolant-filler cap. (*John Osselaer*)

At the rear of the engine deck on the main engine hatch, there would have been two circular armoured caps with handles for the engine air-intake holes; one of the handles has broken off. These replaced the earlier design from May 1943m when the more powerful Maybach HL 230 engine started to replace the Maybach HL 210 engine. (*John Osselaer*)

THE BACK OF THE TANK

The rear of the tank hull was made from a single piece of armour 40 mm thick set at an angle of 30 degrees. The exit holes of the two engine exhaust pipes were protected by two curved armoured guards. There was a large circular engine-access plate bolted to the rear and smaller covers for the starter port, coolant heater, track tensioner, and inertia starter access points. The rear stowage boxes are missing from the Panther Ausf. D at Breda, Holland.

Two vertical exhaust pipes stuck out of individual curved armoured guards at the rear of the tank. A red convoy light was fixed below the left pannier above the track and large stowage bins were fixed to the left and right of the exhaust pipes. These three things are missing on the Panther Ausf. D at Breda, Holland. (*John Osselaer*)

TRANSMISSION (GEARBOX)

It was fitted with a ZF A.K.7/200 transmission, which was produced by the German ZF Friedrichshafen engineering company. The letters 'ZF' are an abbreviation for the German word '*Zahnradfabrik*' (gear factory). It had seven forward gears and one reverse. The following is the official recommended maximum road speed for each gear—first gear: 4.1 km/h; second gear: 8.2 km/h; third gear: 13.1 km/h; fourth gear: 20.4 km/h; fifth gear: 29.5 km/h; sixth gear: 41.6 km/h; and seventh gear: 54.9 km/h. The tank could be driven in reverse gear at a maximum road speed of 4 km/h.

TURRET

On early Panther turrets, there was a *Verstandigungsöffnung* (a circular, side communication hatch). It could be used for loading shells and throwing out used shell casings. The commander's cupola was drum-shaped and had six viewing ports of 90-mm-thick bulletproof glass. There was a circular escape hatch at the rear of the turret with a handle above it. Starting on 1 August 1943, an anti-aircraft machine gun mount was added to the cupola.

There were three pistol ports in the sides of the turret armour: one on each side and one at the rear. The circular cover at the front of the turret roof was to protect the gun gasses exhaust fan. There were two brackets at the front of the turret attached to the roof, one on either side, to mount *Nebelwurfgerät* (smoke grenade dischargers).

Starting in June 1943, they were no longer fitted. A Tiger tank crew battlefield report, dated February 1943, recorded the self-ignition of *nebelkerzen* (smoke rounds) inside the *Nebelwurfgerät* smoke grenade discharger when hit by small arms fire. Wind conditions were calm, and this resulted in a fog around the tank, incapacitating the crew, as well as restricting vision of potential threats and targets.

At the same time, a rain guard was welded over the top of the two binocular gunsight apertures on the gun mantlet, and a gun-laying vane was welded onto the turret roof in front of the commander's cupola. Later production turrets had semi-circular rain guards welded above each pistol port opening, communication hatch, and escape hatch.

◀ The early production on the Panzer V Ausf. D Panther tank turret had small, circular pistol ports in the sides and rear of the turret. The rear large circular crew hatch had a handle above it but not on it. An additional circular communication hatch was fitted to the side of the turret. It could also be used for loading shells and throwing out used shell casings. The commander's cupola was drum-shaped. Later versions had a dome-shaped cupola.

▶ This is a closer view of the larger circular communication hatch (*Verstandigungsöffnung*) and one of the three pistol ports in the sides of the turret armour. Both have semi-circular rain guards fitted above the openings. The three cone-shaped bolts secure the communication hatch hinge to the side of the turret. (*John Osselaer*)

◀ A close-up view of the semi-circular rain guard fitted above a turret pistol port. (*John Osselaer*)

▶ The right side of the turret did not have a large circular communication hatch (*Verstandigungsöffnung*). It did have a pistol port with a rain guard. At the bottom edge of the pannier superstructure sloping armour plate, there are two female brackets. The top section of the skirt armour *Schürzen* plate's inverted L-shaped hanger would have been inserted in these holes.

◀ The early version of the commander's cupola was drum-shaped. It was later replaced by a dome-shaped cupola. On the right side of the turret at the front is the circular armoured guard for the turret exhaust fan that helped extract the fumes caused by the main gun and coaxial machine gun being fired. (*John Osselaer*)

▶ This is the right-hand side radio operator/hull-machine gunner's hatch. Compared with other tanks of this time period, it was quite large, which would have helped the crew exit the tank fast if it was knocked out by enemy fire. (*John Osselaer*)

CREW

The Panther tank had a five-man crew. The turret was large enough for three people: the commander, gunner, and loader. The driver sat on the left-hand side of the tank hull at the front, and next to him on the right-hand side was the hull machine gunner, who also operated the radio.

RADIO

The Panther tank was fitted with a FuG 5 radio and an intercom system. The prefix FuG is an abbreviation for '*Funkgerät*', meaning 'radio device'. The *Funkgerät* 5 radio was a high-band HF/low-band VHF transceiver. It operated in the 27,000–33,3000 kHz (27–33.3 MHz) frequency range with a transmit power of 10 watts. This equipment provided for 125 radio channels at 50 kHz channel spacing. It was fitted in many German tanks and in other vehicles. The FuG 5 was designed to be used for tank-to-tank communication within platoons and companies. It had a range of approximately 2–3 km when using the AM voice frequency and 3–4 km when using CW (continuous wave) frequency.

If the Panther tank was used by a company commander, a second radio was fitted called a *Funkgerät* 2 (FuG 2). This radio was a high-band HF/low-band VHF receiver (not a transmitter). It operated in the 27,000–33,3000 kHz (27–33.3 MHz) range. The FuG 2 was never used on its own but as an additional receiver. It allowed tank commanders to listen on one frequency while transmitting and receiving on the FuG 5. It used the same band as the FuG 5 radio set. This meant that the commander could listen to the regimental command net while talking to other tanks at the same time. This radio receiver could listen into a total of 125 channels, at 50 kHz channel steps in the 27–33.3 MHz range.

FUEL TANKS

The Ausf. D had a fuel capacity of 730 litres. It used petrol. It had an operating range of 200 km on the road and about 100 km across country before it needed to refuel.

CAMOUFLAGE

When the first batch of Panthers left the factory, they were painted *dunkelgrau* (dark-grey, RAL 7021). In February 1943, all factories were instructed to paint all German armoured fighting vehicles *dunkelgelb* (dark sandy yellow, RAL 7028). Each individual Panzer unit then applied its own individual camouflage pattern. They were issued with *olivgrün* (olive-green, RAL 6003), and *rotbraun* (reddy-brown, RAL 8017) paint. In the winter, a covering of whitewash was applied to the tanks.

TANK PROPORTIONS

The Panzer V Ausf. D had an overall length of 8.86 m. The length of the hull without the gun was 6.86 m. It was 3.27 m wide and 2.99 m tall. Its weight with a full combat load was 44.8 metric tons.

New Scotland Yard police detective and tank enthusiast Richard Langdon is 6 feet (1.82 m) tall. This photograph of him standing next to the tank gives a good perspective of the size of the Panther.

PANTHER AUSF. D SPECIFICATIONS

Dimensions (L-W-H)	8.86 m × 3.27 m × 2.99 m (29 feet 1 inch × 10 feet 9 inches × 9 feet 10 inches)
Total weight, battle-ready	44.8 tonnes
Main armament	Main: 7.5-cm KwK 42 L/70, eighty-two rounds
Secondary armament	2 × 7.92-mm MG 34 machine guns
Armour: front upper glacis	80 mm at 55 degrees
Armour: front lower glacis	60 mm at 55 degrees
Armour: hull side	40 mm at 0 degrees
Armour: side superstructure	40 mm at 40 degrees
Armour: rear	40 mm at 30 degrees
Armour: hull deck	16 mm at 90 degrees
Armour: belly	16 mm at 90 degrees
Armour: turret gun mantlet	100 mm at rounded
Armour: turret front	100 mm at 12 degrees
Armour: turret sides	45 mm at 25 degrees
Armour: turret rear	45 mm at 25 degrees
Armour: turret deck	16 mm at 84.5–90 degrees
Crew	Five (commander, driver, gunner, loader, and radioman/machine gunner)
Propulsion	Maybach HL 210 P30 V12 water-cooled 650-hp petrol engine or Maybach HL 230 P30 V12 water-cooled 700-hp petrol engine
Transmission	ZF AK 7-200 7-forward/1-reverse gearbox
Suspensions	Double torsion bars and interleaved wheels
Max Road Speed	55 km/h (34 mph)
Operational range	200 km (124 miles)
Production	842 approx.

3

PANZER V AUSF. A PANTHER TANK (SD.KFZ.171)

The *Ausführung* A is the second version of the Panther tank. The first was the *Ausführung* D as covered in the previous chapter. It can be difficult to identify the *Ausführung* version of a Panzer V Panther tank without knowing its *Fahrgestell-Nummer* (Fgst.Nr.—hull number). Many features of the Ausf. D, like the drum-shaped commander's cupola and the thin rectangular 'letterbox' hull machine gun port, were still present on early production Ausf. A Panthers produced between July to December 1943.

They only changed mid-production and not at the same time. Other modifications were introduced during the production run. Ausf. D and Ausf. A tanks were also upgraded with different features once they had been issued to a Panzer division, when they went to a maintenance or repair unit.

The long name for this tank was *Panzerkampfwagen* 'Panther' (7.5-cm KwK 42 L/70) (Sd.Kfz.171) *Ausführung* A. The hull used for the early production Panzer V Ausf. A was exactly the same as that used for the Ausf. D. This new batch of Panther tanks was given a new version designation, Ausf. A, because they were fitted with an improved turret.

The tank hulls were produced at four different locations: Daimler-Benz produced Fgst.Nr. 151901 to 152575; Maschinenfabrik Niedersachsen Hannover (MNH) produced Fgst.Nr. 154801 to 155630; Demag-Benrath produced 158101 to 158150; and Maschinenfabrik-Augsburg-Nuernberg produced 210255 to 210899.

◀ The early production versions of the Panzer V Ausf. A Panther still had the same features used on the Ausf. D chassis. In this photograph of the front glacis plate on the Panzer V Ausf. A Panther in Thun, Switzerland, you can see the armoured rectangular driver's vision port and next to it the 'letterbox' thin rectangular vision port of the radio operator/machine gunner. (*Massimo Foti*)

▶ In late November 1943, on the later production versions of the Panzer V Ausf. A, the radio operator's thin rectangular 'letterbox' vision port was replaced with a ball-mounted (*Kugelblende*) machine gun with a spherical armoured guard. The forward-looking periscope has now been removed from above the machine gunner's position as he can now look forward through the ball mount optics. (*Massimo Foti*)

THE TURRET

The new Ausf. A turret, like the hull, underwent changes during its production. The 7.5-cm KwK 42 L/70 gun was the same, and so was the binocular T.Z.F.12 gunsight. The external shape of the new turret looked very similar to the older Ausf. D turret, but there were some subtle changes. The gun mantlet on the Ausf. A turret was wider than the one fitted to the older Ausf. D. Directly behind the gun mantlet, the shape of the cast turret side had changed to a dish-shaped protrusion to fit the new seal for the gun mantlet.

On the older Ausf. D turret, the front and side armour plate used a dovetail-angled, carpentry-style welded joint. The new Ausf. A turret plates were welded together using an interlocking squared-off joint, with the top and bottom cut parallel to the turret base.

This Panzer V Ausf. A Panther turret has the interlocking squared-off joint joining the front turret armour with the side. The early production Ausf. A turret gun mantlet had two holes on the left side of the gun to house the binocular gun optics. This was changed in the later production Ausf. A turret to a monocular aperture when a new improved gunsight T.Z.F.12a was gradually introduced in November 1943. You can also see in this photograph a ring fitted to the outside of the commander's cupola. It was used to mount an anti-aircraft machine gun. These were introduced starting on 1 August 1944. Again, there are no pistol ports in the side of the turret armour. (*Massimo Foti*)

The loader had a periscope mounted in the turret roof. The *Rohrausblasevorrichtung* (gun fumes, gas extractor) was improved. The Ausf. D turret had a single-speed power traverse system. A new variable-speed unit was fitted to the Ausf. A. To prevent water from entering into the tank during fording, a new spring-compressed sealing ring was fitted to the turret ring.

Early production Ausf. A Panthers were fitted with the Ausf. D round drum-like commander's cupola. A new dome-shaped cast armour commander's cupola was gradually introduced. It had seven periscopes with armoured protective cowlings. It was fitted with a 1 o'clock to 12 o'clock azimuth indicator ring that moved with the turret. The gunner also had a 1 o'clock to 12 o'clock azimuth indicator mounted to his left. This helped with target acquisition communication. The commander could shout, 'enemy tanks 7 o'clock', and the gunner would know where to look. On 1 August 1943, a ring was mounted on the commander's cupola to enable an anti-aircraft machine gun to be mounted.

The early production Ausf. A turrets had three pistol ports: one on each side and one on the rear. To make production simpler and the armour stronger, the pistol ports were dropped from late production Ausf. A turrets. Instead, a *Nahverteidgungswaffe* (close-defence weapon) was fitted to the roof of the tank to the right of the commander's cupola. It could fire a high-explosive grenade in the direction of attacking infantry. The crew were safe from the shrapnel inside the tank, but the enemy soldiers would be exposed. The *Nahverteidgungswaffe* could also be used to fire smoke grenades and signal flares. It looked like a large flare pistol.

The early production Ausf. A turrets had the same gunner's binocular T.Z.F.12 gunsight with a rain guard over the two lenses that were fitted on the earlier Ausf. D turrets. This was changed to a monocular T.Z.F.12a gunsight starting in late November 1943. There was now only one hole on the gunner's side at the front of the turret, not two. The design of the gun mantlet had to be changed to accommodate this new single-lens gunsight. A smaller semi-circular rain guard was added to the design.

These changes to the turret design were not introduced at the same time. You can see photographs of Ausf. A turrets with the new commander's dome-shaped cupola but the sides still had pistol ports and the binocular gunsight mounted in the gun mantlet.

The new turret design used on the Panzer V Ausf. A was simplified. On turrets built after June 1944, there are no longer small, circular pistol ports in the sides and rear of the turret. The rear large circular crew hatch now has a handle on it as well as above. The additional circular communication hatch (used for loading shells and throwing out used shell casings) was no longer cut into the turret side armour. The earlier production Ausf. A turrets still had the pistol ports. You can also see the new domed cast armour commander's cupola. (*Massimo Foti*)

BELLY AND DECK ARMOUR

The production drawings have shown that the construction of the Panther Ausf. A hull belly armour was not consistent. Some hull belly armour was made from one sheet of 16-mm armour. Others were constructed in two parts with the front part being 30 mm thick to help cope with the damage caused by anti-tank mines. The third variation was formed of three separate armour plates. The front two were 30 mm thick, and the rear one was 16 mm thick. It is not known exactly when these changes were introduced or what factory followed, which authorised plans.

The construction of the deck armour was also not consistent. Some hull deck armour was built from a single piece of 16-mm armoured plate. Others were formed by welding three different pieces of 16-mm thick armoured plate.

SIDE ARMOUR

The eight large double-interleaved rubber-rimmed steel road-wheels on either side of the hull provided more armoured protection for the thin 40-mm-thick, surface-hardened hull sides than the smaller wheel used on the Panzer III and IV. The gap between the top of the wheels and the panniers was covered by plates of skirt armour designed to stop Soviet anti-tank rifle rounds.

On the Panzer V Ausf. A, the gap between the top of the wheels and the panniers was covered by plates of *Schürzen* skirt armour suspended on hangers. They were designed to stop Soviet anti-tank rifle rounds. You can also see in this photograph that the tank has been fitted with the newer replacement production series road wheels with twenty-four rim bolts rather than the earlier sixteen rim bolt version. (*Massimo Foti*)

HULL MACHINE GUN

Early production Ausf. A tanks had the same rectangular 'letterbox' pistol port in the front glacis plate, out of which the radio operator could fire a machine gun. In late November 1943, a *Kugelblende* (ball mount) with a spherical-armoured guard was introduced. The radio operator could now see forward through the machine gunsight. The forward-facing periscope was no longer fitted. His side periscope was repositioned 25 mm further to the right.

SIDE STRAPS

Most metal straps for holding tools, spare parts, and stowage boxes were welded or bolted to the top of the hull or under the pannier, just above the track. Panthers built by Demag-Benrath were the exception. They welded the spare track hangers, base-bar directly to the hull side.

SUSPENSION

The Panzer V Ausf. A hull used the same dual torsion bar suspension system used on the earlier Ausf. D, but numerous changes were introduced during the production run at different times and locations. In August 1943, the road-wheels were strengthened with twenty-four outer rim bolts, but road-wheels with sixteen rim bolts were still being fitted to some Panthers as late as March 1944. When new wheels were damaged, there would be a chance that they could be replaced with the older sixteen rim bolt wheels at the maintenance yard. Some had locking rectangular tabs on the inner face of replacement production-series road-wheels. The design of the armour casing for the final drive housing was altered during the production run of Ausf. A Panthers. The armoured hub cap that went over the centre of the drive sprocket was also changed midway through production. Not all Panzer V Ausf. A Panther tanks looked the same.

EXHAUST PIPES

The early production Panther Ausf. A had the same layout as on the Ausf. D tank with two vertical exhaust pipes sticking out of individual curved armoured guards at the rear of the tank. The red convoy light was fixed below the left pannier above the track.

Later, the left side pipe was altered. Two cooling pipes were added. Now, three long vertical pipes came out of a modified, armoured, curved cover. There was still only one exhaust pipe coming out of the armoured cover on the right side of the tank. The red convoy light was moved from over the left track to the immediate left side of the left exhaust armoured cover at the rear of the tank.

CAMOUFLAGE

In February 1943, all factories were instructed to paint all German armoured fighting vehicles *Dunkelgelb* (RAL 7028). Each individual Panzer unit then applied its own individual camouflage pattern. They were issued with *olivegrün* (RAL 6003) and *Rotbraun* (RAL 8017) paint. In the winter, a covering of whitewash was applied to the tanks.

PANTHER AUSF. A SPECIFICATIONS

Dimensions (L-W-H)	8.86 m × 3.42 m × 3.10 m (29 feet 1 inch × 11 feet 3 inches × 10 feet 2 inches)
Total weight, battle-ready	45.5 tonnes
Main armament	Main: 7.5-cm KwK 42 L/70, seventy-nine rounds
Secondary armament	2 × 7.92-mm MG 34 machine guns
Armour: front upper glacis	80 mm at 55 degrees
Armour: front lower glacis	60 mm at 55 degrees
Armour: hull side	40 mm at 0 degrees
Armour: side superstructure	40 mm at 40 degrees
Armour: rear	40 mm at 30 degrees
Armour: hull deck	16 mm at 90 degrees
Armour: belly	30/16/16 mm (or all 16 mm) at 90 degrees
Armour: turret gun mantlet	100 mm at rounded
Armour: turret front	100 mm at 12 degrees
Armour: turret sides	45 mm at 25 degrees
Armour: turret rear	45 mm at 25 degrees
Armour: turret deck	16 mm at 84.5–90 degrees
Crew	Five (commander, driver, gunner, loader, and radioman/machine gunner)
Propulsion	Maybach HL 230 P30 V12 water-cooled 700-hp gasoline/petrol engine
Max Road Speed	55 km/h (34 mph)
Operational range	200 km (124 miles)
Production	2,200

4

PANZER V AUSF. G PANTHER TANK
(Sᴅ.Kꜰᴢ.171)

The Panzer V Ausf. G driver no longer had an armoured rectangular vision port in the front glacis plate. He had a swivelling periscope fitted to the hull roof above his head. (*Massimo Foti*)

The Panzer V Panther tank was given the Ausf. G version designation to indicate this production run of tanks used a different redesigned hull. The turret and 7.5-cm KwK 42 L/70 tank gun was the same one used on the earlier Ausf. A.

On 4 May 1944, during a meeting at the MAN company, a decision was made to design a new Panther tank hull. Work had already started on developing a new version of the Panther tank called Panther II but that was far from completion. Some of the lessons learnt from that design process were used in formulating the plans for the Ausf. G tank hull.

The side pannier armour that covered the top of the tracks on both sides of the tank was angled at 40 degrees on the Ausf. D and Ausf. A tank hull. The new hull pannier side armour was sloped at 29 degrees. The thickness in the armour was increased from 40 to 50 mm. This increased the weight of the tank by 305 kg.

To compensate for this increase in weight, the designers looked for areas where the thickness of the armour could be reduced. They chose to use 50-mm armour plating on the lower front hull instead of the normal 60 mm. This saved 150 kg.

The forward belly plates were reduced to 25 mm from 30 mm. The front two belly plates were 25 mm thick, and the rear plate was 16 mm thick. This saved a further 100 kg in weight. The rear side armour wedges at the end of the superstructure were not part of the new design. The floor of the pannier was now a straight line. These weight reduction changes meant that the increase inside armour thickness did not result in an increase in weight of the Ausf. G tank hull compared with the older hull.

As the bottom of the pannier was now 50 mm nearer to the top of the track, no weld seams or stowage straps were fixed there. This was to stop them coming into contact with the track as the tank drove fast over undulating ground. Instead, the stowage straps were welded to the side of the pannier armour.

The side armour of the Panzer V Ausf. G chassis was redesigned. The new chassis pannier side armour was sloped at 29 degrees instead of 40 degrees. The thickness in the armour was increased from 40 to 50 mm. It now had a straight bottom edge. (*Massimo Foti*)

There were many other minor changes, but the overall thinking behind the design was to simplify the construction process to enable more tanks to be built as fast as possible. For example, the ventilation systems for the transmission, brakes, engine, and exhaust were redesigned. This meant that the two additional parallel vertical pipes that came out of the left armoured exhaust cover at the rear of the tank on the late production Ausf. A tank hulls were no longer needed.

Starting in May 1944, cast armour exhaust guards gradually replaced welded ones. To help reduce the red glow given off by the exhaust pipes at night, as a temporary solution, sheet metal covers were gradually introduced starting in June 1944. Starting in October 1944, these were replaced gradually with purpose-built *Flammenvernichter* (flame-suppressor exhaust mufflers). When additional supplies became available, they were back-fitted to other Panther tanks.

Another simplification of the production process was to introduce less complicated hinged hatches above the heads of the driver and radio operator. It was found during trials that the performance of the cross-country ride of the tank with or without the rear shock absorber was practically the same. Starting from 7 October 1944, the factories were ordered to stop fitting them to help simplify production.

THE DRIVER'S POSITION

A perceived weak spot was the driver's armoured vision port cut into the front glacis plate. This was deleted in the design of the Ausf. G hull. The driver was provided with a single pivoting traversable periscope that was mounted in the roof of the hull covered by an armoured rain shield. Starting in August 1944, it was covered by a larger hood rain shield. This change in design helped simplify construction. When building the older Ausf. A hull, three features had to be built: the driver's armoured vision port plus the forward and side periscopes. Now, only one periscope had to be fitted.

SCHÜRZEN SIDE SKIRT ARMOUR AND HEADLIGHT

When looking at the side of the Panther Ausf. G hull, it appears that the track guard is jutting out of the steeper angled pannier side armour along the whole length of the tank. This is an optical illusion. It is a fender, introduced on this hull, to enable the *Schürzen* (side skirt armour plates) to be hung in the correct position. They were designed to protect the thinner 40-mm hull side armour, visible above the top of the road-wheels and under the pannier, from Soviet anti-tank rifles. It meets the front track fender.

The single headlight on the Ausf. A hull was mounted on the left side of the upper glacis plate. To make fitting the headlight easier, it was moved to the top of the left front track guard on the Ausf. G hull.

AMMUNITION STOWAGE AND MACHINE GUN BALL MOUNT

Two 4-mm-thick dust cover sliding doors were introduced to close off the sponson ammunition racks. Starting in September 1944, these were no longer installed as it was found they got in the way of ammunition handling. The ammunition stowage area was changed so the tank could now carry eighty-two 7.5-cm main gun rounds.

There was now a distinct 'step' around the bottom of the late production Ausf. G 7.92-mm MG 34 machine gun ball mount armoured cover. This was to reduce enemy bullet splash entering the mount's aperture. The machine gun ball mount was considered a weak spot by enemy infantry and was often targeted. If a bullet hit the sloped glacis plate below the mount, it would ricochet upwards. The 'step' helped reduce the damage they could do.

You can see a distinct lip around the bottom of the late production Panzer V Ausf. G Panther's 7.92-mm MG 34 machine gun ball mount armoured cover. This was to reduce enemy bullet splash entering the mount's aperture, having first hit the sloped glacis plate below the mount and ricocheted upwards. (*Massimo Foti*)

RADIO

Most Panther Ausf. G tanks were fitted with a Fug 5 radio set and an internal intercom. It had a usable range of around 4–6 km depending on the atmospheric conditions and location of the tank. Hills reduced the radio's range. Platoon leaders and company HQ tanks were fitted with an additional FuG 2 radio for a command channel.

PRODUCTION

On 3 April 1944, MAN reported that it had successfully completed trial production runs of the new Ausf. G hull. MAN built about 1,143 Panther Ausf. G tanks between March 1944 and April 1945. Between July 1944 to March 1945, MNH constructed 806 Panther Ausf. G tanks. Daimler-Benz finished 1,004 Panther Ausf. G tanks between May 1944 and April 1945.

There were some minor differences between factory-built tanks. MNH fitted cast steel *Gleitschuh* (skid shoes) instead of a rubber tire return roller behind the front track drive sprocket. The other two factories continued to fit rubber-rimmed return rollers.

Starting in September 1944, MAN replaced the road-wheels on a few Panther Ausf. G tanks, with smaller 800-mm diameter steel tire, rubber-cushioned, road-wheels similar to the ones used on all Tiger II tanks and some Tiger Is. Although this saved on the amount of rubber required to build a new Panther tank, it had the disadvantage of reducing the vehicle's ground clearance by 30 mm. The slightly larger rubber rimmed tires were 860-mm diameter wheels. A few tanks built in April 1945 had rubber-rimmed road-wheels, except for the one next to the idler wheel at the rear of the turret. That was fitted with a smaller steel tire road-wheel, though it is not known why.

Starting in October 1944, a larger diameter self-cleaning idler wheel was fitted. This new idler wheel was introduced to help elevate the problems caused by the build-up of mud and ice.

During the production run, some of the components of the suspension system changed like the swing arms and bump stops.

TURRET

A few minor changes were made to the turret during the production run. The most visible was the introduction of a handle on the circular hatch at the rear of the turret as well as the one above it. A thin rectangular metal sheet was welded across the gap between the front of the turret and the top of the gun mantlet to help stop debris entering the gap and jamming the gun elevation.

A lengthened rain guard over the gunsight aperture was added starting in September 1944. At the same time, a new gun mantlet was gradually introduced. It had a 'chin' guard to stop armour-piercing enemy shells ricocheting off the bottom of the mantlet and penetrating the roof of the hull and killing the driver or radio operator. When allied troops inspected the MNH Panther production factory at the end of the war, they found turrets still being produced with the older curved gun mantlet without the 'chin' guard.

Starting in January 1945, five metal loops were welded to each turret side. Rope or wire was run between these loops to help hold in place branches from trees and bushes used as camouflage.

Some Panzer Ausf. G Panther turrets were fitted with a gun mantlet that had a 'chin guard' to stop ricocheting armour piercing (AP) shells bouncing off the mantlet into the roof of the tank chassis and killing the machine gun operator or the driver. Not all Panzer Ausf. G Panther tanks were fitted with them.

INFRARED SEARCHLIGHT AND SCOPE

To be able to see the enemy at night was a tank commander's dream. To be able to point the tank's gun at a target with the correct elevation as well was cutting-edge technology in late 1944.

Starting in September 1944, a few Panzer V Ausf. G Panther tanks had a F.G.1250 *Ziel und Kommandanten-Optic* (infrared searchlight and scope) mounted on the commander's cupola. When he moved the scope up and down, an attached steel band that had been fed through a hole in the turret roof connected with a new indicator that showed the gunner the correct elevation. The 200-watt screened infrared light and receiver gunsight optic had a range of 600 m in clear weather.

It is not known exactly how many Panther tanks were fitted with this device or used on the battlefield. On 5 October 1944, MNH reported that it had fitted twenty Panther tanks with the new infrared equipment during September. Another thirty were scheduled to be completed in October and a further thirty in December 1944. On 15 January 1945, MNH were instructed to fit them to all of their current order for Panther Ausf. G tanks. It cannot be confirmed if this was done.

CAMOUFLAGE

Early production Panther Ausf. Gs were delivered to the front line painted in *dunkelgelb* (dark sandy yellow, RAL 7028) on top of the *Zimmerit* (anti-magnetic mine) coating. Each individual Panzer unit then applied their own camouflage design. On 19 August 1944, an order was issued to the factories that the tanks should be painted in a new camouflage pattern known as 'Ambush'. Patches of *rotbraun* (reddy-brown, RAL 8017) and *olivgrün* (olive-green, RAL 6003) were spray-painted over the *dunkelgelb* base coat.

Due to Allied and Soviet air supremacy in the later part of the war, Panther tank crews tried to hide their tanks under trees where possible. Dots of *dunkelgelb* were applied to the olive-green and reddy-brown patches to simulate light coming through a tree canopy. Darker dots were applied to the *dunkelgelb* base coat.

On 9 September 1944, because of reports that *Zimmerit* had caused tank fires and the lack of evidence of magnetic mine use by the Soviets and Allies, the factories were ordered to stop applying *Zimmerit*. Panther Ausf. G tanks now left the factory painted in a base coat of red oxide primer. They were only sparingly painted in camouflage patterns using *dunkelgelb* in patches. Paint supplies were getting low and the need to get as many tanks to the front line as fast as possible was urgent.

On 31 October, additional instructions were received at the factories. The inside of the Panther Ausf.G tanks were no longer to be painted a light Ivory white colour. They were just painted in red oxide primer to save time. This would make the inside of the tank a very dark working environment. The outside could be sparingly painted in patches of *rotbraun*, *dunkelgelb*, and *olivgrün*. If supplies of *Dunkelgelb* had run out the factories were authorised to use *Dunkelgrau* (dark grey) instead. On 15 February 1945, the factories were ordered to paint the inside of the turrets *Elfenbein* (ivory white) again.

PANTHER AUSF. G SPECIFICATIONS

Dimensions (L-W-H)	8.86 m × 3.42 m × 3.10 m a(29 feet 1 inch × 11 feet 3 inches × 10 feet 2 inches)
Total weight, battle-ready	45.5 tonnes
Main armament	Main: 7.5-cm KwK 42 L/70, eighty-two rounds
Secondary armament	2 × 7.92-mm MG 34 machine guns
Armour: front upper glacis	80 mm at 55 degrees
Armour: front lower glacis	50 mm at 55 degrees
Armour: hull side	40 mm at 0 degrees
Armour: side superstructure	50 mm at 29 degrees
Armour: rear	30 mm at 30 degrees
Armour: hull deck	40 mm (front section)—16 mm at 90 degrees
Armour: belly	25 mm (front section)—16 mm at 90 degrees
Armour: turret gun mantlet	100-110 mm at rounded
Armour: turret front	100 mm at 12 degrees
Armour: turret sides	45 mm at 25 degrees
Armour: turret rear	45 mm at 25 degrees
Armour: turret deck	16 mm at 84.5–90 degrees
Crew	5 (commander, driver, gunner, loader, radioman/machine gunner)
Propulsion	Maybach HL 230 P30 V12 water-cooled 700-hp gasoline/petrol engine
Transmission	ZF AK 7-200 7-forward/1-reverse gearbox
Suspensions	Double torsion bars and interleaved wheels
Max. road speed	46 km/h (28.5 mph)
Operational range	200 km (124 miles)
Production	2,961 approx.

TOTAL PRODUCTION NUMBERS

The amount of Panzer V Panther tanks produced was recorded by Fgst.Nr. (hull number) for each *Ausführung* (version) and from factory monthly completion figures. The factory completion figures did not record the *Ausführung* information. Panther tank production occurred at factories belonging to the following companies: Daimler-Benz, MAN, Henschel, and MNH. A few were built by Demag. As you can see, the figures do not match.

Total Number Produced Using Hull Number Data (Fgst.Nr.)
Panzer V 'Panther' Ausf. D (Sd.Kfz.171):   Total: 842
Panzer V 'Panther' Ausf. A (Sd.Kfz.171):   Total: 2,200
Panzer V 'Panther' Ausf. G (Sd.Kfz.171):   Approx. total: 2,961
                                            Grand total: 6,003

Total Produced Using Monthly Factory Completion Data
1943   Total 1768
1944   Total 3777
1945   Total 439
              Grand total 5,984

5

THE SOVIET PANTHER TANK REPORT

Panzerkampfwagen Ausf. D Panther (No. 521) was one of the first tanks captured and examined by the Soviets. They sent a report detailing their findings to the Allies. Notice the smoke grenade dischargers on the side of the turret and the hull machine gunner's 'vertical letterbox' vision port to the right of the rectangular driver's armoured vision port on the left of the front glacis plate. All these features were changed in later versions of the Panther. (*Russian Archives*)

Note: The information in this chapter has been transcribed from original wartime documents. The report format and brief notation style of writing has been kept.

SECRET REPORT FROM THE CANADIAN MILITARY ATTACHÉ, USSR

Department of National Defence—Army—Ottawa, Ontario, 21 Oct. 1943 (HQS 9029-1 FD 11)
Equipment—German PzKw V (Panther)
Central Registry Army 166297

This report is compiled from information given by the Russians and from examination, in Moscow, of the tank captured on the Russian front. It was knocked out by a shell which entered the tank between the turret and the hull, almost exactly at a right-angle to the armour, and which passed right through the tank.

The inside of the fighting compartment was burnt out and the gearbox, all controls and most of the transmission had been removed. Nothing could be dismantled for a closer examination.

Number on the outside of turret—521

Number in white painted lettering on offside front hull—210055

DIMENSIONS

Overall length with gun	29.1 feet
Length of tank without gun	22.7 feet
Width of tank	11.3 feet
Height of tank	9.6 feet
Clearance	1.6 feet
Length of hull	22.0 feet
Width of hull, upper part	9.8 feet
Width of hull, lower part	6.0 feet
Inner diameter of the turret ring	5.4 feet
Length of surface in contact with the ground between the centres in rollers	12.8 feet
Length of surface in contact with the ground between outer edges of track plates of those in contact with ground	13.3 feet
Width of track between centres of track plates	8.6 feet
Width of track between edges of track plates	10.8 feet
Track pressure	11.7 lb per sq. in.
Power to weight ratio	13.3 to 14.4 hp per ton
Fuel capacity	81 gallons
Octane value	not less than 74
Weight laden	45 tons

Crew consists of: commander, gun layer, loader, driver and wireless operator.

ENGINE

Engine No. in tank examined 46847. Appears to be exactly the same as in Tiger, *i.e.* 12-cylinder Maybach, consisting of two banks of six cylinders at 60 degrees. It is located in the centre of the rear compartment. It has four carburettors and two 6-cylinder Bosch magnetos (1 to each bank of cylinders and mounted at rear of engine above the camshaft drive).

A 12-volt Vater accumulator was found in the rear of the fighting compartment but there was no indication as to where it was mounted. Electric and inertia starters are fitted. The inertia starter being operated by handle in rear of fighting compartment. Russians give horsepower of engines as 600 to 650.

AUTOMATIC FIRE EXTINGUISHER

An electrically operated fire extinguisher is mounted in the rear of the fighting compartment with tubing leading to six jets around the engine. The fire extinguisher is smaller than our own CO_2 bottles. It is a little larger than a normal pyrene extinguisher.

TRANSMISSION

Transmission shaft passes through a transfer box, situated directly under the fighting compartment, to a gearbox located in the extreme front of the tank. The gearbox had been removed, but the steering breaks still remained and appeared to be exactly the same type as for the Tiger but above each steering brake is a hydraulic cylinder which appears to be for brake operation. This was too far dismantled to say for certain.

The drive passes through a single reduction gear to the forward drive sprocket which is a detachable rim tooth sprocket having seventeen teeth.

Internal diameter of rim	2 feet 4.5 inches
External diameter of rim	2 feet 11 inches
Depth of tooth	2 3/32 inches
Height centre of sprocket from ground	30.5 inches

Suspension is of the inter-leaved bogey and independent torsion bar type as in Tiger. Hydraulic shock absorbers are provided on front and rear suspensions only and these shock absorbers are mounted inside the hull. Greasing of torsion bars is carried out by means of four groups of ten grease nipples mounted on each side of the fighting compartment. One rubber-tired jockey roller on each side carries the track from the front roller to the drive sprocket.

Number of track rollers	For twin rubber-tired rollers to each side
Diameter of roller	2.8 feet
Distance between front sprocket axle and front bogey axle	4.7 inches on each side
Idler wheel diameter	22.5 inches
Height, centre of idler wheel to ground	27 inches
(Has cracked spindle as in Tiger)	
Type of track	Metallic short pitch
Pitch of track	6 inches
Width of track	2.2 feet
Number of track plates	86 per track
Diameter of track pin	0.9 inches

The track examined had the following stampings:

Inner edge	021B	Outer edge	agh
	4838		43.
	0–1		

ARMAMENT AND FIGHTING COMPARTMENT

The main armament is a parallel bore 75-mm tank gun, 1943 pattern, having SA vertical falling block type breech and having muzzle brake as in 88-mm gun on Tiger. The buffer gear is situated on the right of the gun and recuperator on the left. During travel, the gun can be secured to the roof of the turret by means of a clamp. The machine-gun is coaxial: mounted on the right of the main armament. A simple swivel arm is provided inside the commander's cupola for AA machine-gun. No forward hull machine-gun is provided.

Overall length of gun	5,535 mm
From rear of rifling to rear of piece	690 mm
From rear of rifling to rear of breech block	910 mm

The breech block examined had a stamping '1943'on left of breech block and 'R164' on the right. This was also stamped on top of band by the mantlet. The firing mechanism appears to be electrical. The breech block was fitted with three nozzles but owing to destruction there was no indication what these were used for.

The turret floor (diameter approximately 5 feet 2 inches) revolves, and the turret drive is taken through the centre of the turret floor, as in the Tiger tank, to the motor which is situated on floor of the fighting compartment. Power is transmitted mechanically to the traverse gearbox. Elevation and traverse handwheels are situated directly in front of the gunner.

The commander cannot assist the gunner to traverse the turret as in Tiger tank. The commander's cupola is geared to the turret ring as in the Tiger tank so that the gun can be rotated without altering the position of the cupola. There are three smoke dischargers (diameter 1.7 inches) mounted on each side of the turret and set at varying angles. They are electrically fired as in the Tiger. Turret can be locked by wedge and hand wheel on the right side of the loader.

SIGHT

There are amateurs for telescopic sight fitted into the gun mantlet at the left of the gun.

HATCHES

(a) The commander has a raised cupola, 26 cm approximately above the level of the turret, having a singular circular hatch in cupola. The cupola turret bearing is protected by a welded ring, 1.5 inches high by 1.5 inches at base.

(b) Circular, single hinged, escape hatch in rear of turret, approximately 18 inches in diameter.

(c) Revolver ports, one in each side of turret and one in rear. These are approximately 8 cm in diameter and are closed by steel plugs.

(d) Machine-gun port, rear left of gunner, approximately 27 cm in diameter, single hinged.

(e) Two heavy rectangular hatches, one each above driver and co-driver. These are approximately 43 cm by 60 cm and are operated by large hydraulic rams. The rams appear to be operated by oil force pumps which are driven off the transfer box below the fighting compartment and controlled by handle at rear right of driver. The hatches are raised slightly and then swivelled to open. There are no doors in the sides of the hull and no hatch is provided in the roof of the turret for loader.

(f) Large rectangular inspection hatch is provided over engine (approximately 3 feet 4 inches by 2 feet 4.5 inches).

(g) Eight small inspection hatches underneath rear of hull for inspection of engine and buffer gear.

VENTILATION

An electric fan is fitted in the turret roof above coaxial machine-gun, and an adjacent port is fitted between driver and wireless operator's hatches.

OBSERVATION

(a) The commander is provided with six horizontal vision slots around the cupola, the frame being scaled to give sighting arc. These are closed by rotating a steel ring (2.35 inches thick) around the cupola. The ring is operated by a handwheel situated directly in front of the commander.

(b) The driver has a large rectangular observation slot operated by a single spring-loaded lever. There is a fitting for safety glass (9.75 inches by 4 inches).

(c) The wireless operator has a rectangular slot 9.5 inches by 3.75 inches in the front plate. This is close by a single hinged hatch operated by a spring-loaded lever. There is no fitting for safety glass nor can the size of this slot be varied.

(d) Gun-layer is provided with by knocking the gunsight on left of gun.

(e) No observation is provided for the loader.
Two periscopes are provided for the driver, one at 12 o'clock and one at 10.30 o'clock and two for the wireless operator, one at 12 o'clock and one at 1.30 o'clock.

ARMOUR AND VULNERABILITY

Comparing this tank with the Tiger one is immediately struck with the well-sloped armour and good contour. Welded construction is used throughout, and the armour is dovetailed as well as welded. At the front of the hull, the dovetailing is achieved by bending the armour plate around the corners. No angle iron framework appears to be used in the hull construction. The design of the turret includes the fitting of a turret protecting-ring. The gun mantlet is cast in one piece and is semi-circular covering the full height and breadth of the turret.

ARMOUR	THICKNESS	INCLINATION TO VERTICAL
Upper front plate	85 mm	57 degrees
Lower front plate	75 mm	53 degrees
Upper side plate	45 mm	42 degrees

Lower side plate	45 mm	Nil
Rear armour	45 mm	30 degrees
Turret	45 mm	25 degrees
Turret, front plate	100 mm	
Gun mantlet	100 mm	
Turret roof	17 mm	90 degrees
Underside of hull, above track	17 mm	90 degrees
Belly	17 mm	90 degrees

Slots are provided under the side of the hull above track for fitting skirting plates.

STOWAGE

75 rounds are carried which are stowed on each side of the hull and in-floor containers. 2,500 rounds of machine gun ammunition are carried.

PERFORMANCE

Maximum speed	30 mph approximately
Average speed	15 mph approximately
Radius of action	170 kilometres

INTERCOMMUNICATION

An internal intercom telephone is provided. External communication is by RT, WT, flag, etc. Radio set appears to be mounted on the right-hand side of the wireless operator.

CONCLUSION

The Panther seems to be a compromise between the heavy infantry tank and a medium cruiser type machine suitable for both roles. It is an impressive fighting machine, probably with good fighting qualities.

THE SOVIET AIMING POINT PAMPHLET

The Soviets produced a pamphlet that was issued to its troops showing the perceived weak points of the Panther tank and suggested aiming points with minimum distances.

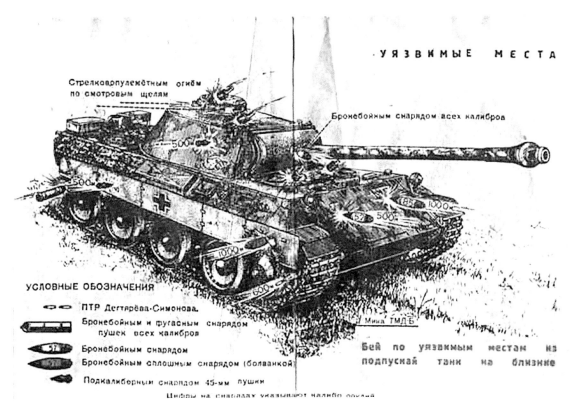

Soviet pamphlet showing aiming points in red on a German Panther tank—front ¾ view. (*Russian Archives*)

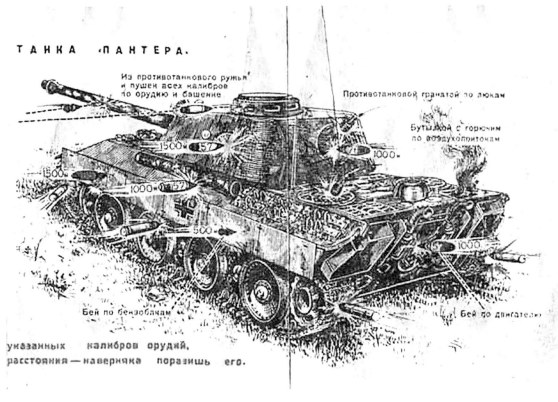

Soviet pamphlet showing aiming points in red on a German Panther tank—rear ¾ view. (Russian Archives)

6

PANTHER ARMOUR–THICKNESS POSTER

In 1943, the following poster was distributed within the British and Commonwealth army showing the known Panther armour thicknesses to help the troops work out weak spots. Most of this information was based on Soviet data from examination of destroyed and captured vehicles on the Eastern Front.

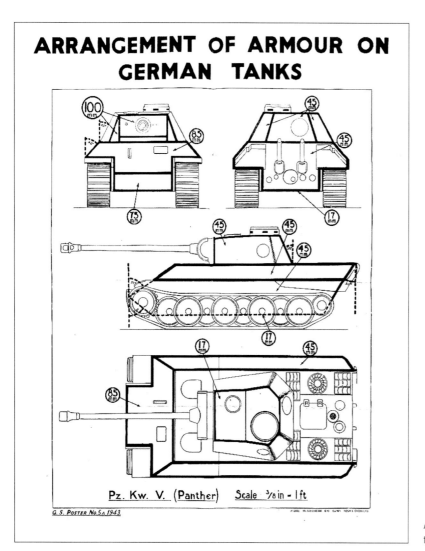

A 1943 poster showing Panther tank armour thickness. (*G.S. Poster No. 5a 1943*)

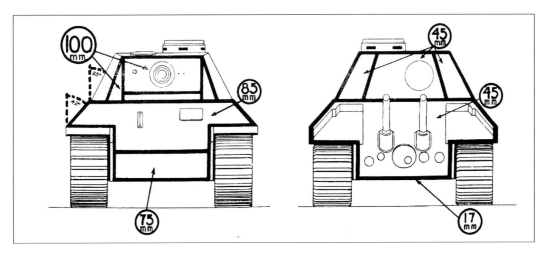

This shows the front and rear views of the panther tank and also the angle of the side pannier armour and the turret side armour. (*G.S. Poster No. 5a 1943*)

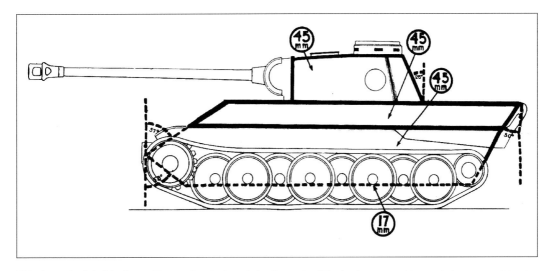

This shows the left side views of the panther tank and also the angle of the front upper and lower glacis armour plate plus the angle of the rear turret armour. (*G.S. Poster No. 5a 1943*)

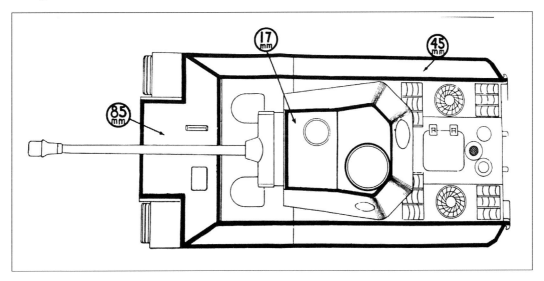

This shows the top view of the Panther. Unusually, it does not show the thickness of the armour used on the chassis deck. (*G.S. Poster No. 5a 1943*)

7

PAMPHLET ON ATTACK ON PANTHER PzKw V AND TIGER PzKw VI

Note: The information in this chapter has been transcribed from original wartime documents. The Pamphlet format and brief notation style of writing has been kept where possible.

SECRET

Prepared for the use of Students of the School of Tank Technology

April 1944 (Copy number B8727)

Amendment No. 1
The issue of an amended R.V. curve for 6-pdr APCBC has made it necessary to revise the figure for this projectile. New half-tone pictures and polar diagrams have been prepared and are enclosed herewith.

The examination of the one Panther that has so far reached this country has supplied slightly different figures for the armour thicknesses and angles to those given in section 3 of the pamphlet. It is not considered that these differences are sufficient to call for a revision of the figures for the other weapons quoted in the pamphlet until other specimens of Panther had been examined in detail. In any case, the errors involved are less than those which will be introduced by inaccuracies in the estimation of range, angle of presentation and the actual MV of the guns under operational conditions. The new figures for the 6-pdr APCBC have been based on the increased thickness and angle data.

Section 1

1. This paper is an attempt to define the conditions under which Panther (PzKw V) and Tiger (PzKw VI) may be attacked successfully by British and American A/T guns. The information is given in the form of marked photographs and polar diagrams. It is limited to the attack of certain prominent plates on each vehicle, and in making the necessary calculations, the conditions stated in paragraphs 2, 3 and 4 have been assumed.

2. Armour on Tiger
The armour is assumed to be of rolled machineable quality of a standard similar to that required for British machineable quality plate, and of the following thickness and tilts.

PLATE	THICKNESS	TILT
Driver's visor	102 mm	10 deg.
Front of turret	102 mm	5 deg.
Side of turret	82 mm	Vertical
Rear of turret	82 mm	Vertical
Hull, side superstructure	82 mm	Vertical
Hull side, below mudguard	62 mm	Vertical
Rear of hull	82 mm	8 deg.

3. Armour on Panther

The armour is assumed to be of rolled machineable quality of the standard similar to that required for British machineable quality plate, and of the following thicknesses and tilts.

PLATE	THICKNESS	TILT
Glacis plate	85 mm	57 deg.
Front of turret	102 mm	Vertical
Side of turret	45 mm	25 deg.
Rear of turret	45 mm	25 deg.
Side of hull	45 mm	Vertical
Hull, side superstructure	45 mm	42 deg.
Rear of hull	45 mm	30 deg.

4. Guns and Projectiles

The data refer also only to the following guns and projectiles with muzzle velocities as stated below. The following approximate corrections for muzzle velocity are suggested.

GUN	TYPE OF PROJECTILE	WEIGHT OF PROJECTILE	MUZZLE VELOCITY
37-mm	APCBC (M51)	1.92 lb	2,900 f.s.
6-pdr Mk IV	APCBC	7.19 lb	2,725 f.s.
75-mm M3	APCBC (M61)	14.36 lb	2,030 f.s.
3-inch	APCBC (M62)	14.89 lb	2,600 f.s.
17-pdr	APCBC	17.00 lb	2,900 f.s.

5. A small difference in the weight of a projectile will not have a marked influence on its performance. On the other hand, the performance decreases somewhat rapidly as the muzzle velocity decreases.

	M.V. CORRECTION	PROJECTILE
	50 f.s.	37-mm APCBC
Decrease each range by	40 f.s.	6-pdr APCBC
100 yards for a fall	30 f.s.	75-mm APCBC
In muzzle velocity of:-	30 f.s.	3-inch APCBC
	30 f.s.	17-pdr APCBC

6. The information is given primarily in the form of a set of seven marked photographs for each combination of the projectile and tank. The photographs have been chosen to represent typical orientations at which enemy tanks may be found. The relationship of gun and observer and the general appearance of Tiger at these presentations are given below. The arrow indicates the direction in which the tank is moving and is also the normal to the front (or rear) of the tanks, in the horizontal plane the hatched line indicates the normal to the side.

 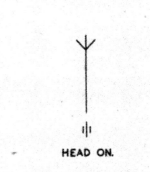

Fig. 1: Head-On Angle of Impact in Horizontal Plane—Front Normal. (*School of Tank Technology*)

 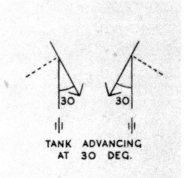

Fig. 2: Tank advancing at 30-degree Angles of Impact in Horizontal Plane—Front 30 degrees. Sides 60 degrees. (*School of Tank Technology*)

 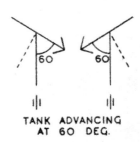

Fig. 3: Tank advancing at 60-degree Angles of Impact in Horizontal Plane—Front 60 degrees. Sides 30 degrees. (*School of Tank Technology)*

 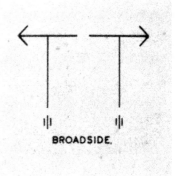

Fig. 4: Broadside Angle of Impact in Horizontal Plane—Sides Normal. (*School of Tank Technology*)

 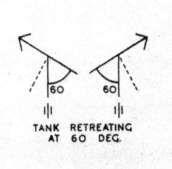

Fig. 5: Tank retreating at 60-degree Angles of Impact in Horizontal Plane—Sides 30 degrees. Rear 60 degrees. (*School of Tank Technology*)

 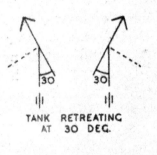

Fig. 6: Tank retreating at 30-degree Angles of Impact in Horizontal Plane—Sides 60 degrees. Rear 30 degrees. (*School of Tank Technology*)

Fig. 7: Rear Angle of Impact in Horizontal Plane—Rear Normal.

It should be realised that, because the turret of a tank can rotate, photographs and diagrams given must be regarded as being in two distinct parts, one for the turret and the other for the hull. To take the extreme case, the photograph and diagram for attack on the rear (Fig. 7) will apply to the hull only. Those for the head-on position (Fig. 1) will apply to the turret. Similarly, if a tank has halted broadside to a gun and is firing at it, the broadside photograph and diagram (Fig. 4) will apply to the hull: the head-on photograph and diagram (Fig. 1) will apply to the turret, and so on for other combinations.

Some Notes on the Attack of Enemy Tanks

Explanation of Photographs and Diagrams

Section II

9. Damage to enemy tanks can be divided into two classes:
   (a) Primary, where a main plate is holed.
   (b) Secondary, where damage is done to the tracks and suspensions, the turret is jammed, etc., but the projectile does not enter the tank.

10. The data supplied refer only to primary damage. It does not follow that when a shot is shown as failing against the main plate under a given set of conditions that it is useless to fire at the tank. While it is unlikely that the shot will enter the tank if it strikes fairly on the main plate, a certain number of hits will do secondary damage and may even violently dislodged fittings inside the vehicle.

Nonetheless, it is always better, if circumstances allow, to waiting until the conditions are such that there is a reasonable probability of hitting and of the hit penetrating a main plate.

11. The quality of German plate varies considerably, and that used for our shoot is not consistent. It is, therefore, impossible to do more than indicate conditions under which average shot are likely to prove successful against plate of average quality. If the shot is rather poor and the plate is exceptionally tough, the ranges stated may have to be shortened, perhaps by 200 yards or more. On the other hand, if there is a favourable combination of shot and plate, the tank may be defeated at ranges longer by perhaps 200 yards or more than those indicated.

12. The performance figures have been produced on the assumption that the tank is standing on level ground and that fire is in the horizontal plane, that is angle of descent and angle of site have been neglected. With high-velocity guns at short ranges, the angle of descent will always be small and will usually be negligible in comparison with the angle of site. The corrections are usually quite small and cannot be made without introducing complications. The general effect, however, can be indicated.

Thus, if the tank is on level ground and the gun is firing downhill at it, the driver's visor plate of the Tiger, which is tilted back at an angle of 10 degrees, will be struck at an angle of less than 10 degrees (unless the gun is very high indeed) and will prove more vulnerable than usual. The same will be true if tank and gun are at the same height and with the tank coming downhill towards the gun. (The tank is here tilted forwards towards the gun). In the above cases, the increase in effective range will not be large, perhaps not more than 200 yards with 6-pdr APCBC.

If the plates on the tank have a considerable backward tilt, conditions such as those indicated above will be relatively more favourable to the gun, the contrary conditions, however, being relatively less favourable. The greater the tilt of a plate, the greater the change in resistance caused by a small change in the angle of impact.

The further away from the condition of horizontal fire and the more the tank is off an even keel, the more difficult it is to get through a vertical plate, but the effect is again usually small under ordinary practical conditions.

13. Attack on Turret Fronts

The resistance of the armour on the front of a turret varies from point to point and is difficult to assess. The ranges given are those at which performance or severe secondary damage should be obtained, but it must be realised that an occasional hit under the conditions defined may be almost ineffective. On the other hand, a hit at a longer range will sometimes put the tank out of action.

When a tank has a turret front and a main front hull plate, of approximate the same thickness and tilts, as on the Tiger, a hit on the main plate will probably prove the more effective.

When the gun mantlet is curved, as on the Panther, the vulnerability of the turret front depends still more on the point of strike, and any range must still more be taken only as a general guide. The hull front on the Panther, however, is so strong that the gunner's best chance in a head-on attack is to go for the turret.

14. Attack on the Turret Sides

When the turret side is straight or nearly straight, as on the Panther, the ranges given hold, with the usual reservations. When the side is curved, however, as on the Tiger, the ranges refer to the area halfway between the mantlet and turret rear. When the turret is broadside to the gun a hit in any other position will only perforate at a shorter range. On the other hand, when the turret is not square to the gun, as when the tank is advancing or retreating at 60 degrees, there will be a small area round about the centre of the target as presented, where a hit near normal and favourable to the gun can be obtained on the turret. Thus, as the ranges given for the above conditions refer to the real mid-position, and not to the apparent mid-position, they will be somewhat pessimistic when applied to the special area.

15. Remarks on Attack on Tiger

(a) The nose plate is thick (100 mm), tilted forward (25 degrees) and is often covered with shoes. The 6-pdr will almost invariably fail against it, and it is definitely a less promising target than the visor plate for the 17-pdr or M10.

(b) When the tank is broadside, there is a small area of vertical plate 62-mm thick on the hull side just above the track and below the superstructure. This can be perforated quite easily by the 75-mm and 6-pdr at moderate ranges even at unfavourable angles. However, as a target, this area is very small. A hit still lower on the side of the tank will strike the bogies. Whether shot will enter the hull or not will then depend to a considerable extent on the exact point of strike, but sometimes the wheels will add only slightly to the resistance of the main armour which is still the vertical plate only 60 mm thick.

(c) The various fittings on the rear of the hull and turret add little to the resistance of the main plates.

(d) When the visor plate seems to be as long as the hull superstructure side plate, the tank is advancing at slightly more than 30 degrees, when the rear and side superstructure appears to be of equal length the tank is retreating at about 30 degrees.

16. Remarks on Attack on Panther

(a) The armour on this tank is out of balance, the hull front being a very strong and the turret front being an awkward target, but all the other plates on the tanks have only a moderate resistance. It follows, therefore, that the flanks and rear of this tank should be engaged where ever possible. It should be noted, however, that a lucky hit at quite long ranges low down on the turret front may result in a ricochet through the roof of the hull.

(b) The hull side superstructure is tilted back at the awkward angle of 42 degrees, but the plate is comparatively thin (45 mm). It follows that although the side superstructure is very resistant to a small gun its resistance to a gun of moderate size, such as the 6-pdr, is not good, and that the 17-pdr, is able to perforate it under a wide range of conditions.

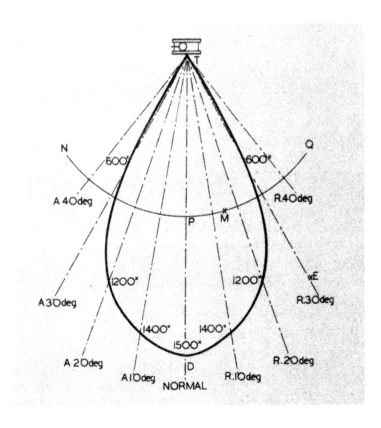

Fig. 8: Polar Diagram—Illustrated attack on side of tank with APCBC shot. (*School of Tank Technology*)

17. Explanation of a Polar Diagram

The polar diagram is simply a crude map of the ground. Unlike the ordinary map, the ruling direction is not north, but the direction at right angles to the front, side or rear of the tank, as the case may be. Instead of all distances being measured from an agreed and stationary datum point, they are measured from the tank, and mixed co-ordinates, arrange and in angle, are used instead of the ordinary rectangular co-ordination.

18. Fig. 8., A scale diagram to express the attack on the side of the tank using APCBC Shot illustrates. The line, DT, is the ruling direction and is the normal to the side of the tank. The vehicle would be broadside to an observer standing at any point along TD, and would appear as in Fig.4. The rays coming out from the tank are at intervals of 10 degrees and give the angle of attack on the side plates. Thus to an observer standing somewhere on the R30 degree ray along the TE the tank would appear to be retreating at 60 degrees and would appear as in Fig. 5. A shot fired from a gun along this Ray would strike the side at 30 degrees. The tank would appear to an observer along the A30 degree ray to be advancing at 60 degrees (Fig. 3) but a shot from a gun sited along this ray would again strike the side at 30 degrees. In other words, from the point of view of striking the side, there is no material difference between the rays at A30 degree and R30 degree.

19. Ranges on the diagram can be represented by arcs of circles with their centres at the tank. Thus in Fig. 8., NPQ is the arc representing a range of 800 yards. These arcs are used in the construction of a diagram but, as they become unnecessary and tend to confuse the finished map, often they are later removed. In an alternative form of diagram, the arc representing the principal ranges are left in, but the ranges in yards at which the plate can be perforated at particular angles are then not stated numerically.

20. In illustration of how the position of a point with respect to a tank can be defined in terms of range and angle, consider point M. M is clearly 800 yards, R15 deg., and any position on the ground in front of the side of the tank can be stated in this a similar manner.

21. The performance of a gun against a plate depends on the range and angle as well as on the nature of the ammunition used. The effective range decreases as the angle of attack increases, the change sometimes being very fast. It is possible by using the polar diagrams system to show this somewhat complicated connection between range and angle. Thus for a particular gun firing APCBC, The relationship which might be much as shown in Fig. 8. If the gun is square to the side of the tank, the tank will appear to the gunner as in Fig. 4, the gun will be along TD, and if the range is less than 1,500 yards, the gun will be successful. If the range is longer than 1,500 yards, the gun will fail to do primary damage. If the gun cannot hit the tank quite squarely as at 10 degrees, the critical range shortens to 1,400 yards. In this particular case there is a further small decrease in effective range to 1,200 yards as the angle increases to R20 degrees, but the effective ranges halved as the angle increases from R20 degrees to R30 degrees and disappears altogether at about R35 degrees.

At R30 degrees the tank will appear as in Fig. 5. An area, or wing, is obtained by joining these critical positions. When the gun is inside the area, it can defeat the tank: when outside, it will fail. Thus, every hit will probably perforate if the gun is at M while it is unlikely that a gun cited at E will ever be successful.

22. While the general shape of the polar diagram remains fairly constant, the actual ranges and angles depend very much on the size and muzzle velocity of the projectiles, the thickness of the target, and on other factors. If, however, the gunner is supplied with information, perhaps in the form of marked photographs, telling him how his shot will perform against a particular tank at certain definite angles (e.g. broadside, advancing at 60 degrees, advancing at 30 degrees), and this information is supplemented by one or two polar diagrams typically of particular plates on the tank, he can usually tell with reasonable accuracy what the critical ranges are at other angles of attack.

For example, marked photographs may tell him that he can get through the side of the tank at 1,200 yards provided the tank presents itself squarely. Another may tell him that if he can hit the side only at 30 degrees, his shot will probably fail at any range. In the absence of a polar diagram, a special photograph would be required to state the position at 20 degrees attack but a polar diagram of a plate of about the same thickness gives the information that in this special case the effective range does not change very much from normal up to perhaps 20 degrees. When this critical Angle is passed, his chances of holing the plate at any range are small. If, however, the plate on the front of the tank is much thicker than that on the side, the polar diagram for the side will be useless as a guide to the behaviour of the shot against the front of the tank, and a more suitable diagram would have to be used.

23. The polar diagram differs from an ordinary map but only as stated in para. 17, but also in another very important aspect as explained below. The vulnerable area or wing of the diagram is a property of the tank and not of the ground. As the tank shown in Fig. Eight moves to the left, so does the wing move with it. As the tank turns, so does the wing turn. The wing, indeed, may be regarded as an imaginary shadow attached to the tank. When the wing or shadow falls over the gun, then a hit from the gun will perforate the tank. Thus an A/T gun at N (Fig. 8) is not under the wing and therefore will not be able to do the side of the tank primary damage. But if the tank moves left, it will carry its shadow with it: N will then be covered, and the gun can win. In exactly the same way, if the tank does not advance but swings around clockwise to retreat, the wing will again swing over the gun, which can then succeed.

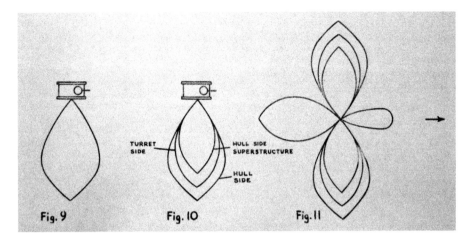

Polar Diagrams.
(*School of Tank Technology*)

24. A single polar diagram, as Fig. 9, can apply only to a single plate. However, the aspect of the tank may consist of several plates, each of a different resistance, and each requiring a polar diagram for itself. Thus the side (hull and turret) of Panther has three main plates, each 45-mm thick, but of different resistance to horizontal fire, because they are mounted on the tank at different tilts—namely, hull side vertical, hull side superstructure, at 42 degrees, and turret side at 25 degrees. These can be shown as a family of polar diagrams as in Fig. 10.

Further, a family such as that given in Fig. 10, is required for each aspect of the tank, front, sides and rear. These can be assembled as in Fig. 11 to give a 'butterfly' which gives an idea of the vulnerability of the tank as a whole. In Fig. 11, the arrow indicates the direction in which the tank is moving. As the areas often overlap, the tank must be shown to scale (*i.e.* as a point) and not of grossly exaggerated size as in Figs. 9 and 10.

Alternatively, the 'butterfly' can be simplified by taking the most prominent or strongest or weakest plate to represent a particular aspect. It should be realised clearly that the polar diagram as given define only the conditions under which a hit will be successful. They say nothing about the probability of a hit being obtained. In order to obtain a complete picture of the attack on a tank the two factors, the probability of a hit and the probability of a hit perforating, must be considered together. It is obvious that the probability of a hit will increase as the range shortens. The lesson seems to be moderately short range as squarely as possible to the aspect of the tank under attack.

26. In the polar diagrams prepared, the vulnerable and in vulnerable areas are shown as being separated by lines. It would be more correct to replace the lines by bands, the inner side of the band representing the attack of worst British shot on best German plate, and the outside that of best British shot on worst German plate. The lack of data does not permit this to be done.

As the available Soviet firing-trial results only cover a small fraction of the conditions which must be defined, much of the data used in the construction of the diagrams has had perforce to be obtained indirectly by calculation and assessment, and unsatisfactory process at best. An attempt has been made to put the lines through the centre of the bends. That is, if a gun is sited on, and is firing shot of average quality against plate of average quality, it is calculated that 50 per cent of the hits under the conditions set out in para. 12 above will be through is. A small error in a calculation, particularly as the loss in energy of APCBC Projectiles with increasing range is not marked, may result in a substantial error in the position of the line and its displacement from the centre of the band. Further, the vulnerable areas will swell or contract pending on whether the ground level favours or does not favour the gun (see para. 12).

For these reasons, the data given both on the photographs and in the form of polar diagrams can at best be accepted only as a crude guide.

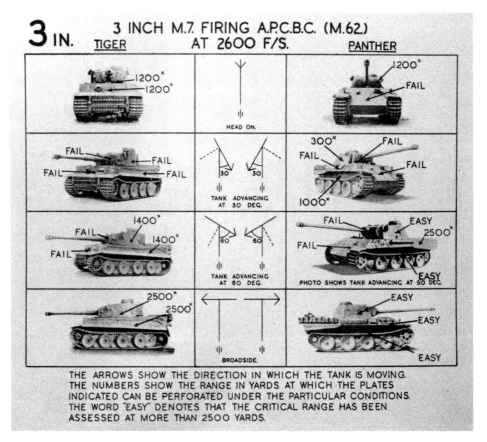

(*School of Tank Technology*)

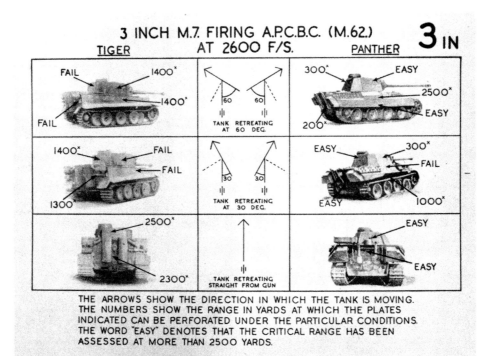

(*School of Tank Technology*)

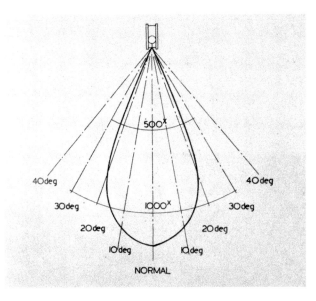

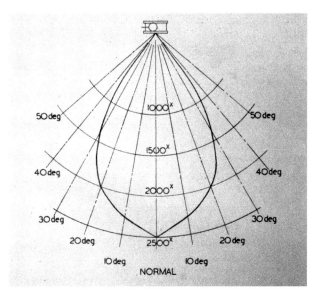

◀ Polar Diagram—3-inch M7 gun (M62 APCBC) at 2,600 f.s. *v.* vision plate of Tiger (Pz.Kw.VI) and turret front of Tiger and Panther (Pz.KW.V). This projectile is not expected to succeed against the glacis plate of Panther. (*School of Tank Technology*)

▶ Polar Diagram—3-inch M7 gun (M62 APCBC) at 2,600 f.s. *v.* hull side superstructure of Tiger (Pz.Kw.VI). This diagram applies also to hull rear of Tiger provided all ranges are shortened by 200 yards. (*School of Tank Technology*)

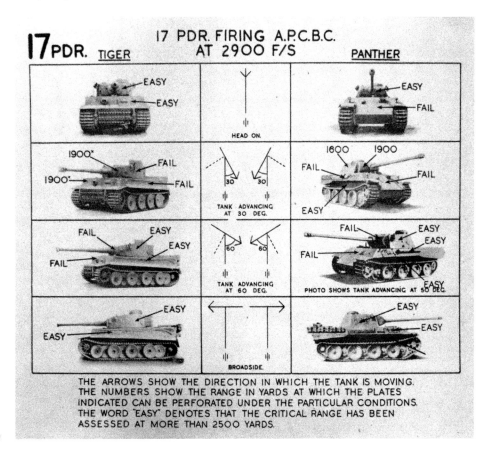

(*School of Tank Technology*)

27. No attempt has been made to estimate performances at ranges over 2,500 yards. If it is judged that the projectile will succeed under the stated conditions at a longer range, the plate on the photographs is marked 'Easy', and the polar diagram is left open. The fact that the diagram is open means no more than this, and in these cases, it will not normally be possible to estimate the critical range at normal from the information given.

28. Changes in the armour of the enemy A.F.V.'s may cause the information to become obsolete and misleading. For example, there is at the time of writing a report that the Tiger has been strengthened, but what plates are affected and the amount of the strengthening, is not yet known.

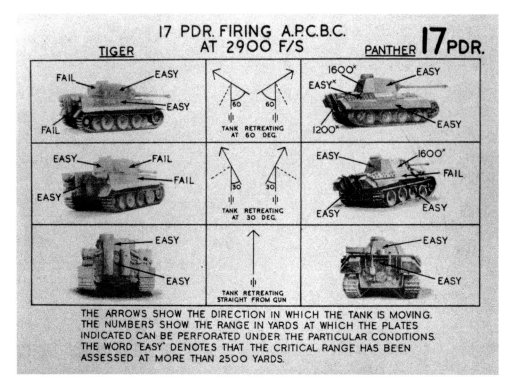

(*School of Tank Technology*)

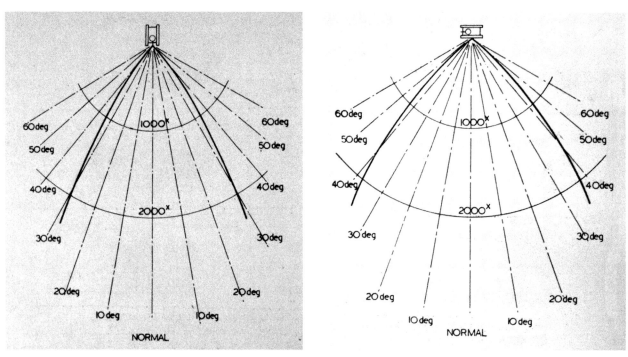

◀ Polar Diagram—17-pdr firing APCBC at 2,900 f.s. *v.* turret front of Tiger (Pz.Kw.VI) and Panther (Pz.Kw.V). Also driver's visor plate of Tiger. The 17-pdr is not expected to succeed against the glacis plate of Panther. (*School of Tank Technology*)

▶ Polar Diagram—17-pdr firing APCBC at 2,900 f.s. *v.* hull side superstructure and side and rear of Tiger (Pz.Kw.VI) and Panther (Pz.Kw.V). This diagram applies with reasonable accuracy to hull and rear of Tiger. (*School of Tank Technology*)

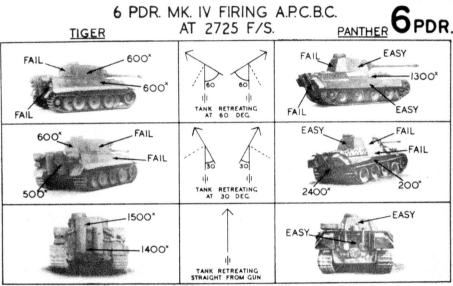

THE ARROWS SHOW THE DIRECTION IN WHICH THE TANK IS MOVING.
THE NUMBERS SHOW THE RANGE IN YARDS AT WHICH THE PLATES
INDICATED CAN BE PERFORATED UNDER THE PARTICULAR CONDITIONS.
THE WORD "EASY" DENOTES THAT THE CRITICAL RANGE HAS BEEN
ASSESSED AT MORE THAN 2500 YARDS.

(*School of Tank Technology*)

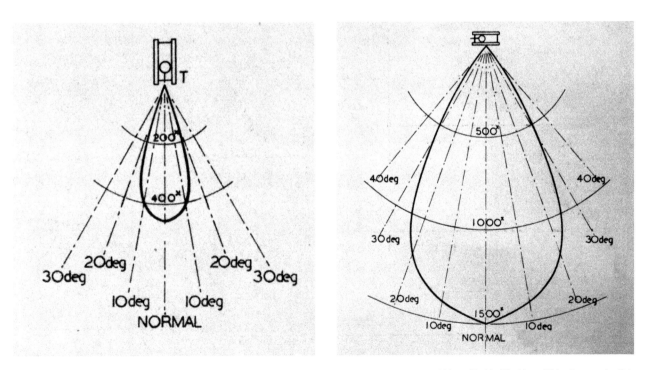

◀ Polar Diagram—6-pdr Mk IV firing APCBC at 2,725 f.s. *v.* driver's visor plate and front of turret of Tiger (Pz.Kw.VI). Note: This diagram for this projectile applies to the front of the turret of the Panther Pz.Kw.V. The shot cannot be expected to succeed against the glacis plate of Panther. (*School of Tank Technology*)

▶ Polar Diagram—6-pdr Mk IV firing APCBC at 2,725 f.s. *v.* side of hull superstructure and side and rear of turret of Tiger (Pz.Kw.VI). Note: This diagram applies with slight modifications to attack on hull rear of Tiger. (*School of Tank Technology*)

(*School of Tank Technology*)

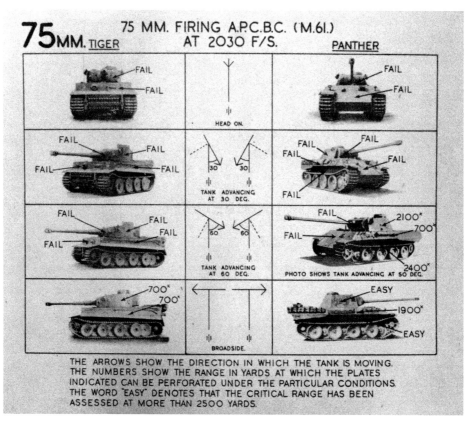

(*School of Tank Technology*)

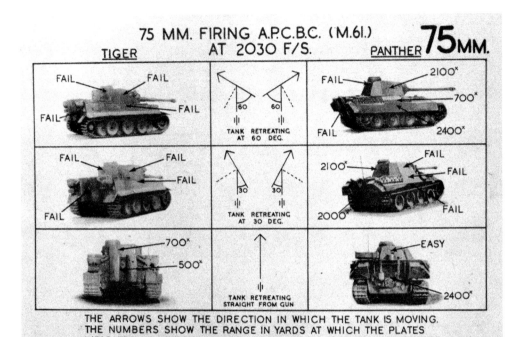

(*School of Tank Technology*)

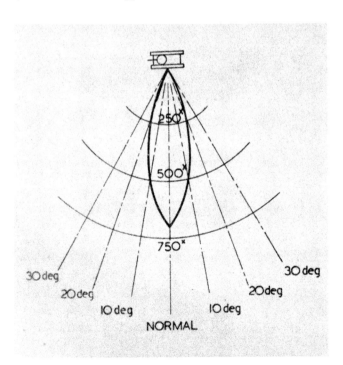

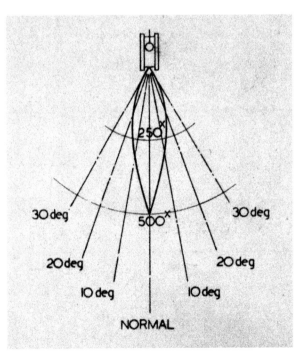

◀ Polar Diagram—75-mm M61 APCBC at 2,030 f.s. *v.* turret side and rear and hull side superstructure of Tiger (Pz.Kw.VI). It is not expected that the projectile will succeed against the front of either hull or turret of either Tiger or Panther. (*School of Tank Technology*)

▶ Polar Diagram—6-pdr Mk IV firing APCBC at 2,725 f.s. *v.* side of hull superstructure and side and rear of turret of Tiger (Pz.Kw.VI). Note: This diagram applies with slight modifications to attack on hull rear of Tiger. (*School of Tank Technology*)

(School of Tank Technology)

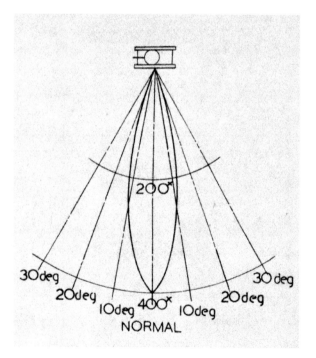

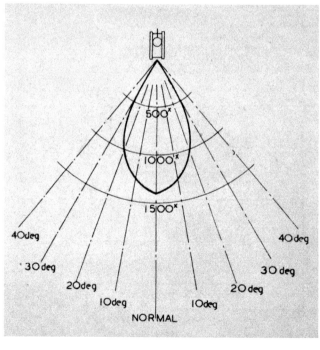

◀ Polar Diagram—37-mm M51 APCBC at 2,900 f.s. *v.* hull side superstructure and rear of turret of Tiger (Pz.Kw.VI). The projectile has a small chance against the hull side superstructure and the side and rear of the turret, but only at very short ranges and angles very near to normal. It has a similar, though smaller, chance against the rear of the hull. It is unlikely to perforate either the front of the turret or the front of the hull of this tank. There is a small strip between the side superstructure and the top of the bogy wheels where the shot will succeed at about 1,300 yards when the tank is broadside to the gun and at 500 yards when the tank is advancing or retreating at 60 degrees, but as a target, this area is very small. (*School of Tank Technology*)

▶ Polar Diagram—37-mm M51 APCBC at 2,900 f.s. *v.* hull rear of Panther (Pz.Kw.V). (*School of Tank Technology*)

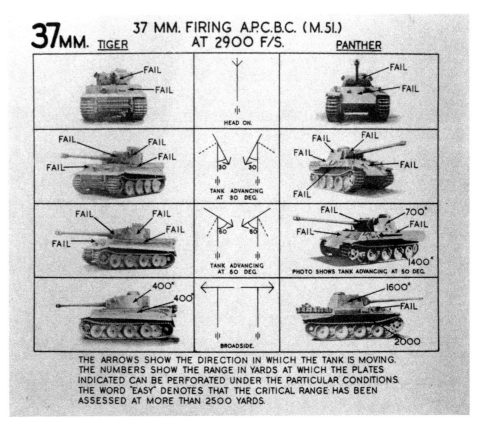

(School of Tank Technology)

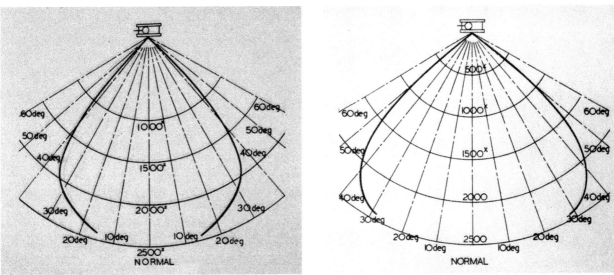

◀ Polar Diagram—75-mm M61 APCBC at 2,030 f.s. *v.* side and rear of turret of Panther (Pz.Kw.V). (*School of Tank Technology*)

▶ Polar Diagram—75-mm M61 APCBC at 2,030 f.s. *v.* hull side of Panther (Pz.Kw.V). (*School of Tank Technology*)

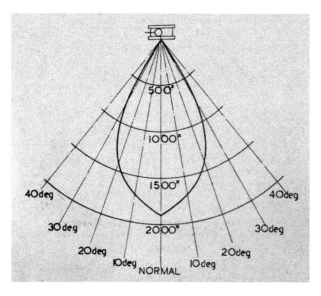

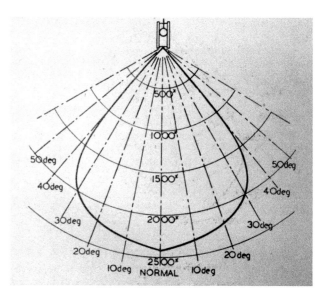

◀ Polar Diagram—75-mm M61 APCBC at 2,030 f.s. *v.* hull side superstructure of Panther (Pz.Kw.V). (*School of Tank Technology*)

▶ Polar Diagram—75-mm M61 APCBC at 2,030 f.s. *v.* hull rear of Panther (Pz.Kw.V). (*School of Tank Technology*)

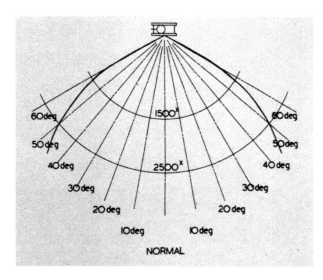

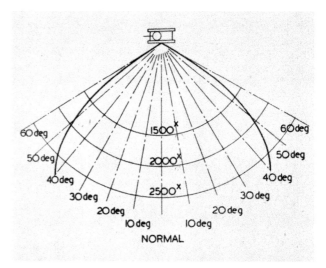

◀ Polar Diagram—3-inch M7 Gun M62 APCBC at 2,600 f.s. *v.* hull side of Panther (Pz.Kw.V). (*School of Tank Technology*)

▶ Polar Diagram—3-inch M7 Gun M62 APCBC at 2600 f.s. *v.* side and rear of turret of Panther (Pz.Kw.V). This diagram applies with reasonable accuracy to the attack of this projectile on the rear hull of Panther. (*School of Tank Technology*)

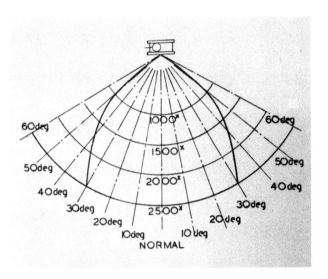
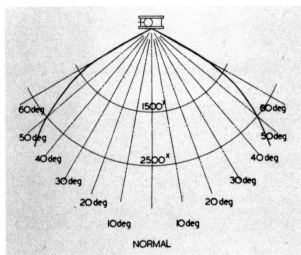

◄ Polar Diagram—3-inch M7 Gun M62 APCBC at 2,600 f.s. *v.* hull side superstructure of Panther (Pz.Kw.V). (*School of Tank Technology*)

❯ Polar Diagram—3-inch M7 Gun M62 APCBC at 2,600 f.s. *v.* hull side of Panther (Pz.Kw.V). (*School of Tank Technology*)

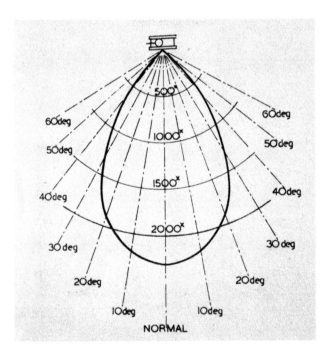
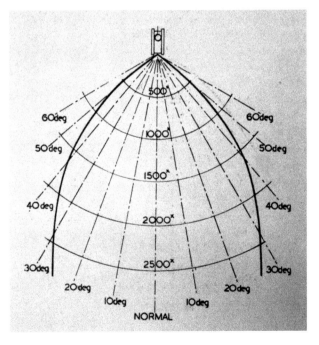

◄ A 6-pdr Mk IV firing APCBC at 2,725 f.s. *v.* hull side superstructure of Panther (Pz.Kw.V). (*School of Tank Technology*)

❯ A 6-pdr Mk IV firing APCBC at 2,725 f.s. *v.* hull rear of Panther (Pz.Kw.V). (*School of Tank Technology*)

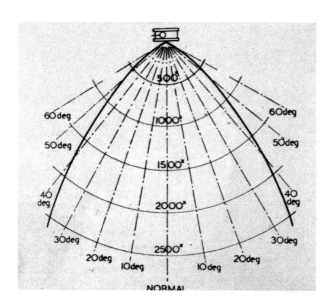

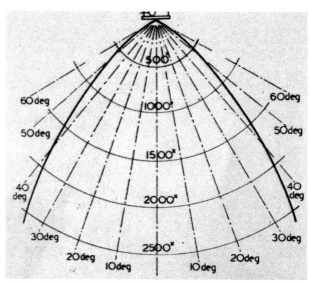

◀ A 6-pdr Mk IV firing APCBC at 2,725 f.s. *v.* side of turret of Panther (Pz.Kw.V). (*School of Tank Technology*)

▶ A 6-pdr Mk IV firing APCBC at 2,725 f.s. *v.* hull side of Panther (Pz.Kw.V). (*School of Tank Technology*)

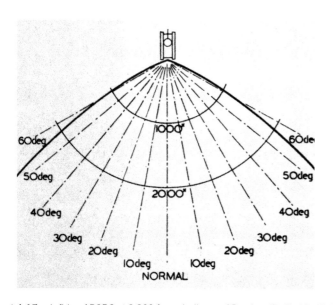

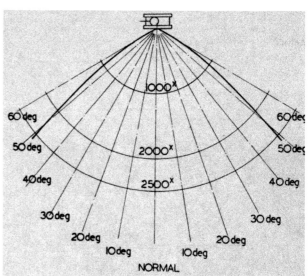

◀ A 17-pdr firing APCBC at 2,900 f.s. *v.* hull rear of Panther (Pz.Kw.V). (*School of Tank Technology*)

▶ A 17-pdr firing APCBC at 2,900 f.s. *v.* hull side superstructure of Panther (Pz.Kw.V). (*School of Tank Technology*)

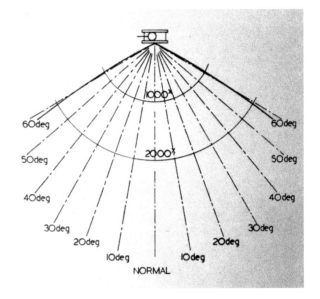

A 17-pdr firing APCBC at 2,900 f.s. *v.* side and rear of turret of Panther (Pz.Kw.V). It is expected that against the vertical hull side of Panther, the diagram will be similar, but that the 17-pdr will always fail at 70 degrees and will succeed against it at 60 degrees at any range at least up to 2,500 yards. (*School of Tank Technology*)

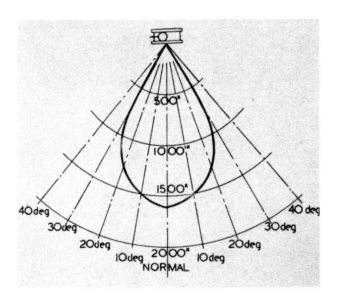

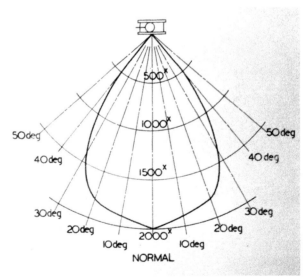

◄ A 37-mm M51 APCBC at 2,900 f.s. *v.* side and rear of turret of Panther (Pz.Kw.V). (*School of Tank Technology*)

▶ A 37-mm M51 APCBC at 2,900 f.s. *v.* hull side of Panther (Pz.Kw.V). This projectile is most unlikely to defeat either the glacis plate or the front of the turret of Panther, neither is it expected to succeed against the hull side superstructure. (*School of Tank Technology*)

8

US ARMY PAMPHLET: HOW TO KILL A PANTHER

The Ordinance Service, 1st US Army, produced a pamphlet called 'How to kill a Panther'. It was designed to fit into a tank crewman's uniform chest pocket. It was dated 28 December 1944. This example of the pamphlet belongs to Rob Cogan, Curator of the US Army Armor and Cavalry Collection and is reproduced here with his kind permission.

INTRODUCTION

Actual tests against captured German Mark V Panther tanks have definitely proven that it can be engaged by American tanks and tank destroyer guns and knocked out. Due to the fact that the Panther has 80 mm of armour plate in front, and a gun of extreme range and high muzzle velocity, every advantage of tactics must be utilised. Head-on engagements must be avoided if at all possible.

Contained in this pamphlet are the weapons, maximum range and aiming point of each at which the Panther can be knocked out. This document should be carried by all tank and anti-tank gunners until a thorough knowledge of the vulnerable points of fire and range are known. If the directions contained herein are followed, the Panther need not be deemed as superior or unconquerable.

NOTE: Red dots on the silhouette indicate aiming point. Reproduced by 654th Engineers. First U.S. Army, 1944.

Front cover of the 'restricted' Ordinance Service—1st US Army produced a pamphlet called 'How to kill a Panther'. (© *US Army Armor and Cavalry Collection*)

1. Will penetrate turret below shield or will ricochet downward through the top plate of hull: will penetrate sides of hull and turret: will penetrate rear of engine compartment or turret: will break track or suspension.

2. Will pierce front plate and jam final drive: will penetrate front belly plate: will break gun shield or penetrate the turret.

3. Will penetrate front plate, gun shield, turret or break track: will penetrate sides or rear. Range does not affect penetration: however, trajectory affects ability to aim.

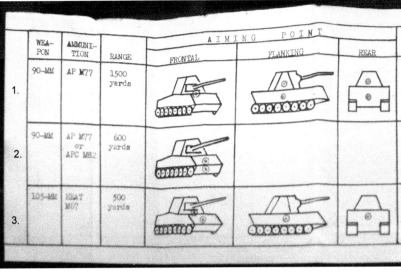

(© *US Army Armor and Cavalry Collection*)

4. Will penetrate sponson: lower hull side: turret side or rear and may jam suspension.

5. Will penetrate turret below gun shield.

6. Will penetrate gun shield and partially pierce the turret behind the shield. Will penetrate turret where not protected by gun shield.

(© *US Army Armor and Cavalry Collection*)

7. Will penetrate sponson: lower hull side; turret side; or rear. Will penetrate turret below gun shield or will ricochet downward through top plate of hull.

8. Will penetrate front belly plate.

9. Will penetrate front slope plate about 25 per cent of the time.

(© *US Army Armor and Cavalry Collection*)

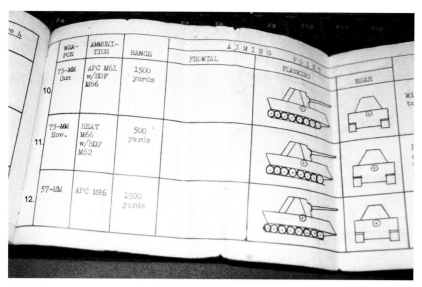

(© US Army Armor and Cavalry Collection)

10. Will penetrate sponson; lower hull side, turret side or rear: may jam suspension.

11. Penetrate will be affected wherever side armour is struck. Spaced armour, baggage containers or skirting may initiate detonation and protect the tank from full effects of the projectile.

12. Will penetrate sponson: lower hull side, turret side or rear.

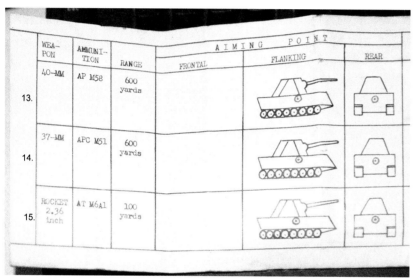

(© US Army Armor and Cavalry Collection)

13. Will penetrate sponson; lower hull side; turret side or rear.

14. Will penetrate sponson; lower hull side; turret side or rear.

15. Penetration will be effective wherever side armour is struck. Spaced armour, baggage containers or skirting may initiate detonation and protect the tank from full effects of the projectile.

16. Penetrate will be effected wherever side armour is struck. Spaced armour, baggage containers or skirting may initiate detonation and protect the tank from full effects of the projectile.

17. Top plate of tank or turret will be penetrated by grenade placed on top. Grenade will not adhere to side plates covered with anti-magnetic substance.

18. (1) Will sever tank track when track covers mine. It is recommended that 10 per cent of minefield be laid with double mines.

(2) The 'Daisy chain' is operated from concealed positions by pulling rope to place mines in immediate path of tank just prior to its arrival. An adequate warning system is necessary.

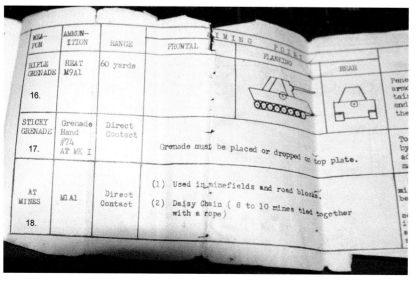

(© US Army Armor and Cavalry Collection)

9

PERFORMANCE TRIALS
AND WORKSHOP REPORT

Photograph of captured Panther Ausf. D tank 433 passing over the first ramp on the suspension course at the Fighting Vehicle Proving Establishment in Chobham, England. The tank was sent to Britain from Russia. This tank had the chassis number of 213101. It was one of thirty-six Panther tanks built by MNH (*Maschinenfabrik Niedersachsen* Hannover) in June 1943. The Panzer *Abteilung* 51 (51st Tank Battalion—Pz. Abt. 51) was reconstituted completely anew in July 1943 with ninety-six new Panther dispatched from the *Heeres Zeugamt*, 17–18 July 1944. Panther Ausf. D tank 433 was one of these ninety-six tanks. It was later captured by Soviet troops. The early Ausf. D models suffered from a number of mechanical problems. Many of these issues were resolved in later models of the Panther. This vehicle suffered from transmission problems during the tests; in particular, the third gear became inoperable. This was not an uncommon complaint regarding early Panther gearboxes. (*Fighting Vehicle Proving Establishment*)

Note: The information in this chapter has been transcribed from original wartime documents. The report format and brief notation style of writing has been kept.

DTD COVER SHEET AND JOINT FVPE/DTD
Conclusions to FVPE Reports NOS.FT.1391 and WS.413 on German (Pz.Kpfw) Panther

Origin
These trials were initiated by DTD in order to obtain Performance data on a Panther tank when running with various British and American machines.

Comment
It will be noted in the Field Trial report that the mileage recorded on the Panther prior to the performance trials was comparatively small. It was not possible to verify the actual figure; nevertheless, a considerable amount of repair and maintenance work was necessary to obtain the performance data. A total of 20 miles was covered by the machine during the trials. A transporter was used to convey the machine to the test courses in order that the performance figures could obtain under the most favourable conditions.

The behaviour of the engine did not permit a proper assessment of the vehicle's performance. It was evident that the engine was mechanically unsound and without adequate spare parts, it was not possible to restore the unit to a satisfactory standard, since certain of the engine components appeared to be of a sub-standard or obsolete type.

The almost complete lack of accessibility to the engine compartment rendered difficult the amount of maintenance the power unit required.

During the cross country trials, a fire occurred in the engine compartment and due to the considerable internal damage sustained the trials were abandoned.

Conclusions
The results of the trials on this single machine suggest that the Panther compares with British Tanks as follows:

Speed
Across country, the average speed is rather less than that of the Churchill VII. Note 3rd gear was not available on Panther. On roads the maximum speed has not yet been established but 30 mph is claimed by the Germans.

Reliability
The amount of mechanical trouble experienced on this trial suggest that the Panther compares very unfavourably with any British tank now in the service.

Suspension
Whilst the camera pitch records show a marked ability to damp out oscillations the opinion of all members of F.V.P.E Staff who have ridden across country on the tank is that the suspension is not good.

Further Action
Since the completion of these trials a later model of the Panther Tank has been received from Normandy, this machine will be submitted for performance trials as soon as possible.

This project will remain open until the new trials are completed.
(A.T. Sweeney)
Assistant Director (General Design)
(A. A. M. Durrant)
Director

Fighting Vehicles Proving Establishment Field Trials Report on German Panther (PzKw V)

FVPE Report No. F.T.1391
REFERENCE
DTD Project No. DE 9736
DTD File No. 160/78/7

Statement

Trials were undertaken in order to establish the performance of a German Panther tank in direct comparison with various British and American tanks. It was originally intended to include the Russian T.34, but this tank could not be made available.

A great deal of mechanical trouble has been experienced on the Panther during the trial but no attempt is made to give details of all the defects in this report.

The Panther has been seriously damaged by fire before the trials were completed. As there is no early prospect of completing the performance data this interim report is now published.

Conditions

Panther No. 213101 was received at F.V.P.E. from S.T.T. for these trials. The tank had originally been sent to this country from Russia. On receipt, the engine and steering system were found to be defective and were repaired and tested in F.V.P.E. Workshops report No. W.S.413.

The following tanks were run during these trials.

TANK	BATTLE WEIGHT	PREVIOUS MILEAGE
Panther	44 tons 5 cwts	Approx. 500 miles
Churchill VII	39 tons 10 cwts	3232 miles
T.14	43 tons 10 cwts	393 miles
Cromwell	28 tons 3 cwts	46 miles
Sherman II	30 tons 11 cwts	1821 miles
Comet	32 tons 13 cwts	1853 miles

Each tank was driven by an experienced F.V.P.E. driver.

Ground conditions throughout the trial were very dry, the Long Valley course offering extra dusty conditions.

The following tests were attempted in order named:

(a) 12 June 1944, Miles Hill slopes, Beacon Hill climb, and Ively Farm suspension course.

(b) 14 June 1944, Farnham Park Slopes, Ively Farm suspension course and Long Valley speed, fuel consumption, and cooling trials.

(c) 28 July 1944, Long Valley speed, fuel consumption and cooling trials.

Observations

12 June 1944

(a) Miles Hill Slopes (Gravel and Concrete)

Climbs of No. 4 slope (22.5 degrees) and Concrete 'A' (24 degrees) were attempted with the following results.

TANK	GEAR USED.	NO. 4 SLOPE	CONCRETE 'A'	REMARKS
Panther	1st	Successful	Successful	Engine misfiring slightly
T.14	1st	Successful	Not attempted	Prop shaft broke after climb of the slope
Churchill VII	1st 2nd	Successful Failed at 18 degrees	Successful	Lack of torque in 2nd gear
Sherman II	1st 2nd	Successful Failed 21 degrees	Failed	Track slip on concrete 'A' 19 feet from bottom of slope Lack of torque in 2nd gear

Cromwell (3.7:1 Final Drive Ratio)	1st 2nd	Successful Failed at 22 degrees	Failed	Track slip on concrete 'A' 31 feet from bottom of slope Lack of torque in 2nd gear
Cromwell (4.5:1 Final Drive Ratio)	2nd 3rd	Successful Failed at 22 degrees		Lack of torque in 3rd gear

Notes

(i) The second Cromwell with a 4.5:1 final drive ratio was used for comparative purposes on this test only.

(ii) Stop and restart tests were attempted by all tanks on No. 4 slope with the exception of Panther. As trouble with the hydraulic assistance to the steering had been experienced in was decided not to attempt this test with the Panther in order not to overload the hydraulic system which was found to be leaking badly at the rear swash pump.

(b) Flying Climbs of Beacon Hill

Two runs were made up the Hill with the Panther. Between runs the hydraulic reservoir had to be refilled, having emptied itself on each run. The engine was observed to be misfiring badly so that the results recorded below are not fully representative of the tanks true performance.

TANK	GEAR USED	AVERAGE SPEED
Panther	5, 4, 3	8.19 mph
Cromwell (3.7:1 Final Drive)	5 & 4	20.6 mph
Churchill VII	4 & 3	8.19 mph
Sherman II	4 & 3	10.4 mph

Before further trials were undertaken, work was done in F.V.P.E Workshops to cure the engine misfiring and leaking rear swash pump. Details of this work are contained in F.V.P.E. Workshops report No. W.S. 413.

14 June 1944

(a) Farnham Park Slopes

Trials were first carried out on the 35-degree grass slope, each tank climbing in 1st gear. Later attempting to climb up a 40-degree slope, the Panther stalled through lack of engine torque, (misfiring was again prevalent).

The tank ran backwards with the engine turning over in the reverse direction. When the tank reached the foot of the slope, an explosion occurred in the engine compartment, and a petrol fire was started around the petrol pumps at the front nearside corner of the engine. This was quickly put out with Pyrene fire extinguishers. The force of the explosion was sufficient to lift the engine compartment cover hatch, breaking the thermometer bracket above it. On examination of the engine, no serious defects were found as a result of the explosion and the tank continued its trials.

The results of the test are recorded below:

TANK	SLOPE	RESULT	REMARKS
Panther	35 degrees	Successful	
	40 degrees	Failed	Lack of torque, engine misfiring
T.14	34 degrees	Successful	
	35 degrees	Failed	Track slip
Comet	34 degrees	Successful	
	40 degrees	Failed	Track slip

(b) Ively Farm Suspension Course

The test here consisted of driving each tank over a ramp and sleepers at various speeds. A pitch and roll camera was fitted in turn to the top of the turret of each tank, and the time taken to cover the fixed length of the course recorded electrically. The speeds chosen for these tests were approximately 10, 15 and 20 mph for each tank. The results of these tests recorded by camera are shown graphically in an Appendix attached to this report. A photograph (No. 6331/8) showing the tank going over the first ramp of the suspension course is attached to this report.

During these tests with the Panther, the Belville washer travel stops of the drop arms of No. 7 road-wheel stations of both sides, broke away, the washers being scattered over the suspension course.

Although the pitch and roll records show that the Panther suspension damps out quicker than that of the other tanks tested, it was found that in cross country going it was harder than the others. The nose of the tank dipped right down until the front suspension was 'solid' when riding over the larger bumps, and this gave an uncomfortable ride for the crew.

(c) Long Valley fuel consumption test

Thermometers with remote reading dials were fitted as follows:

(i) To the inlet to the rear radiator on each side to record hot water temperature.

(ii) To the water header tank, to record cold water temperature.

(iii) To the inlet and outlet to the oil cooler, to record hot and cold engine oil temperatures respectively.

(iv) To the gearbox main filter cap to record transmission temperature.

Only two laps were completed before the trial was abandoned, due to the misfiring of the engine. This was now so prevalent that the speed and cross-country performance of the Panther was seriously affected. It was also found on the second lap that 3rd gear could not be retained, continual jumping out taking place. Up to the time of the publication of this report, this gearbox defect has not been investigated. On being loaded on to the transporter for the return to F.V.P.E. it was observed that steam was blowing from the off-side exhaust pipe.

(c) Long Valley fuel consumption test

Subsequently, the engine was removed from the tank in F.V.P.E. Workshops for examination and was found to be in need of major repairs. Details of the defects and the repair work carried out are contained in F.V.P.E. workshops Report No W. S. 413, 28 July 1944

After the Panther had been restored to running order, the speed, fuel consumption and cooling tests on Long Valley (2.8-mile course) were again attempted. The engine was now running evenly, the misfiring having been overcome. 3rd gear, however, was still defective and was not used on this trial.

After one lap had been completed a light misfiring developed on the 6/3 bank, but the performance of the tank was not seriously affected. The following speeds were recorded on the first lap for each tank:

Panther	9.5 mph
Churchill VII	10.2 mph
Comet	15.7 mph
Cromwell	16.4 mph

When another half lap had been run, the right-hand steering was in need of adjustment and the tank was halted and switched off. Simultaneously thick smoke filled the turret, coming from the engine compartment. A few seconds later, an explosion took place in the engine compartment, and the floor of the compartment was seen to be on fire. The probable cause of the fire is given in an Appendix attached to this report. The tank was burnt out and the trials on this machine abandoned.

(L.G. KIMBERLEY) Major
For O'Dye Field Trials
(W.P. MORROGH) Brigadier
Commandant, Fighting Vehicle Proving Establishment.

APPENDIX

Results of Workshop Investigations into Cause of Fire on Panther Tank PzKw V

The fire, which occurred after the engine had been switched off and backfired, started with an explosion in the engine compartment. The actual cause of the backfire is not known, but it is assumed that some incandescent substance, such as sparking plug points or a piece of carbon, provided the means of ignition. The very high compression ratio would render the engine more liable to reverse direction than would be experienced with orthodox practice. A backfire would cause petrol and oil vapour to be blown through the air cleaners, (oil bath type), which are situated centrally on the engine. The inlets to the air cleaners are underneath the unit, and oil and petrol vapour would be sprayed over the valve covers on to the exhaust manifold cowls which, with the engine hot, would ignite the vapour. The explosion was extremely heavy, and it is assumed that one of the flexible petrol pipes burst and the petrol caught fire.

10

PRELIMINARY REPORT ON ARMOUR QUALITY AND VULNERABILITY OF THE PANTHER TANK

Note: The information in this chapter has been transcribed from original wartime documents. The report format and brief notation style of writing has been kept.

Pzkw V (PANTHER)

Preliminary Report on Armour Quality and Vulnerability

Top Secret: Report No. M.6815A/3 No. 1

General

The report is based on an examination of Vehicle No. 213101 made available to the DTD on Monday 22nd instant.

Construction

The hull and turret are of a single skin all welded construction. The welding appears sound and adequate. The interlocking system of plate jointing as used on the PzKw VI has been generously employed. While not fitted on the present vehicle, provision has been made for fitting detachable skirting plates of some 6 mm in thickness to give cover to the vertical hull sides through their length and over a depth estimated to extend from the lower edge of the hull side superstructure to some six inches below the top of the bogie wheels.

Armour Quality

An appreciation of the quality of the armour, in so far as a superficial

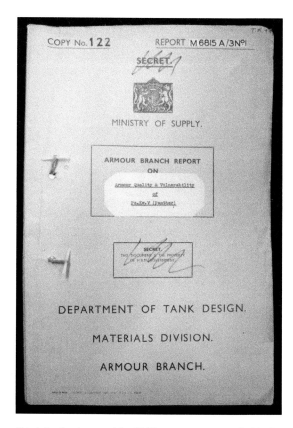

This is the front cover of the 1944 secret report compiled by the Department of Tank Design, Materials Division, Armour Branch's Preliminary Report on Armour Quality and Vulnerability of the Panther Tank. (*DTD Report M6815 A/3No. 1 Copy No. 122*)

examination would allow, is given in Part I of this report. From this, it will be noted that the armour is of the homogeneous type throughout, and in general, some 10 tons per square inch harder that the corresponding British type.

Reports from Russia (War Office Technical Intelligence Summary No. 126) had indicated that certain plates (including the glacis plate) had been of flame-hardened type, and as previously noted (DTD Report No. M6816A/2 No. 1.) it had always been considered that the analysis of the steel, now apparently used by Germany for the bulk production of tank armour, was chosen with this possible view. It must be assumed, therefore, that Panther (and probably Tiger) will variously contain flame-hardened and/or homogeneous armour.

Trials on Tiger armour (DTD Reports No. M.6816A/2 and M.6816A/4 No. 1), which is assumed to be of comparable quality to that used in Panthers have shown it to have variable ballistic properties, and, according to heat treatment, etc.. slightly superior, equal to, or inferior to British machineable quality.

Trials carried out on differentially-hardened British armour which may be assumed comparable with the German flame-hardened type (DTD Report No. M.6303A/6 No. 1) would indicate that the effect of the latter on British shot is not appreciably different from that of the homogeneous machineable variety. This test, not by any means conclusive, is the only evidence immediately available, and accordingly, in making the estimations as to vulnerability ranges against British weapons, the quality of the German Armour on Panther has been assumed to be equal to that of British machineable quality to Specifications I.T.89D.

Vulnerability

The vulnerability of Panther to British tank and anti-tank weapons is described in Part II and III of the report, the former dealing in detail with effective ranges and angles of attack, the latter with the effect on structure and personnel.

The information in these sections, although necessarily qualitative in nature, is considered to be reasonably reliable, and may, therefore, be used with some confidence in tactical considerations.

Some general observations relating to the vulnerability of Panther are noted below.

In the first place, it will be appreciated that a tank having the weight fire-power and speed characteristics of Panther cannot (with the existing state of the art and science of armour quality and disposition) profess all-round immunity to up-to-date anti-tank weapons. Faced with this problem the German designers have followed a course which we ourselves would recommend for a tank of this description, namely, make the hull and turret front immune as far as possible against most common anti-tank gun, and having decided from considerations of mine blast, HE attack, and structural strength, the thickness of the belly roof and rear plates, allot the remainder to the hull and turret sides.

The hull front of Panther, then, is immune to 6-pdr APCBC shot 75-mm APCBC M.61. shell. The turret front and gun mantlet (unless the latter is struck almost dead on its traverse centre line) are likewise immune. Further, the glacis plate covering the most vulnerable part of the hull front is nominally immune to 17-pdr APCBC shot. The gun mantlet, except when struck at normal within a few inches of either side of the transverse centre line, is likewise nominally immune to this latter attack.

Having regard to the above factors, therefore, frontal attack by our 6-pdr, 75-mm, and 17-pdr, weapons would normally be expected to be ineffective, but, as stressed in this report, a strike either by 6-pdr, 75-mm, or 17-pdr. Below the transverse centre line of the gun mantlet is, on account of the design adapted, likely to be deflected through the relatively thin hull roof, thus causing damage and casualties.

If 25-pdr or 105-mm HE shells are fired so as to detonate on the lower half of turret mantlet, it is considered that the weak roof structure over the driver's and co-driver's compartment would collapse to the extent of allowing dangerous blast to enter, and severely injure or kill the driver and co-driver.

It would seem, therefore, that from the point of view of a direct frontal attack, whether by AP or HE, the 'Achilles Heel' of the Panther is the relatively weak hull roof structure in combination with the peculiar design of the external mantlet.

The hull and turret sides of Panther, even having regard to the up-armouring of the front at their expense, appear weaker than would have been expected in a tank of its weight. The reasons for this are not readily forth-coming without a detailed weight distribution investigation, but the fact remains that the hull and turret sides are weak to 6-pdr, 75-mm, and 17-pdr attack, as will be seen from a study of the Vulnerable Range Table in Part II of the report.

In addition to the vulnerability of the hull sides per se, the danger of cordite fires arising from penetrations is high, since the ammunition is stowed unprotected in the panniers.

As noted in Part III, it cannot be said with certainty that British anti-tank mines Mk IV or Mk V. HC bursting singly under the tracks will immobilise the vehicle. Casualties to crew are not likely to result from such attack. On the other hand, two Mk IV or Mk V HC mines detonated simultaneously and bursting on the inner edge of the track would almost certainly immobilise the vehicle, and would probably rupture the belly plate.

Summing up, the following conclusion may be drawn from preliminary investigations which have been made as to vulnerability:

(1) The hull and turret front provide, as they were specifically designed to do, a high degree of protection to attack from current British tank and anti-tank weapons firing APCBC shot or HE shell. Accordingly, head-on attack, except by HE shell, should be avoided where possible. But if it must be undertaken, the principal weakness of the design should be exploited by concentrating fire on the area contained between the traverse centre line of the mantlet and the hull roof. Attack by HE shell is, in fact, likely to be most effective when directed at this area from direct or near direct ahead.

(2) AP attack should if possible be directed on the hull and turret sides, and should where possible be withheld in order that the angle of incidence favourable to the type of weapon and range, as indicated in Part II of the report, is obtained.

(3) Damage and casualties resulting from single standard British Mk IV or Mk V HC anti-tank mines bursting under the tracks is likely to be of a minor order. To be effective, it is considered that such mines should be laid in pairs, one above the other, so as to detonate simultaneously.

Fighting Qualities

A short appreciation of the fighting qualities of the Panther prepared by the Fighting Equipment Division of DTD is attached to this report.

A.T. Bowdon

Assistant Director (Armour)

A.A.M. Durrant

Director

DTD (Ascot 1160)

Chobham Lane, Chertsey. 24/5/44 DW. M.417(a)

Distribution

Immediate

CAFV	1
DGAFV	2
DDGFV(D)	3
DDAFV(T) (Cairo)	4
DTD	5
DD(Mats)	6
DD(F)	7
M/AQ.	8
DG of A	9
OB	10
DRAC	11
DMI	12

Future

As directed by DGAFV in consultation with DRAC

Preliminary Report of Armour Quality and Vulnerability of PzKw Mk V (Panther) examined at Chobham on May 22nd and 23rd 1944.

Report M6815A/3 No. 1.

Department of Tank Design

Armour Branch

Part I–Armour Quality

Introduction

Quality

Rolled Armour

Cast Armour

Discussion

Part II–Effective Ranges for Attack by British and Allied Tank and Anti-Tank Weapons

Part III–Effect of Attack on Structure and Personnel

APPENDICES

Part I–Armour Quality

Introduction

At this stage, the quality of the armour can only be inferred from tests made with a portable hardness tester, supplemented by information obtained from Russia, and from the results of the examination in Britain of plates from vehicles of other types.

On this vehicle, the turret front and gun mantlet are castings, the turret sides and turret roof are bent plates, and the remainder of the armour consists of flat plates, with the exception of the cupola, which may be casting or forging.

The first reports from Russia suggest that all the plate on this vehicle were of homogeneous machineable quality, but a later report stated that the superstructure side plates, the hull side plates and the lower front plates were face-hardened (presumably by flame-hardening). Tests with the portable hardness tester on the main plates accessible to the test on the vehicle now at the DTD have shown all the plates to be of homogeneous machineable quality.

Quality of Armour
(a) Rolled Armour
In the following table the important plates are shown in the order of increasing thickness, and for each thickness is given, (a), the actual thickness as measured on the vehicle at DTD, (b), the Brinell hardness as reported from Russia, (c), the Poldi hardness as actually measured on the vehicle at DTD, (d), the Poldi hardness corrected on the basis of the information previously obtained about the differences between Poldi tests and laboratory Brinell tests on the same plates, and, (s), the hardness that the plates would be expected to have from consideration of what has previously been found from a large number of laboratory tests on German machineable quality plate of different thickness.

	(A) ACTUAL THICKNESS	(B) RUSSIAN HARDNESS	(C) POLDI HARDNESS	(D) CORRECTED POLDI	(E) HARDNESS EXPECTED
Turret Roof	15 mm	313	307	337	305 – 410
Top Front	17 mm	298	313	343	345 – 405
Top Rear	17 mm	298	-	-	345 – 405
Belly Plate	18 mm Front 15 mm Rear	344 311	-	-	345 – 405
Superstructure Side	41.5 mm	F.H.*	320	350	325 – 385
Hull Side	42 mm	F.H.*	**	-	325 – 385
Tail Plate	43 mm	282	250	280	325 – 385
Turret Side	47 mm	308	285	315	320 – 380
Turret Rear	47 mm	300	272	302	320 – 380
Lower Front Plate	65 mm	F.H.*	276	306	305 – 365
Glacis Plate	84.5 mm	290	270	300	285 - 345

F.H.* means face-hardened.   ** Poldi hardness could not be measured accurately.

It will be seen that there is close agreement between the result in columns (d) and (e), and that the Russian results are rather lower. It is probably correct to infer from this table, (a), that the hardness ranges given in column (e) are the ranges within which the Germans work for plates of different thicknesses, (b), that the machineable quality plates of the Panther have been treated to hardness levels which conform to the usual German practice, and, (c), that in general, German machineable quality armour is about 40–50 points Brinell harder than British.

At a later stage, information about the chemical composition of the plates and the quality of the steel from which they are made will be obtained, but it is not likely that this will add anything to what can already be inferred about plate quality in relation to the Panther as a fighting vehicle. Experience has shown that the chemical composition of armour may be varied within wide limits without affecting the ballistic properties of plates made from steel of the same qualities and treated in the same way to the same final hardness. Enough information about German armour has been obtained to indicate the types of composition that are used, and to show that good quality steel is employed. Consequently, once it is known that the machineable quality plates on the Panther are treated to the same hardness levels as other German machineable plates which have been subjected to firing trials, the ballistic quality of the Panther plates can be inferred from previous results.

Practically all German armour examined in this country has had a substantially high carbon content than British and American armour, and recent analyses here and in America on plates from Tiger have shown that this high carbon content is being maintained since all the carbon contents were between 0.41 and 0.57 per cent. There are both advantages and disadvantages in the use of a high carbon content, but one important point, relevant to the present purpose, is that all German armour is suitable for flame-hardening. When The Tiger was first examined by DTD it was considered that although all the plates about which information was obtained were of homogeneous machineable quality, there was the possibility that on a proportion of the vehicles some flame-hardened plates would be used. Comparison of the information obtained from Russia about the Panther with that obtained at DTD shows that some Panthers have flame-hardened plates, while others have none, and the same may be true of the Tiger.

It has not been possible to carry out Poldi hardness tests on the belly plates, but the hardness values obtained from Russia, 311 – 344 Brinell, are probably substantially correct, and those show the belly plates to be substantially harder than those now being provided for British vehicles, i.e. 187 – 212 Brinell. It should be added that the belly plate on the Tiger had a hardness of about 330 Brinell.

(b) Cast Armour
The two castings on the Panther had the following hardness:

Turret Front   Poldi hardness 257   Corrected 287
Gun Mantlet   Poldi hardness 213   Corrected 243

The hardness of the turret front is within the range used in British armour castings; the mantlet was rather softer than British castings.

The cupola, which may be either a casting or a forging, had a Poldi hardness of 276 (corrected 306)

Discussion

With the exception of the turret front and gun mantlet which are castings, and the cupola, which may be a casting or forging, all the armour of the Panther tank examined at DTD is rolled plate of homogeneous machineable quality.

Tests carried out with a portable hardness tester on the main accessible plates, show that the hardness values of the plates are in the same ranges as those of German machineable quality plates previously examined.

As there is little likelihood that there is any feature of the composition or quality of the plates on the Panther which would make them differ substantially from German machineable plates previously examined and subjected to firing trials, it can be concluded with considerable assurance that the ballistic properties of the machineable quality plates on the Panther are of the same order as those of German machineable quality plates previously tested.

Practically all German armour examined in this country has had a higher carbon content than British or American armour, and the results of recent analysis in this country and America on plates from the Tiger have shown that the carbon content is being maintained in the range of 0.41–0.57 per cent. A flame-hardening, and although none of the Tiger plates which have been examined have been flame-hardened, it has been considered probable that a proportion of Tigers were fitted with some flame-hardened plates.

Although the Panther examined at DTD had no flame-hardened plates, the vehicle examined in Russia had certain flame-hardened plates. This indicates that some of the Panthers have flame-hardened plates and suggests that some of the Tigers may also be fitted with them.

One of the armour castings on the Panther had a similar hardness to the British armour castings, the other was softer.

The belly plates on the Panther are much harder, according to Russian information, than those now being provided for British tanks.

G. M. Robertson
O. i/c Armour Quality Section
DTD (Ascot 1160)
Chobham Lane, Chertsey.
24/5/1944.

Part II–Effective Ranges for Attack by British and Allied Tanks and Anti–Tank Weapons Armour on Kpfw V (Panther) Serial No. 213101

Introduction

1. This tank was examined at DTD, Chobham. Details of armour thicknesses and tilts were established as follows (see also attached sketch at Appendix A):

PLATE		TILT IN DEGREES	NOMINAL THICKNESS IN MM	ACTUAL THICKNESS IN MM
(1)		(2)	(3)	(4)
Hull:	Glacis	55	80	84-85
	Nose plate	55	60	63
	Superstructure side	40	40	42
	Lower side	0	40	42
	Rear	30	40	43
	Top	90	15	17
Turret:	Front	11	110	-
	Mantlet	Curved	100	102
	Sides	25	42	41
	Rear	25	42	-
	Top Front	83	15	17

Notes:

(a) The tilt of the plates as determined with a clinometer agrees with those given in the last report received from Russia. (War Office Technical Intelligence Summary, No. 126. 20 March 1944)

(b) The normal thickness at column (3) quoted are from the same Russian report.

(c) It was found impossible to determine the thickness of the turret front plate. Those thicknesses actually determined are shown in column (4).

2. Vulnerability of the armour

In the attached table are shown vulnerability figures of plates under varying conditions and weights of attack. The figure under each projectile show:

(a) The range at which the plate is vulnerable to normal attack, that is, to attack under the most unfavourable conditions from the point of view of the plate. In this case, the angle of attack is the same as the angle of tilt of the plate.

(b) The range at which the plate is vulnerable to an attack displaced from the normal through 30 degrees. The angle of impact on a vertical plate will be a compound angle formed by 30 degrees and the angle of tilt.

(c) The greatest angle from the normal at which the plate will be vulnerable to attack from a given range.

It is stressed that these figures are in most cases reasonably intelligent guesses, but some of them may be wrong by as much as 500 yards. Reliable figures can only be obtained by firing the projectiles against the plates *in situ*.

The guesses are based on:

(A) Thickness of the plates

The actual thicknesses given in section 1, column 4, show that these are liable to be some 5 per cent greater than the nominal thicknesses. It is presumed that the Germans have a thickness tolerance of this order. The vulnerable figures quoted are for the maximum thicknesses that the plates are likely to be with this tolerance.

(B) Type and quality of the armour

The Brinell hardness figures quoted in Part I of this report reveal that all the plates are of homogeneous machineable type, somewhat harder in general than the corresponding British type.

Trials carried out on Tiger armour showed it to have ballistic qualities which were, under varying conditions of attack, slightly superior, equal, or inferior to British armour of like type and so in the present analysis it has been assumed that the Panther offers, in general, resistance under all conditions of attack comparable to that of armour to Specification I.T. 80 D.

(C) Equipment, ammunition and muzzle velocities.

The figures are quoted for:

(1) 6-pdr, Mk II and IV, firing APCBC shot at MVs of 2,600 and 2,725 f.s. respectively.
(2) 75-mm M3 firing M.61 APCBC/HE at MV 2,050 f.s.
(3) 17-pdr firing APCBC shot at MV 2,900 f.s.

Vulnerable ranges for the 77-mm Firing APCBC Shot can be readily obtained by deducting 600 yards from the ranges quoted for the 17-pdr. The critical angles will be some 2–3 degrees less.

3. Vulnerability of the Hull and Turret Front

The immunity of the big frontal glacis plate to even 17-pdr APCBC attack presents a serious problem. There appear to be two possible solutions:

(a) Use of 17-pdr DS (Sabot) projectile. In a recent trial this projectile defeated an 80-mm I.T. 80 D plate at 50 degrees at a striking velocity of about 3,400 f.s., with no shot through. At high velocities, some portion of the shot went through. Though no official R/V figures have yet been issued, it is possible to estimate that the projectile will start driving out plugs at a range of 1,500–1,600 yards, attack being from direct ahead. There should be more lethal successes at ranges below 1,000 yards.

(b) Confine the attack to APCBC to the small areas that are vulnerable, that is, (1) the nose plate and (2) the area between the horizontal centre line of the mantlet and top of the hull.

This is illustrated in the sketch below.

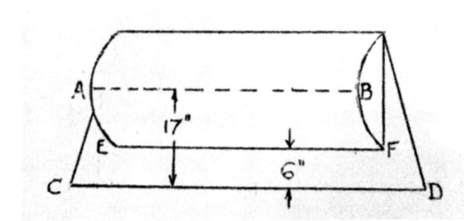

AB: horizontal centre line
of mantlet. CD: top of hull.
(*Department of Tank Design*)

The shot may do one of three things:

 (a) hit in the area close to AB. and so hole the mantlet.
 (b) ricochet from the area ABEF through the thin (15-mm) top plate of the hull.
 (c) hit in the area EFCD and so hole the turret plate and/or jam the turret ring.

It is considered that concentrated attack in this region has the best chance of disabling the tank.

 4. Air Attack

Beam attack obviously offers the best chance of success. The following conclusions were drawn from a recent Ordnance Board trial on a 45-mm plate at 40 degrees:–

 (a) 40-mm Class S shot will not defeat the plate at ranges over 400 yards. It will win at ranges up to 800 yards if the plane dives
    at 10 degrees.
 (b) The Littlejohn AP Mk II shot will defeat the plate at ranges up to 750 yards provided the attack is from dead abeam.
 (c) The 6-pdr APC will win up to ranges of 1,150 yards at angles from the beam to 40 degrees and up to ranges of 550 yards if the
    arc is increased to 50 degrees.

The actual targets on the tank, 42 mm at 40 degrees (Hull side Superstructure), 48 mm at 25 (turret side) are easier than the trial targets referred to above, and should therefore prove vulnerable at greater ranges than those indicated. The lower hull side plate, even though it may be fronted by a 5–6 mm skirting plate will be vulnerable to the 40-mm 'S' shot and to the 6-pdr APC over a wide arc of fire. There is insufficient data on which to assess the effectiveness of the Littlejohn AP Mk II against the same plate combination.

H. Harris-Jones Maj. R.A.
O. i/c Ballistics Section.
DTD (Ascot 1160)
Chobham Lane, Chertsey.
24/5/1944.
ID.

Pz.Kpfw.V. (Panther)

Based on Data Received from Russia.

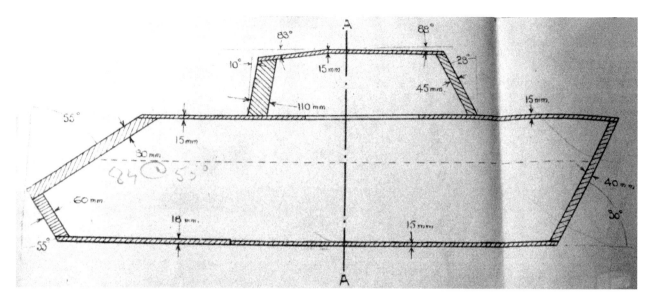

Pz.Kpfw.V. (Panther) based on data received from Russia, not to scale. Ref. MI 10 A/BM/3728. These details have been checked on a vehicle at DTD Chobham, 22 May 1944. Note: the original drawing included in the report was a poor copy. Recorded angles and thicknesses of the turret armour were hard to see and have been typed over in white for ease of reference. The centre line has a capital 'A' at the top and one of the bottom. This shows where the following cross-section AA diagram was taken from. (*Department of Tank Design 10.3.44 Armour Branch*)

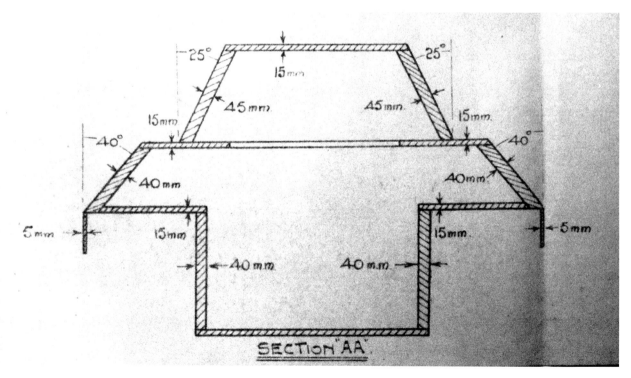

Cross-section AA Note. Thicknesses shown are nominal. Actual thicknesses are in general some 5 per cent more due to thickness tolerance. (*Department of Tank Design 10.3.44 Armour Branch*)

VULNERABLE RANGES OF GERMAN KPFW V. (PANTHER) VERSUS: **6-PDR APCBC MK IV GUN.**
MV 2,725 F.S.

Plate	Slope (degrees)	Nominal Thickness in mm	Actual Thickness in mm	N	30 degrees	Critical Angle at 750 yards Range (degrees)
Hull Front Glacis	55	80	84		Immune	
Hull Front Nose	55	60	63		Immune	
Hull Side Superstructure	40	40	42	>2,500	2,200	46
Hull Side Lower	Vertical	40	42	>2,500	>2,500	58
Hull Rear	30	40	42	>2,500	>2,500	52
Turret Front (Cast Armour)	11	110	115	220	Immune	-
Turret mantlet (Cast Armour)	Curved	100	102	1,250	Immune	15
Turret Sides and Rear	25	45	47	>2,500	2,400	48

VULNERABLE RANGES OF GERMAN KPFW V. (PANTHER) VERSUS: **6-PDR APCBC MK II GUN.**
MV 2600 F.S.

Plate	Slope (degrees)	Nominal Thickness in mm	Actual Thickness in mm	N	30 degrees	Critical Angle at 750 yards Range (degrees)
Hull Front Glacis	55	80	84		Immune	
Hull Front Nose	55	60	63		Immune	
Hull Side Superstructure	40	40	42	>2,500	1,900	42
Hull Side Lower	Vertical	40	42	>2,500	>2,500	55
Hull Rear	30	40	42	>2,500	2,400	48
Turret Front (Cast Armour)	11	110	115	Immune	Immune	-
Turret mantlet (Cast Armour)	Curved	100	102	1,000	Immune	-
Turret Sides and Rear	25	45	47	>2,500	220	44

VULNERABLE RANGES OF GERMAN KPFW V. (PANTHER) VERSUS: **17-PDR APCBC**

Plate	Slope (degrees)	Nominal Thickness in mm	Actual Thickness in mm	N	30 degrees	Critical Angle at 750 yards Range (degrees)
Hull Front Glacis	55	80	84		Immune	
Hull Front Nose	55	60	63	1,400	400	25
Hull Side Superstructure	40	40	42	>2,500	>2,500	56
Hull Side Lower	Vertical	40	42	>2,500	>2,500	65
Hull Rear	30	40	42	>2,500	>2,500	60
Turret Front (Cast Armour)	11	110	115	>2,500	1,600	33
Turret mantlet (Cast Armour)	Curved	100	102	>2,500	>2,500	37
Turret Sides and Rear	25	45	47	>2,500	>2,500	56

VULNERABLE RANGES OF GERMAN KPFW V. (PANTHER) VERSUS: **75-MM APCBC**
M.61

Plate	Slope (degrees)	Nominal Thickness in mm	Actual Thickness in mm	N	30 degrees	Critical Angle at 750 yards Range (degrees)
Hull Front Glacis	55	80	84		Immune	
Hull Front Nose	55	60	63		Immune	
Hull Side Superstructure	40	40	42	2,100	1,100	35
Hull Side Lower	Vertical	40	42	>2,500	>2,500	50

Hull Rear	30	40	42	>2,500	2,000	44
Turret Front (Cast Armour)	11	110	115	Immune	Immune	-
Turret mantlet (Cast Armour)	Curved	100	102	Immune	Immune	-
Turret Sides and Rear	25	45	47	2,500	1,700	40

Part III—Effect of Attack on Structure and Personnel Offensive Weapons Considered

(a) Small Arms up to 15-mm Besa.
(b) 25-pdr, 105-mm HE Airburst.
(c) 25-pdr, 105-mm HE Contact Burst.
(d) 6-pdr, 17-pdr APCBC
(e) Mortar Bombs 4.2-inch
(f) Land Mines A/T Mk V HC

Observations Regarding Vulnerability

(a) Small Arms Attack
Protection offered by fittings against this attack is good, and casualties to crew by splash entry would be rare. Frontal attack with Ball ammunition on the underside of the turret gun mantlet and flank attack on the rear edges of the mantlet are most likely to cause splash entry, but accurate shooting would be necessary, and in the former, attack would have to be made from a height of at least 6 feet.

SAAP would be ineffective except against periscope prisms above the driver's position and those in the commander's cupola. 15-mm Besa attack would be mainly ineffective, although with accurate shooting at close range the turret could be jammed by shots directed at the bottom edge. The machine-gun in the turret could be put out of action by a shot striking the muzzle.

(b) HE Airburst
It would appear that the only areas on the roof of the vehicle vulnerable to this form of attack are the air inlet and outlet louvres set in the engine compartment roof, and occupying 35 per cent of its total area.

The engine compartment is divided into three sections by two bulkheads running fore and aft; the centre watertight compartment houses the engine, and each outer section, two water radiators and fuel tanks. In the roof of each outer section, at the front and the rear, are rectangular air inlet grilles, and at the centre is the circular air outlet grille, beneath which is a circulating fan. The radiators are set vertically between the inlet and the outlet grilles, the airflow being directed through them by means of curved ducts below the inlets, and expelled through the centre outlet. Fuel tanks are located in the panniers and below the radiators and apparently extend for the full length of the engine compartment.

It is thus apparent that fragments from HE airbursts (25-pdr and 105-mm) Occurring at heights between 10 and 30 feet, or possibly higher, may enter the grilles and cause damage to radiators or fuel tanks. Fragments from bursts occurring below 10 feet are unlikely to enter the grilles unless the point of detonation is on or immediately above the hull roof.

It is improbable that the tank would be put out of action immediately by any damage to the radiators or the fuel tanks, which could be caused as a result of HE airbursts. It is considered that fire risk from this form of attack is slight.

(c) Contact HE
With the tank advancing head-on, HE Attack would be effective if directed on the lower half of the turret gun mantlet. This attack on the upper half would probably be ineffective. 25-pdr HE detonations occurring within a height of 12 inches above the hull roof would result in extensive dishing of the roof plate and in considerable admission of blast below the escape doors. There is little doubt that the driver and the co-driver would become casualties.

It is also probable that the turret would be jammed as the result of shell fragments lodging in the clearance between the turret bottom and the hull roof.

Attack with 105-mm HE in the same position would result in still heavier damage to the roof. Should strikes occur with either 25-pdr or 105-mm. HE below the mantlet close to the hull roof, the roof would be holed or blown in, and it is considered that the majority of the crew would become casualties either from blast fragments, or both.

Attack against the turret cupola with 25-pdr HE would probably result in the dislodgement of the outer armour ring and would most certainly rupture the roof, causing casualties in the fighting compartment. A similar attack with 105-mm HE would cause more serious damage.

With the hull broadside on and without outer skirting plates, attack opposite the driver's and the fighting compartments, between the upper length of track and the floor of the sponson, would be effective in bursting open the weld joint between the side plate and the sponson bottom. The resulting admission of blast may cause casualties to the crew in the vicinity.

Should the vehicle be fitted with skirting plates, HE will detonate on the faces of these plates and would not be effective.

The track is sufficiently robust to withstand HE attack of this nature, and it is considered that although it would not be completely severed, it would be damaged locally.

The radiators and petrol tanks located within the rear engine compartment are likely to be seriously damaged by blast or shell fragments resulting from detonation of 25-pdr HE against the turret site in the vicinity of the forward air louvres.

It is considered that a detonation of this kind occurring within 6 inches of the hull roof would cause sufficient damage to eventually stop the vehicle.

(d) AP Attack

The underside of the turret gun mantlet would appear to be the most vulnerable position for frontal attack to be made with either 6-pdr or 17-pdr. Shots striking here are liable to be deflected downwards and penetrate the hull roof causing casualties in the fighting compartment.

Shots directed against the side of the gun mantlet would cause such damage as to render the mounting unserviceable. There is ample evidence to indicate that even relatively light impacts directed at the side of the gun mantlet would jam the elevating movement.

17-pdr attack directed into the corner of the re-entrant angles of each side of the gun mantlet even from extreme ranges would penetrate, causing heavy damage and casualties.

Attack from either 6-pdr or 17-pdr on the bottom of the turret sides would cause jamming of the traverse by bulging the lower edge of the armour into contact with the hull roof.

With the tank advancing at angles of between 30 and 60 degrees to gun normal, attack by either 6-pdr or 17-pdr in the corner of the pocket at each side of the hull nose would damage the final drive, affect the steering and possibly immobilise the vehicle.

The front of the vehicle gives a high standard of immunity to AP Attack, whilst that of the sides is relatively low. The ranges at which penetration from AP projectiles occur are detailed fully in Part II of this report.

The brief statement given above is intended to emphasise certain structural features which are known to be weak when subjected to AP attack.

(e) 4.2-inch Mortar Bomb

The side plates of the vehicle are capable of withstanding an attack with 4.2-inch Mortar Bombs. Should these bombs detonate on the turret sides near to the hull roof this would most likely be ruptured by blast.

Direct hits upon the hull roof, engine covers, or turret top, including the cupola, would probably result in serious plate rupture and entry of blast and fragments.

It is unlikely that hits upon the tracks and suspension would completely immobilise the vehicle.

(f) British A/T. Mines

The Panther as examined is equipped with 26-inch wide tracks, join together with pins through for lugs on the one side and five mugs on the other, which allows the pins to take the shear through eight sections. The drive is through twin sprockets engaging the tracks at one quarter their width from the centre line.

The belly plates measured 18 mm at the front and 15 mm at the rear and had a ground clearance of 21.5 inches at the rear and 22 inches at the front. The horizontal distance from the inner edge of the track to the side of the hull is 2.25 inches, and the side plates are 42 mm thick. All plates adjacent to the belly plate are welded to it, and the junction between the side and belly plates is such that each plate is cut back alternatively so as to allow them to interlock.

Torsion bars for the suspension are carried across the full width of the vehicle clear of the floor. At the forward and a relatively small stiffener is carried across the floor, but it would require some stripping of the vehicle to obtain full details. The driver's seat is not fitted direct to the floorplate and is well above it.

A British Mk V HC A/T Mine detonated under an outer edge of the tracks is not likely to completely cut the belt, although a piece would be blown out. It is probable that half would remain in a driveable condition and on account of the disposition of the driving sprockets the tension on this from the drive would be fairly evenly distributed. It cannot be definitely stated that at any point a single Mk V HC A/T Mine would be sure of completely severing the track, since tracks of this width have not yet been subjected to trial. Damage to the road-wheels is not likely to immobilise the vehicle.

There would be no effect upon the belly plate from single Mk V HC A/T Mines detonating under the tracks, except in the case of those under the inner edge when a slight bulge might be caused, but it is most unlikely that the plate would fracture. Mines detonating under the centre line of the vehicle from a position slightly below the level of tracks would induce at least a permanent bulge in the plates, but would not be certain of fracturing them. In suitable material, a fracture would be unlikely, and the torsion bars would tend to restrict the extent of the bulging.

The effect of the Mk V HC A/T Mines in pairs, detonated simultaneously under the tracks would be likely to completely sever the belt, and the same charge would seriously overmatch the belly plate if detonated well underneath it.

The good ground clearance and medium thickness belly plates give good protection against the single British Mk V HC A/T Mine, and the wide tracks make it possible for some single mines to be detonated without immobilising the vehicle. Mk V HC A/T Mines in pairs would be likely to immobilise the vehicle. Similar results would be obtained from Mk IV Mines, but Mk V Mines L.C. would not be effective.

(g) Air Attack

The air inlet and outlet louvres in the engine compartment roof appear to be the most vulnerable areas against small arms attack (up to 20 mm) from the air. Otherwise, the roof of both the turret and hull are proof.

Absence of first-hand experience of this attack, however, renders it impossible to offer any reliable data.

Effect of Attack on Internal Fittings and Personnel

All internal fittings and small stowage items are mounted on frames made from the steel strip 24 mm × 3 mm thick, with the exception of the switch box between the driver's and co-driver's compartments. These strips are welded directly to the roof to support roof fittings and the side frames are welded to the roof and floor, leaving a gap of 16 mm between the frame and the side plates. This resilient mounting makes the fittings immune from displacement, except where complete penetration of the side armour occurs. The only week attachment is the hull nose where a large switch box is suspended from the hull roof, between the escape hatches, by a rolled steel angle to which the switch box is bolted. Detonation of 25-pdr HE on the turret front will undoubtedly dislodge this.

Ammunition for the 75-mm gun is stowed in the panniers and in the vacant floor space between the turntable and the fighting compartment walls. Shells in the panniers are stowed horizontally and held in position by wooden battens and those on the hull floor are vertically supported by wooden frames. Heavy impact on the pannier side may break the fixings of these battens and free the ammunition. If skirting plates were not fitted the detonation of 25-pdr HE under the pannier floor would have a similar effect.

Fire Risks–Cordite and Fuel

Cordite

As indicated in section (d) of this report, the side armour can be penetrated by both 6-pdr and 17-pdr AP.

All ammunition is stowed unprotected, those in the panniers being stacked horizontally and shells on the turret turntable vertically.

It is difficult to conceive how a cordite fire could be avoided if the side armour of the fighting compartment is penetrated by AP.

Petrol

The fuel tanks are situated on either side of the engine compartment under the radiator and are completely partitioned off from the rest of the vehicle by bulkheads. They can only be punctured after penetration of the side armour, and even then no fuel will enter the other parts of the vehicle unless the bulkheads are also penetrated.

There is a fire extinguisher located against the bulkhead in the fighting compartment which is thermostatically controlled and will operate immediately if fire breaks out in the engine compartment.

The vehicle is well designed against an outbreak of fire. Should fire occur, it is probable that the extinguisher would be effective. The layout of the engine compartment is such that with engines stopped, there is insufficient air to support combustion.

Discussion

It may be stated with reasonable certainty that the hull roof forward of the turret gun mantlet is ballistically weak and if subjected to AP attack by shots deflected off the lower side of the mantlet plate or by HE shell directed into the pocket formed by the outer mantlet and the hull roof, the results obtained would, it is considered, be effective in mobilising the vehicle and causing serious casualties to members of the crew.

This vehicle could not be employed tactically by advancing it through, and HE barrage designed to keep British AT gunners to earth, without serious risk of immobilisation. The vulnerability of the radiators and fuel tanks renders its use in this role hazardous, as serious damage is liable to be caused to both radiators and petrol tanks through, HE splinters entering the air inlet and outlet ducts. Further, the vulnerability of these ducks to contact HE bursting on the rear of the turret has been stressed in this report.

The protection afforded by the frontal armour of this machine is of a high order. Penetration of the side armour of the fighting compartment by AP projectiles will no doubt result in cordite fires. Owing to the excellent design layout of the engine compartment, however, it is improbable that petrol fires would be of a serious nature and it is quite possible that the fire extinguishers provided would be able to cope with any outbreaks.

The enemy have taken considerable care to avoid the direct attachment of fittings to the inner armour face. It is therefore unlikely that internal fittings will be dislodged under attack.

Provision is made for the attachment of external skirting plates at each side. With these in place, HE against the hull side will be ineffective. Without these, however, HE detonating against the side below the pannier will burst a length of side weld admitting blasts. Resultant damage to the track is not likely to be so serious as to immobilise the vehicle.

It is considered that the roof structure of both hull and turret would be vulnerable to attack by the 4.2-inch mortar bomb. Such bombs detonating on the sides of the hull, however, would be unlikely to cause serious damage.

It can be stated with reasonable certainty that one British Mk V HC A/T mine detonating under either track or belly would be ineffective.

To such mines, detonating in parallel below the inner edge of the track will probably rupture the belly and casualties may result. Should these mines detonate under the track centre or at the outer edge, it is considered that no serious damage would result to the hull structure, although the vehicle may be immobilised owing to damage to track and suspension.

G. Guthrie, Major, R.E.M.E.
Officer i/c Armour Trials Section
Armour Branch
DTD (Ascot 1160)
Chobham Lane,
Chertsey
24.5.1944

PzKw V (PANTHER): APPENDIX A

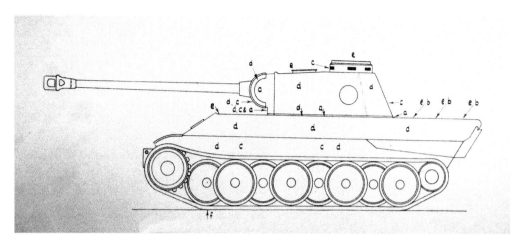

Letters have been used to indicate the vulnerable parts of the tank and by what type of weapon as follows: a—small arms up to 15-mm BESA; b—25-pdr, 105-mm HE airburst; c—25-pdr, 105-mm HE contact burst; d—6-pdr, 17-pdr APCBC; e—mortar bomb 4.2-inch; and f—land mine: AT Mk V HC. (*Department of Tank Design*)

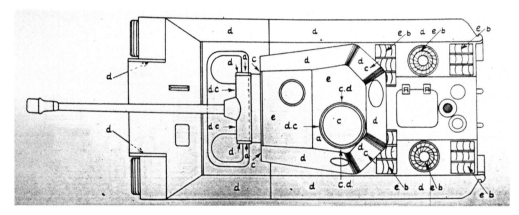

Letters have been used to indicate the vulnerable parts of the tank and by what type of weapon as follows: a—small arms up to 15-mm BESA; b—25-pdr, 105-mm HE airburst; c—25-pdr, 105-mm HE contact burst; d—6-pdr, 17-pdr APCBC; e—mortar bomb 4.2-inch; and f—land mine: AT Mk V HC. (*Department of Tank Design*)

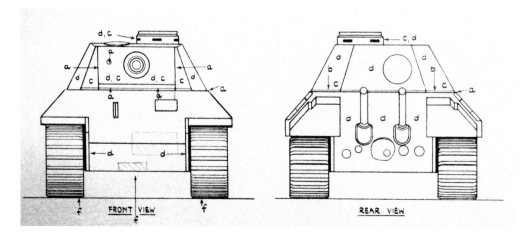

Letters have been used to indicate the vulnerable parts of the tank and by what type of weapon as follows: a—small arms up to 15 mm BESA; b—25-pdr, 105-mm HE airburst; c—25-pdr, 105-mm HE contact burst; d—6-pdr, 17-pdr APCBC; e—mortar bomb 4.2-inch; and f—land mine: AT Mk V HC. (*Department of Tank Design*)

PzKw V (PANTHER): APPENDIX B

Fig. 1: Right-side three-quarter front view of Panther 433 at the Fighting Vehicle Proving Establishment, Chobham, England. (*Department of Tank Design*)

‹ Fig. 2: Front view of Panther 433 at the Fighting Vehicle Proving Establishment, Chobham, England. (*Department of Tank Design*)

› Fig. 3: Left-side three-quarter front view of Panther 433 at the Fighting Vehicle Proving Establishment, Chobham, England. (*Department of Tank Design*)

Fig. 4: Left-side view of Panther 433 at the Fighting Vehicle Proving Establishment, Chobham, England. (*Department of Tank Design*)

❮ Fig. 5: Rear view of Panther 433 at the Fighting Vehicle Proving Establishment, Chobham, England. (*Department of Tank Design*)

❯ Fig. 6: Right-side view of Panther 433 at the Fighting Vehicle Proving Establishment, Chobham, England. (*Department of Tank Design*)

Fig. 7: Left-side rear view of turret of Panther 433 at the Fighting Vehicle Proving Establishment, Chobham, England. (Department of Tank Design)

◀ Fig. 8: Left-side rear view of engine compartment roof of Panther 433 at the Fighting Vehicle Proving Establishment, Chobham, England. (*Department of Tank Design*)

▶ Fig. 9: Internal view of turret front of Panther 433 at the Fighting Vehicle Proving Establishment, Chobham, England. (*Department of Tank Design*)

◀ Fig. 10: Internal view of left side of turret of Panther 433 at the Fighting Vehicle Proving Establishment, Chobham, England. (*Department of Tank Design*)

▶ Fig. 11: Internal view of escape door in turret rear of Panther 433 at the Fighting Vehicle Proving Establishment, Chobham, England. (*Department of Tank Design*)

Fig. 12: Internal view of left side of the driver's compartment of Panther 433 at the Fighting Vehicle Proving Establishment, Chobham, England. Note the pressed steel cross girder supporting tank top. (*Department of Tank Design*)

◀ Fig. 13: Internal view of ammunition stowage arrangements in the left-side pannier of Panther 433 at the Fighting Vehicle Proving Establishment, Chobham, England. (*Department of Tank Design*)

▶ Fig. 14: Internal view of ammunition stowage arrangements in right side pannier in fighting compartment of Panther 433 at the Fighting Vehicle Proving Establishment, Chobham, England. (*Department of Tank Design*)

Showing Panther Tank tilted 30 degrees for attacks on turret and hull roofs. Firing point is on a railway truck 10 meters away on the left. (*O.G.44/ PC(T)32E. Report Number A.T.320 Photograph No. 3. (18232/B.2) Department of Tank Design*)

View of turret and engine compartment roofs before attack. (*O.G.44/PC(T)32E. Report Number A.T.320 Photograph No. 4. (18232/B.3) Department of Tank Design*)

11

PANTHER, BRIEF NOTES ON FIGHTING QUALITIES: DTD FIGHTING EQUIPMENT DIVISION

Note: The information in this chapter has been transcribed from original wartime documents. The report format and brief notation style of writing has been kept.

The vehicle available is neither complete enough nor insufficient good condition to enable anything very definite regarding fighting qualities to be given. The following, however, constitutes a summary of notable features –

(A) RATE OF FIRE

The turret ring is only 66 inches clear, which does not give much space for the turret crew. As in Tiger, the loader is fairly well off, but the commander and layer are pretty badly cramped. It is estimated that a rate of fire of roughly 8 rounds per minute could be maintained up to about 10 rounds, when the difficulty of filling up from stowage would cause a slowing up. It is noted that there are 10 ready rounds positioned near the loader with gun pointing forward, in addition there are 26 rounds which could be considered 'ready' when the gun is in other positions. The remaining rounds are clamped down in the panniers. The loader's position appears to be comfortable and, when the rounds in the panniers are conveniently situated in relation to the turret, loading is easy.

It is observed that very little deflector guard is provided on the loader's side, and the design would definitely be considered dangerous in British vehicles.

(B) ELEVATING GEAR

This is so stiff that it is almost impossible to operate, and the gun feels very much out of balance, but there may be damage to the mounting. The rate of elevation is 2 ½ turns of the handwheel for 1. There is no sign of any balancing gear for the mounting.

(C) MANTLET AND FRONT PLATE

This appears very vulnerable to jamming by crossfire. There is some kind of gear behind the mantlet, the function of which we are unable to ascertain, but it would appear to be a wadding seal which can be screwed into position. The design of the mantlet provides a bad pocket for HE between the mantlet and hull top.

(D) TRAVERSE GEAR

The power traverse for this tank is in an unusable condition. The rate appears to be about 2.5 turns of the handwheel per degree of traverse. A shaft with universal joints is carried across under the mounting for the layer's side to a duplicate handle for the loader. This arrangement, combined with a very large well attached elevating gear, robs the loader of much space.

(E) TRAVELLING LOCK IN ELEVATION

This does not appear good and fails to rigidly lock the gun to the turret. The design appears to be as complicated as it is ineffective.

(F) FIRING GEAR

Electrical (primer) operated from elevating handwheel through the loader's safety switch. Foot mechanical firing is provided for the machine gun. The layer's seat and sighting gear are missing and it is therefore impossible to give an opinion on this aspect.

(G) AIR BLAST

Pipes are provided around the breech ring which are coupled up to the output of a small belt-driven compressor through an air bottle. Parts are missing, but the function of this equipment would appear to be on the same lines as those we are developing from British A.F.Vs.

(H) STOWAGE

This would appear to be about 48 rounds. The stowage bins are not armoured.

(I) VISION

All-round vision cupola seems to provide the only means of vision. The glass blocks of this are only 5 inches above the rooftop but, since the cupola is located well to the nearside, the offside at its best position must be blind for some 54 feet. The all-round vision cupola appears to be the same as that on Tiger, and generally speaking, vision from it is poor as regards fields of view.

(J) ESCAPE DOORS

Facilities for escape are scarcely up to British standards. Doors in the all-round vision cupola are reasonably big. The only other means of escape is through the circular door in the back of the turret. The fact that this is sloping greatly facilitates movement through it.

(K) SIGHTING

There is no sighting equipment left in the machine. Direct sighting would appear to be provided by the usual by knocking the telescopes. There was nothing to indicate how to lay indirect for elevation, but possibly an arc like the Tiger may have been fitted.

The remains of the traverse indicator exist, which had two dials. It is smaller than the British instrument.

The commander's cupola is marked in clock hours from 1 - 12, with quarter divisions between the hours.

G. Wilks
Deputy Director
Fighting Equipment Division
DTD
Chertsey, Surrey,
24/5/1944
DA 454(s)

12

REPORT OF COMPREHENSIVE FIRING TRIALS AGAINST THE GERMAN PANTHER PzKw V

Note: The information in this chapter has been transcribed from original wartime documents. The report format and brief notation style of writing has been kept.

SECRET
Department of Tank Design,
Materials Division,
Armour Branch Report AT No. 232 Parts I IV

Project Nos.M.6815A/4

Subject
Comprehensive Firing Trials against German Panther.
PzKw V.

Origin
The trials were originated by the Armour Branch of the Department of Tank Design.

Remarks
A. Three vehicles were used during the trials, all the ballistic trials being directed against a Model G. Panther.

The trial was carried out in four parts, and weapons and ammunition used wore as follows:-

Part I.	.303-inch Rifle	Ball and AP
	20-mm Hispano	AP
	25-pdr	HE (air-burst)
Part II.	6-pdr	APCBC; APDS
	17-pdr	APCBC; APDS; AP
	75-mm	APCBCHE; HE
	25-pdr	HE (Direct hits)
	PIAT	3.5 lb
	AT Grenade Mine	No. 75 (used as mine)
	AT Mine	Mk V HC (Standard)
Part III.	6-pdr	AP; APC

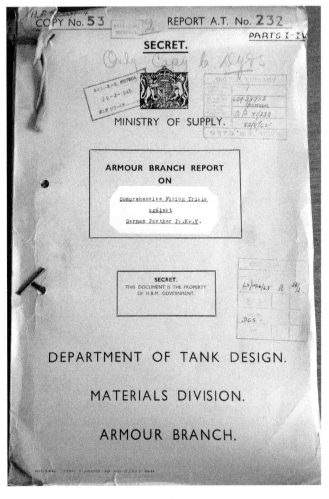

This is the front cover of the 1945 secret report compiled by the Department of Tank Design, Materials Division, Armour Branch Report of Comprehensive Firing trials against the German Panther tank. This copy came from the DCS—DHQ Pretoria, South Africa. (*DGTD Shelf number A.P. 71/232 22/8/45 Class number 629.229 × 2—DTD Report A.T. No. 232 Copy No. 53*)

	17-pdr	AP
	AT Grenade Mine	No. 75 (used as grenade)
Part IV.	AT Mines	4 lb (non-detectable)
		Mk V (reduced depth)
		Mk V HC (standard)
		5.5 lb (Asbestos Cement)
		10 lb
		15 lb

For the attacks in Parts III and IV, and the 20-mm attack, the vehicles used were stripped of engines and equipment.

B. Results may be summarized briefly as follows:

1. The vehicle is virtually immune to small arms fire from ground level.
2. Small arms attack directed downward at 30 degrees into the inlet louvres of the engine compartment causes severe damage to radiators.
3. Even more severe damage to the radiators may result from 20-mm attack from the air or from fragments of HE shell bursting in the air above the vehicle or against the turret above the engine compartment roof.
4. Projectiles of calibre 6-pdr and upwards, whether AP or HE, which strike below the horizontal centre line of the gun mantlet, are likely to penetrate or blow in the roof of the driving compartment and may jam the turret traverse.
5. Penetrations through the sides of the vehicle will very probably cause cordite or petrol fires.
6. The rolled armour proved brittle and flaky.
7. The use of interlocking joints provides a structure which has considerable stability even when the main welds are fractured.
8. The brittle nature of the roof plates makes these vulnerable to attack from HE grenades or shell which burst in contact with or within a few inches of the plate.
9. Frontal attack with PIAT is unprofitable, flank attack against pannier (or turret) is effective.
10. Mine with explosive charges between 4 and 15 lb are likely to break the track if detonated at the centre of its width, but may not do so if detonated by its edge. Detonations under any part of the track are unlikely to affect the floorplates or their joints with the hull side.
11. It is probable that a combination of three No. 75 grenade mines will have an effect on the tract similar to that produced by a single Mk V HC (Standard) AT mine. Either will break the track when detonated below the middle third of the track. Fuller discussion of the above conclusions will be found in the various parts of this report.

C. The trial has confirmed in general the assessment of vulnerability given in DTD Report No. M.6815A/3 No. 1, differences between certain predicted vulnerable ranges and actual results being due to the brittle nature of the armour. Though evidence is available that many Panther tanks damaged in battle have had armour which has shown similar defects, it should be not be assumed that this form of weakness will always exist.

The design of the vehicle is such that its structural stability is considerable; the effective use of interlocking joints being chiefly responsible.

The Panther tank, judged on the results of this trial alone, remains a most formidable weapon with few weaknesses: and its value if used with adequate flank protection should not be underrated.

A.T. Bowden
Assistant Director (Armour)
A.A.M. Durrant
Director
12.1.1945

DTD EXPERIMENTAL REPORT
AT No. 232
Part 1

Project No: M.6815A/4.
Trial Nos: X.789, X.616.
File No: 250/14/5.

Report of firing trial against PzKw V (Panther) held at S. of E. Range, Shoeburyness, on 11, 12 and 13 October and 27 November 1944.

Present at Trial

Name	Representing	Date Present Oct	Nov
Mr. Sankey	DTD (Armour Branch)	11 and 12.	
Mr. Cole	DTD (Armour Branch)	12 and 13.	
Mr. Wilde	DTD (Armour Branch)	11, 12 and 13.	27
Mr. Gray	DTD (Armour Branch)	11, 12 and 13.	27
Lieut. Tredinnick	of E. Range Officer	11, 12 and 13.	27
Range Personnel			

Report

Complied by: -	Mr. G.W. Gray	DTD (Armour Branch)
	Mr. M. D. Wilds	DTD (Armour Branch)
Checked by:-	Major G. Guthrie R.E.M.E.	DTD (Armour Branch)
	Mr. J.B. Sankey	DTD (Armour Branch)

References

Section I.	Object of Trial
Section II.	Target Details
Section III.	Method of Attack
Section IV.	Small Arms Attack
	(a) 0.303-inch Ball and AP
	(b) Conclusions from this attack
Section V.	Airburst HE
	(a) 25-pdr HE attack
	(b) Conclusions from this attack
Section VI.	Air AP
	(a) 20-mm AP attack
	(b) Conclusions from this attack

Appendices

Appendix A.	Detailed Results.
Appendix B.	Photographic Record.

NOTE

This report must not be reproduced in full or in part without the written authority of the Director of Tank Design.

SECTION I

Object of Trial

1. To determine the degree of immunity of various fitments against 0.303-inch ball and AP attack.
2. To determine the effect of 25-pdr HE Airburst against the engine cooling radiators.
3. To determine the effect of 20-mm AP on the hull roof and the engine cooling radiators.

SECTION II

Target Details

PzKw V (Panther) Tank DTD No. 3040 complete, but less stowage. Vehicle in running condition. Fuel tanks were approximately half full.

SECTION III

Method of Attack

1. Small Arms

Various details were attacked with 0.303-inch ball, full-service charges at angles calculated to give the least resistance to splash entry. 0.303-inch AP full-service charge was also used for attack against certain details, to obtain a measure of their immunity to jamming.

2. Airburst HE

25-pdr HE shell (Charge II) TNT filled, were detonated at heights of approximately 5 feet, 13 feet, and 23 feet, above the forward louvres, and in positions forward of the engine covers, as would ensure that the maximum zone of fragmentation was over the engine air louvres. Diagrams 1 and 2 in Section V show how the attack was carried out.

The means used for detonating the shell was wooden boards 3 feet square 1 inch thick, slung by means of wire cables from tubular steel towers erected at a suitable distance either side of the target.

3. Air Attack AP

In order to simulate attack by aircraft, the Engine Air Louvres, and engine roof, were attacked with 20-mm AP full-service charge from an angle of 27 degrees above the horizontal.

SECTION IV

Small Arms Attack

Two items were omitted from those attacked, for the following reasons.

A periscope for the Driver's position was not available. The turret Cupola hatch was jammed in a partially open position.

(a) 0.303-inch Ball and AP

1. Co-Driver's MG Ball Mounting.
    Attack by 0.303-inch Ball, disclosed only very slight marking of the witness cards and in no way affected the function of the mounting.
    0.303-inch AP attack against the mounting in an attempt to cause jamming failed.
2. 75-mm Gun—Annulus between Barrel and Mantlet.
    Splash from 0.303-inch Ball entering is not likely to cause damage to the mounting or harm to the crew.
3. 75-mm Gun Mantlet. Clearance Between Moving and Fixed Cheeks.
    0.303-inch Ball splash entered opposite the right-hand trunnion cheeks, causing two slight perforations, and slightly marked the witness card.
    0.303-inch AP directed into this clearance failed to join the mantlet.
4. Turret Escape Door.
    The witness card in this case was severely torn and perforated adjacent to the edge of the aperture by 0.303-inch Ball splash which entered freely.

It was noted after this attack that the door did not fit closely and it is thought that the catch worked slightly loose.

5. Turret fan Cowl.

Attack with 0.303-inch Ball against rear half of the cowl did not cause any splash entry into the turret.

6. Co-Driver's Hatch.

Slight lead splash entered and marked the witness card when .303-inch ball impinged on the edge of hatch cover, but this would not give any trouble.

7. Turret Ring.

0.303-inch Ball caused a very slight dusting of the witness cards. When the attack was directed at the clearance between the turret and hull roof.

0.303-inch AP attack showed the turret ring to be immune from jamming.

8. Hull Fan Cowl. (Intake full open)

The only effect of 0.303-inch Ball against this detail was to slightly mark the witness card.

(b). Conclusion from Small Arms Attack.

Splash (0.303-inch Ball)

It is concluded that the extent of splash entry, with one exception, is too slight to cause any damage, or inconvenience to the crew.

This exception is the turret escape door which allowed free entry. It should be borne in mind, however, that this door was not a good fit on its seating.

AP (0.303-inch)

Generally, jamming of the gun Mantlet, turret traverse and the m.g. mounting, would not be likely, although core fragments may possibly enter the turret ring.

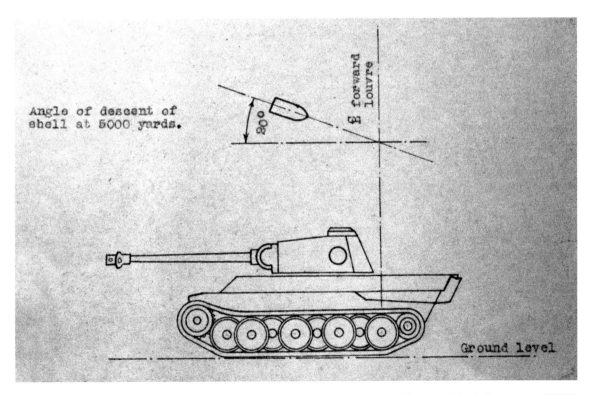

Diagram 1 indicates the angle at which the tank was set in order to simulate the angle of descent of the shell at a range of 5,000 yards. (*Department of Tank Design*)

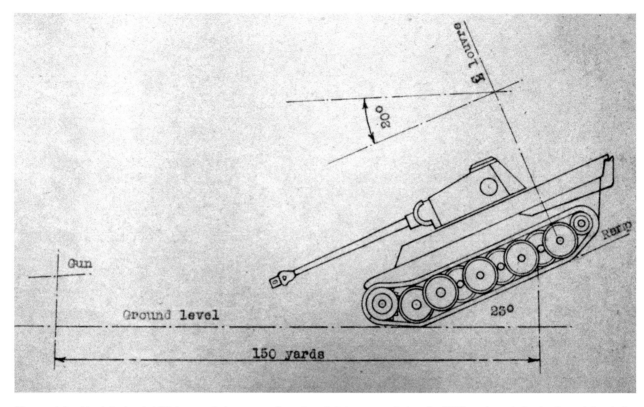

Diagram 1 (part two): tank set at 23 degrees, being a mean figure to suit distance, gun to target, of 150 yards, and allowing for variation in the inclination of line of flight to suit heights of 5 feet, 13 feet, and 23 feet above the forward louvres. (*Department of Tank Design*)

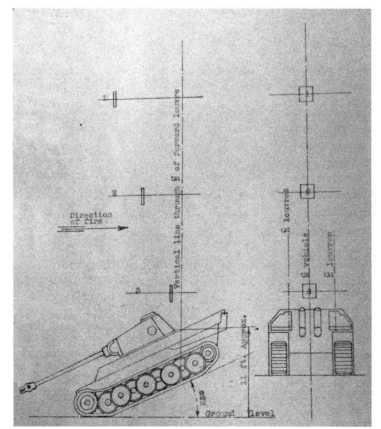

Diagram 2 indicates the points of burst in relation to the louvres. The position of the boards in the direction of the line of fire was derived from the results obtained during Trial X.581 reported under A.T.164, Part II, and was used as a guide for this attack. (*Department of Tank Design*)

Diagram 2 Key

Position of Burst	Height above louvre	Distance forward of louvre
1	23 feet	10 feet
2	13 feet	6 feet
3	5 feet	2 feet

SECTION V

Airburst HE Attack

25-pdr HE (Charge II) was fired from a range of 150 yards and detonated above the tank, so that fragments would enter the air louvres.

Diagram I and II indicate the conditions required to be met, with the tank advancing and at a range of 5,000 yards.

The tank engine was not running during the attack, but an estimate of the effect on the engine from attack given.

(a) 25-pdr HE Attack

Position 1. Burster Board 23 Feet Above Louvre

Round 1 detonating 10 feet in front of the forward louvres failed to penetrate the radiators. Round 2 detonating 11 feet in front caused several perforations in forward and rear radiators. The loss of water would have caused over-heating and ultimate stoppage.

Position 2. Burster Board 13 Feet Above Louvre

Round 3 detonating 6 feet in front of the forward louvres, caused extensive damage to the forward left-hand radiator, with consequent free leakage of water. The remaining radiators were not further damaged. Ultimate stoppage of the engine would have been caused by this attack.

Position 3. Burster Board 5 Feet Above Louvre

Round 4 detonating 2 feet in front of the forward louvre caused only one perforation of the forward right-hand radiator. Over-heating would have resulted with possible engine stoppage. Round 5 detonating 1 foot in front produced further perforation of both of the forward radiators causing extensive damage, with considerable water loss. The engine would quickly have over-heated and stopped.

The results are summarised as follows:-

SUMMARY OF RESULTS

Tank: On ramp—nose down, and front-facing gun. Angle on ramp 23 degrees to horizontal.

Airburst Attack:- 25-pdr HE TNT filled. Charge II adjusted. Fuse 119. Range 150 yards.

Round No.	POSITION OF BURSTER BOARD. Height above forward louvre.	POSITION OF BURSTER BOARD. Distance forward of louvre.	Damage to louvre, Guide vanes etc.	Damage to radiators, fuel tanks, etc.	Effect on tank.
1.	23 feet	10 feet	1 severe strike on left-hand circular outlet grille.	Nil.	Nil.
2.	23 feet	11 feet	2 strikes on rear left-hand inlet grille. 3 strikes on forward left-hand radiator grille. 1 large strike on left-hand circular outlet grille. Right-hand fan one blade perforated.	1 perforation in rear left-hand radiator. Five perforations in forward left-hand side cooling radiator. Water leaking from four perforations. 1 perforation in rear right-hand radiator - forward right-hand side radiator not leaking. 3 perforations in rear right-hand radiator caused by fragments entering right-hand circular outlet grille.	Engine would have overheated and ultimately stopped.
3.	13 feet	6 feet		2 perforations in forward left-hand radiator—largest 3 inches and 2.5 inches. Water leaking freely.	Engine would have overheated and ultimately stopped.

4.	5 feet	2 feet	2 strikes on forward left-hand grille. 4 strikes on forward right-hand grille. 1 strike on right-hand circular outlet grille. 1 strike on left-hand circular outlet grille. four perforations of guide vanes - forward right-hand grille. Some strikes on left-hand forward grille guide vanes.	1 perforation in forward right-hand radiator.	Engine would have overheated after a time and possibly stopped.
5.	5 feet	1 foot	Heavy pitting of forward intake grilles. 1 strike on each circular outlet grille. 2 strikes on rear right-hand intake grille.	Several fragments entered forward intake grilles and perforated radiators. Extensive water leakage.	Engine would have overheated and quickly stopped.

(b) Conclusion from Airburst Attack

It is concluded that the water-cooling system is vulnerable to 25-pdr HE airburst, and that damage to the radiator is liable to occur from detonations occurring within the range of positions selected for this trial.

The degree of vulnerability for each height is difficult to define, but evidence points to heights above the louvre within 13 feet as being the most likely to cause extensive damage radiator perforation.

The loss of cooling water would be such that it is doubtful whether the tank could continue to run other than a short time.

SECTION VI

Air AP Attack (Tank No. 3041)

(a) 20-mm AP Attack

The attack was directed from an angle of 27 degrees above the horizontal against the engine cooling system grilles and engine covers.

It should be noted that no engine radiators or fans were in position but substantial witness cards were fitted in these positions and the probable damage to the system estimated therefrom.

1. Left-handed rear intake grille.

Round 1 striking this grille sheared away two transverse crossbars. Extensive perforation of the witness card representing the rear radiator resulted. Considerable water loss would have been caused with ultimate engine stoppage.

Round 2 striking the same grille caused extensive perforation of the witness cards representing the forward and rear radiators. In the case of the forward card it is thought that with the fan in position damage may not have resulted. The results from this round would have been similar to those from round 1.

2. Left-hand front intake grille.

Round 5 striking this grille, sheared out metal and caused extensive perforation of the rear card. This damage was comparable to that caused by attack against the rear grille and confirmed the vulnerability of the system.

3. Left-hand fan grille.

Two rounds against this grille indicated that fragments are liable to perforate both the front and rear radiators. But to a less degree.

4. Right-hand rear intake grille.

One round of crossfire to endeavour to obtain strikes on the petrol tank failed to cause anything greater than shallow strikes on the rear end of the right-hand tank.

5. Engine roof covers (17 mm thick).

Five rounds directed against the roof showed the plate to be immune to 20-mm attack at this angle and only slight local damage was caused.

(b) Conclusion from 20-mm AP Attack

It is concluded that the water cooling system is vulnerable to attack from 20-mm AP directed into the cooling system grilles from an angle of 27 degrees above the horizontal and considerable damage to the radiators with consequent water loss would result, causing the ultimate stoppage of the engine.

G. Guthrie, Major, R.E.M.E.
O. i/c Armour Trials Section,
Armour Branch.
12.1.45
OWG/YC
GB.

APPENDIX A: TRIAL NO. X.816

Detailed Results: 20-mm Air Attack

TARGET	ATTACK	OBSERVATIONS
Tank No. 3041 on ramp. Rear of tank to gun. Left side air intakes and fan. Cards fitted in positions normally occupied by radiator.	20-mm Hispano AP Mk II. FSC At 27 degrees above horizontal. Range 30 feet	
Rear Intake.	Round 1	Two transverse bars from grille broken away. Left-hand petrol tank untouched. Shot penetrated first bar (11/16) thick and struck second bar. Both bars recovered below grille each in two pieces. 20 perforations on witness card. Largest perforation 0.5 × 0.25 inches—most of which would have struck on radiator tubes. Considerable loss of water would have resulted. Engine would ultimately have stopped. Fuel tank intact.
Rear Intake.	Ditto. Round 2	Shot struck fourth crossbar scooping out metal and carried witness card severely torn and perforated. Top right-hand corner perforated over area 4 × 0.375 inches max. Lower main perforation 2 × 0.25 inches. Sixteen other perforations. Most would have perforated radiator and considerable loss of water would have resulted with ultimate stoppage of engine. Front card torn in two places and perforated in three places. Main perforation 1 × 0.25 inches in top right-hand corner. With fan normally in position the extent to which this damage would have taken place is unknown. Fuel tank intact.
Tank No. 3041 on ramp. Rear of tank to gun. Left-hand front intake.	Round 3. 20-mm Hispano AP Mk II. FSC At 27 degrees above horizontal. Range 30 feet	Struck back bar and passed through into fighting compartment. Witness card not affected.
Tank No. 3041 on ramp. Rear of tank to gun. Left-hand front intake.	Round 4. 20-mm Hispano AP Mk II. FSC At 27 degrees above horizontal. Range 30 feet	Struck top edge of crossbar and passed through shot hole of round 3.
	Round 5.	Struck third central crossbar shearing metal 3 × 1.5 inches. 18 perforations on witness card. Largest 0.5 × 0.375 inches. Radiator would have been perforated resulting in considerable loss of water and ultimate stoppage of engine. Fuel tank intact.
Tank No. 3041 on ramp Rear of tank to gun. Left-hand fan grille. Cards fitted in positions normally occupied by radiator.	Round 6. 20-mm Hispano AP Mk II. FSC At 27 degrees above horizontal. Range 30 feet	Struck centre circumferential bar and perforated same and entered fan hub casting. Two strikes on rear card, one strike on front card.
	Round 7.	Both cards unmarked. Struck central circumferential bar and struck fan hub casting. Fuel tank intact.
Tank No. 3041 on ramp. Rear of tank to gun. Engine roof cover (17 mm)	Round 8. 20-mm Hispano AP Mk II. FSC At 27 degrees above horizontal. Range 30 feet	Code B. Roof not defeated.

	Round 9.	Code B. Struck weld joint between water filler cover and hull roof. Split in throat of weld 9 inches long.
	Round 10.	Code B. Scoop on engine cover.
	Round 11.	Code B. Struck engine hatch lower hinge shearing out one rivet and metal from hinge block over 1 × 0.5 inches.
Tank No. 3041 on ramp. Rear of tank to gun. Right-hand rear intake. Attack against right-hand petrol tank.	Round 12. 20-mm Hispano AP Mk II. FSC At 27 degrees above horizontal. Range 30 feet	Numerous shallow strikes on rear end of Petrol tank, no perforations.

APPENDIX B: TRIAL NO. X.789

AT No. 232: Part I: PzKw V Panther

Small Arms Attack

Front three-quarter view of vehicle in position in butt before attack. (*Department of Tank Design*)

Rear three-quarter view of vehicle in position in butt before attack. (*Department of Tank Design*)

 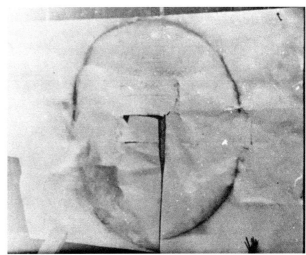

◀ Item No. 2: Showing 0.303-inch ball attack on 75-mm gun aperture. Seven rounds effective. No splash entered. (*Department of Tank Design*)

▶ Item No. 4: 0.303-inch ball attack at normal against turret escape door, showing condition of witness card fitted behind door. Note: Splash entered freely, tearing and marking card. (*Department of Tank Design*)

◀ Item No. 10: Showing 0.303-inch ball attack against hull fan cowl. Four rounds effective. No splash entered. (*Department of Tank Design*)

▶ Item No. 11: Showing 0.303-inch AP attack at 20 degrees to normal against turret gun mantlet side. (*Department of Tank Design*)

Airburst HE Attack

Showing vehicle in position on ramp. (*Department of Tank Design*)

> View from rear of ramp, showing vehicle on ramp and burster board in position above. Burster boards are sheets of wood suspended in the air at set heights that when hit by a shell explode it to simulate an airburst. (*Department of Tank Design*)

< Round two: Burster board 23 feet above and 11 feet forward of louvre, showing perforations in forward left-hand side radiator. (*Department of Tank Design*)

Round two: Burster board 23 feet above and 11 feet forward of louvre, showing perforations in the rear left-hand radiator and guide vanes. (*Department of Tank Design*)

Round five: Burster board 5 feet above and 1 foot forward of louvre, showing strikes on forward left-hand inlet louvre and perforations in guide vanes. (*Department of Tank Design*)

Round five: Burster board 5 feet above and 1 foot forward of louvre, showing strikes on forward right-hand inlet louvre. (*Department of Tank Design*)

20-mm Hispano Attack

Showing engine compartment roof after attack with 20-mm Hispano A.P. from 27 degrees above horizontal. (*Department of Tank Design*)

Showing damage to rear left-hand inlet louvre caused by 20-mm Hispano AP rounds one and two. (*Department of Tank Design*)

Showing condition of rear left-hand witness card
representing radiator after round one.
(*Department of Tank Design*)

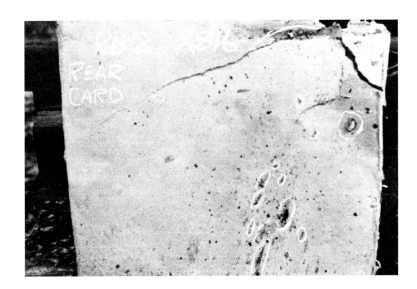

Showing condition of rear left-hand witness card
representing radiator after round two.
(*Department of Tank Design*)

Showing condition of front left-hand witness card
representing radiator after round two.
(*Department of Tank Design*)

Showing damage to forward left-hand louvre caused by 20-mm Hispano AP rounds three, four, and five. (*Department of Tank Design*)

Showing damage to forward left-hand louvre caused by 20-mm Hispano AP rounds three, four, and five. (*Department of Tank Design*)

Showing damage to left-hand circular outlet louvre caused by 20-mm Hispano AP rounds six and seven. Witness card only slightly marked. (*Department of Tank Design*)

DTD EXPERIMENTAL REPORT

AT No. 232: Part II

Project No: M.6815A/4
Sheet 2.
Trial No: X.794
File No: 250/14/5

REPORT OF FIRING TRIAL

Against PzKw V (Model G.) DTD No. 3040 held at Shoeburyness Range on October 16–20 1944.

Present at Trial	Representing	Date attended
Lt. Tredinnick	of E.	All dates.
Col. McNair	Ordnance Board	18.10.44
Capt. Martin	C.E.A.D.	19.10.44
Capt. Ryan	A.3.	19.10.44
Mr. Service	Messrs. Wm. Beardmore & Co. Ltd	17.10.44
Major Fowler	DTD Welding Branch	18.10.44
Mr. Redhead	DTD Welding Branch	16-19.10.44
Mr. Snodgrass	DTD Welding Branch	19.10.44
Dr. Bowden	DTD Armour Branch	17.10.44
Mr. Turner	DTD Armour Branch	17.10.44
Major Martin	DTD Armour Branch	17-18.10.44
Major Guthrie	DTD Armour Branch	17-18.10.44
Mr. Cole	DTD Armour Branch	17,18,20.10.44
Mr. Goodlad	DTD Armour Branch	19.10.44
Mr. Barker	DTD Armour Branch	All dates
Mr. Young	DTD Armour Branch	All dates

Report		
Compiled by:-	Mr. A.Young	DTD (Armour Branch)
	Mr. F. Barker	DTD (Armour Branch)
Checked by:-	Major G. Guthrie	DTD (Armour Branch)
	Mr. J.B. Sankey	DTD (Armour Branch)

References		
Section I.	Objects of Trial.	
Section II.	Target Details.	
Section III.	Method of Attack.	
Section IV.	Trial Commentary	(6-pdr APCBC and DS)
Section V.	Trial Commentary	(17-pdr APCBC and DS)
Section VI.	Trial Commentary	(75-mm and 25-pdr HE)
Section VII.	Trial Commentary	(3-lb PIAT)
Section VIII.	Trial Commentary	(AT Mines and Grenades)
Section IX.	Summary	
Section X.	Conclusion	

Appendices	
Appendix A.	Details of Damage (AP Shot and HE Shell)

Note:
This report must not be reproduced in full or in part without the written authority of the Director of Tank Design.

SECTION I

Objects of Trial

(i) To determine the general battle-worthiness of the hull and turret of a Model G. Panther against 6-pdr and 17-pdr APCBC and DS shot, and against 75-mm APCBC and HE shell, and 25-pdr HE Shell.

(ii) To determine the probable effect of frontal and flank attack from 3-lb PIAT on stowed ammunition.

(iii) To determine what minimum combination of Grenades AT No. 75, or of AT Mines (British Mk V HC) is required to break the track.

SECTION II

Target Details

The target was a German Panther Tank 135 (PzKw V Model G. No. 120404) complete with tracks and suspension units, engine and transmission, and all permanent equipment. No Stowage, either internal or external, was provided. The fuel tanks were filled but as the radiators had been severely damaged during airburst HE attack in Part I of the trial, the engines could not be run.

Diagrams giving the thickness and angles of presentation of various plates are to be found in Appendix C, and details of Brinell Hardness figures for various plates and castings are given hereunder.

N.B. The turret fitted to the hull at the time of capture was badly damaged and was removed at FVPE Workshops. A turret from another vehicle (DTD No. 3041) was fitted to this hull for the purposes of the firing trial. The DTD number of this hull was 3040.

	Turret Roof	Nearside of Turret	Offside of turret	Turret Rear plate	Mantlet
Corrected Poldi Hardness Figures	319	277	315	297	237

	Hull roof front	Nearside Pannier	Offside Pannier	Vertical Hull sides	Rear plate of hull	Glacis Plate	Nose Plate
Corrected Poldi Hardness Figures	309	289	263	316	308	270	304

Photographs in Appendix B illustrate the target.

SECTION III

Method of Attack

The target was situated on level ground and was attacked from 100 yards. Range with the following projectiles.

	NO. OF ROUNDS FIRED	NO. OF STRIKES
6-pdr APDS shot	29	24
6-pdr APCBC shot	17	17
75-mm APCBC shot	1	1

17-pdr APDS shot	5	5
17-pdr APCBC shot	2	2
17-pdr AP shot	1	1
75-mm HE shell	4	4
25-pdr HE shell	3	3
3-lb PIAT (range 10–20 yards)		

The front of the vehicle was attacked at normal, the nearside at angles approximating to 50 degrees and the offside at normal, the tank being turned to give the required presentations.

The attack from AT mines and grenades was carried out on meadowland.

Details of presentation and conditions for each form of attack are given in Appendix A.

SECTION IV

Trial Commentary (6-pdr APDS and APCBC attacks)

1. Turret Front and Mantlet

(a) 6-pdr APCBC

Five rounds of 6-pdr APCBC were directed at the offside half of the mantlet, the thickness of which could not be measured. Strikes at velocities above 2,300 f.s. holed the mantlet at its centre line and 7.5 inches above it, while a strike 4 inches below the centre line at a velocity 125 f.s. lower did not penetrate the mantlet, but was deflected downwards through the hull roof. The damage thus caused to the ammunition bin behind the hull gunner indicated that a cordite fire would probably have resulted had ammunition been stowed, and there is little doubt that the gunner would have been severely wounded by fragments of shot or roof plate.

It is thus apparent that damage likely to arrest the vehicle may be caused by head-on attack from 6-pdr APCDC at a range of 1,270 yards if hits are obtained on the mantlet, especially below the centre line, where the dangerous range is approximately 1,780 yards.

(b) 6-pdr APDS

Ten rounds of 6-pdr APDS were directed at the nearside half of the mantlet and it was apparent that perforations are unlikely to be caused by this form of attack at striking velocities less than 2,500 f.s., i.e. at ranges greater than 2,500 yards. Chance rounds such as Rounds 7 and 14, however, which struck in the clearance round the gun barrel and on the edge of the turret front below the mantlet respectively, may wedge the gun barrel or jam the turret by pegging it to the hull roof. Rounds deflected downward from the mantlet are unlikely to perforate the hull roof, as they will shatter on impact.

Lack of space prevented further data being obtained from the turret mantlet under this form of attack. (Rds. 6–15.)

(N.B. The turret was released by cutting out armour around the lodged core round 14 with an oxy-acetylene flame.)

2. Turret side at 50 and 60 Degrees (Thickness 47 mm)

(a) 6-pdr APCBC

Rounds 37 to 43 directed at the nearside of the turret at an angle of 50 degrees indicated that the ballistic limit and W/R limit were 2,205 f.s. and 2,243 f.s. respectively. Round 43 passed through the turret wall, crossed the fighting compartment, perforated the transverse bulkhead in the offside pannier at the rear of the compartment, and entered the fuel tank behind the bulkhead. A severe fire resulted which was kept under control with some difficulty by means of water from fire hoses, and although some time elapsed before it was extinguished, the armour was not heated above 100 degrees C. The whole round, except for the caps, was recovered from the fuel tank. (Rds. 37–43.)

(b) 6-pdr APDS

Eight rounds were directed at the turret side, two at 50 degrees defeated the plate and indicated that perforations are likely at ranges up to 2,500 yards. As it is highly improbable that hits could be made with any degree of accuracy at such ranges, the angle of presentation of the plate was increased to 60 degrees to normal in order that striking velocities corresponding to a shorter range might be employed. Of six rounds fired with charges reduced to give striking velocities between 2,900 and 3,700 f.s., only two struck the turret. These scooped harmlessly at 2,977 f.s. and 3,629 f.s., indicating that the plate is immune at this angle for ranges approximating to 700 yards.

For some reason, the accuracy from this form of attack deteriorated during the firing of Round 21 to 28, possibly due to the employment of reduced charges or the fact that the cartridge cases were not crimped. (Rds. 21–28)

3. Pannier at 50 Degrees (Thickness 50 mm)
(a) 6-pdr APCBC

Five rounds were fired at the nearside pannier and revealed that the critical velocity at this angle was approximately 2,360 f.s. (Equivalent range 120 yards). The area attacked cracked very severely after each impact and the weld to the pannier floor was fractured for almost the entire length of the vehicle, although attack was confined to the front half of the plate (Rds. 44–48)

(b) 6-pdr APDS

Seven rounds were directed at the rear portion of the nearside pannier, but one strike was obtained on the plate, and that was so wide of the mark that it failed to influence the velocity recording camera. In view of the extreme inaccuracy of this ammunition, the attack was discontinued.

The last round fired went low and penetrated into the fuel tank behind the hull side and caused a violent outbreak of fire, which was eventually brought under control and extinguished without heating the armour enough to affect its temper. (Rds. 69-75 mm)

4. Hull nose at 53 Degrees (Thickness 51.5 mm)
6-pdr APDS

Four rounds were directed at this plate, but two scooped harmlessly off the glacis plate. The others, striking on the nose plate at velocities of 3,330 f.s. and 3,635 f.s., caused a scoop and a perforation respectively, indicating that this plate is vulnerable at ranges under 700 yards against this form of attack. (Rds. 17–20)

SECTION V

Trial Commentary (Contd.)
17-pdr APDS and APCBC Attacks
Glacis plate at 55 degrees
(Thickness 80 mm)

(a) 17-pdr APDS

Five rounds of 17-pdr APDS were directed at the glacis plate and a critical velocity of approximately 3,410 f.s. was estimated from Rounds 31 and 33. The plate was shown to be brittle and flaked severely on being overmatched.

The indication is that the plate is likely to be defeated with this form of frontal attack at ranges not exceeding 1,500 yards (Rds. 29–33)

(b) 17-pdr APCBC

Two rounds only were fired at the glacis plate and both caused excessive cracking over wide areas. Round 35, striking at 2,443 f.s., was deflected upwards but the plate was forced in 0.625 inches along a crack through the point of impact. Round 34 did not penetrate at 2,673 f.s., but dislodged a flake 1 foot 10 inches × 1 foot 6 inches, which however was retained about 1 inch behind the armour by the steering shaft and the left-hand support for the final drive housing.

The plate was so badly cracked by these two rounds that the only areas remaining whole were those covering the pannier fronts. (Rds. 34 and 35.)

(c) 17-pdr AP

One round of 17-pdr AP directed at the glacis plate in front of the offside-pannier at a striking velocity corresponding to a range of 900–1,000 yards, holed the plate and dislodged in pieces a flake 13 × 11 × 2 inches. Further severe cracking resulted and attack against this place was discontinued. (Rd. 36.)

SECTION VI

Trial Commentary (Contd.) 75-mm M.61, HE and 25-pdr HE attacks

1. Turret mantlet
75-mm APCBC shell attack

One round of American M.61 APCBC shell was directed at the lower half of the turret mantlet at the near side. The round detonated, scooped downward, shattered the roof plate behind the driver's hatch, and passed into the hull with large pieces of roof plate. Considerable internal damage was caused, and it is probable that severe injury would have incapacitated the driver even if a cordite fire did not occur in the damage bin behind his back. (Rd. 16.)

2. Turret
75-mm HE attack.

(a) Mantlet

One round, directed at the cupola, detonated on the mantlet which it struck at normal on its centre line to the left of the gun. As the turret was traversed approximately 40 degrees left, no appreciable damage resulted. The mantlet was not attacked with the whole tank facing the gun as the damage already caused to the hull roof by Round 5 and 16 made it impossible to determine the resistance of portion over the driving compartment to HE attack. The brittleness of the roof plate suggests, however, that a round of 75-mm or 25-pdr HE detonated low on the mantlet would probably blow a hole in the roof and displace hatches.

(b) Cupola

One round of 75-mm HE was detonated on the front of the cupola at a point 4 inches above the roof. The roof plate was severely cracked over an area 2 feet 9 inches × 2 feet 6 inches and forced inward 2.5 inches at a point 4 inches in front of the cupola. Blast would have entered the turret, and fittings attached to the roof below the deformed area were dislodged, and would have caused injuries to members of the crew. No periscopes were fitted in the cupola; it was, therefore, impossible to determine whether they would have been dislodged by this type of attack. (Rd. 60)

(c) Rear escape door

The detonation of Round 62 at the centre of the rear escape door on the turret caused negligible damage inside the turret. The door catch was bent but could still be operated and the door was not jammed. The forward radiators were damaged by fragments of the shell which passed through the grills, and the roof of the engine compartment was forced down 0.75 inches adjacent to the front edge of the main hatch. (Rd. 61)

25-pdr HE attack

(d) Turret rear plate

A round of 25-pdr HE was detonated on the turret rear plate towards the near side. The escape door was jammed due to the distortion of the catch, which could not be withdrawn, and damage to the hinge attachments also resulted. As for the previous round, damage to the forward radiators was increased by shell fragments; otherwise the round appeared to have little further effect on the engine compartment roof and fittings. (Rd. 62)

(e) Turret Side

The turret was traversed left to expose the butt-weld in the hull roof at the offside and a round of 25-pdr HE was detonated on the turret side 12 inches above the roof plate. The roof plate was cracked and set downward beneath the point of impact, but no appreciable damage was caused inside the turret. The displacement of the roof plate at the time of detonation caused the top guide rail for the ammunition rack cover to be dislodged from the roof, together with the sheet steel cover. (Rd. 63)

3. Hull
(a) Hull side 75-mm HE

One round of 75-mm HE struck 6 inches below the pannier floor on the offside of the hull at a point immediately below the central bulkhead between the ammunition racks. The detonation cracked the weld to the lower armour for 38 inches but the presence of the bulkheads and a stiffening rib running over the joint prevented any severe distortion of the pannier floorplate. Damage to the track was slight. (Rd. 64)

(b) Hull side 25-pdr HE

Severe damage to the pannier floor resulted when a round of 25-pdr HE was detonated against the hull side opposite the hull-gunner's position. The joint to the lower armour was torn open for more than 7 feet, and blast and fragments entered the hull through the gap, which was 2 inches wide nearest to the point of impact. This round struck 14 inches below the pannier floor, very close to the track and destroyed the inner third of one track link. Damage to the track and bumper bracket might have resulted in the severing of the track had the vehicle been moving. There is little doubt but that the hull-gunner and the driver would have been injured. (Rd. 65)

N.B. No skirting plates were fitted to the hull side.

SECTION VII

Trial Commentary (Contd.)

3-lb PIAT Attack

1. Pannier side

Two rounds were directed at the pannier side opposite the driver's position and struck at 30 degrees to the normal, the tank being broadside onto the attack. Both rounds detonated, but the first failed to pierce the armour and had apparently been affected by the presence of external fittings for securing stowage. The second caused a perforation 0.5 inches in diameter and dislodged a flake of 1.75 inches in diameter. Fragments damaged the casing over the gearbox, and pitted the back of the offside armour. (It was not possible to stow 75-mm ammunition for this attack as the bins and racks had been severely damaged by previous shooting.) Had ammunition been stowed in the pannier racks, it is probable that a cordite fire would have resulted. (Rds. 49–50)

2. Glacis Plate

Three rounds struck on the glacis plate, and all failed to detonate on impact. One detonated after scooping upward and striking a thin plate which had been laid to project forward from the hull roof, but caused no damage to the hull. Attack against this plate was discontinued. (Rds. 51–53)

3. Cupola

Five rounds were directed at the front of the cupola and of these, three failed to detonate. The two which detonated struck on the front edge of a periscope protector and on the protector around the hinge pillar for the hatch. The second caused no internal damage. The first caused fragment entry downwards through the periscope aperture into the turret. Whether this would have occurred had a periscope been fitted is not known, but it is probable that the periscope would have been driven in by the blast. (Rds 54–58)

As 60 per cent of the projectiles used failed to detonate on impact, further attack was considered unprofitable.

SECTION VIII

Attack from AT Grenades and Mines

1. Offside Track

AT Grenades No. 75

(a) Two grenades placed one above the other with detonating plates in contact were statically detonated beneath the leading road-wheel with their centres eight inches from the outer edge of the track. The track was not severed and would probably have continued to give service unless subjected to excessive strain if the tank encountered heavy going. (Rd. 66)

(b) Three grenades, arranged as described in Appendix A (Rd. 67), were detonated statically under the last pair of road-wheels which corresponded in type to the leading pair. The centre of the arrangement of grenades was 8 inches from the outer edge of the track. The detonation severed the track completely by fracturing one link through all its webs. Three links immediately above the grenades were less severely damaged, the broken link was below the road-wheels behind those attacked, and another link (fourth from that fractured) situated under the wheels forward of the attack was broken halfway across. At least five new links would have been required to repair the track. (Rd. 67.)

SECTION IX

Summary

1. 6-pdr Attack

The following table gives details of critical velocities of the plates attacked.

The equivalent ranges are approximate and refer to 6-pdr, 7-cwt Mks IV and V.

Plate	Thickness	Presentation	Angle of strike	APCBC f.s.	Equivalent Range yards	APDS f.s.	Equivalent Range yards
Mantlet	110 mm	Front of turret at normal.	Various	2,300 on centre line	1,280	2,500	2,500+
Turret Side	47 mm	Side Turret at					
		45 degrees	50 degrees	2,243 (2,290)	1,500		2,500+ 675-
		56 degrees	60 degrees	-	-	3,629+ Immune	
Hull Nose	51.5 mm	Front of hull at normal	53 degrees	-	-	3,600	725
Pannier side	50 mm*	Side of hull at 45 degrees	50 degrees	2,360 (2,410)	1,040	-	-

* Nominal thicknesses.

(Velocities in brackets are average ballistic limit figures obtained under similar conditions of attack from British machineable quality armour.)

2. 17-pdr Attack

The following table summarises the results obtained during this trial. Critical velocities are quoted.

Plate	Thickness	Presentation	Angle of strike	APCBC f.s.	Equivalent Range yards	APDS f.s.	Equivalent Range yards
Glacis plate	80 mm	Front of tank at normal	57 degrees	2,670	800	3,410	1,500

The plate was holed by 17-pdr AP at a striking velocity corresponding to a range of 900–1,000 yards.

3. 75-mm APCBC Shell

A shot striking low on the mantlet entered the hull roof and caused considerable internal damage.

4. HE Attack

Detonations of 75-mm or 25-pdr HE within 12 inches of the roof plates of hull or turret, or below the panniers (without skirting plates fitted), caused severe cracking of roof plates and entry of blast into the vehicle. Detonations within 6 inches of the thin plates may drive portions of the plates into the vehicle. Internal fittings are liable to be dislodged from the thin plates by this form of attack.

The most vulnerable area is that below the mantlet where detonations will cause severe damage to the hatches and frames of the driving compartment roof.

Detonations above the roof of the engine compartment, e.g. from strikes on the back of the turret, will cause fragmentation damage to the radiators.

It is improbable that attack from either type of shell will sever a track unless the detonation occurs, from head-on attack, between the driving sprocket and the ground when the fragments will probably cut the track or damage it sufficiently to cause it to break when moved.

5. 3-lb PIAT

The pannier side, the glacis plate, and the cupola were attacked. Results from head-on suggest that this form of frontal attack is likely to be unprofitable. Flank attack against the pannier side will be very effective, provided that the projectile is not deflected by external stowage or fittings.

6. AT Grenades No. 75 and AT Mines Mk V

Two No. 75 grenades laid one above the other and detonated simultaneously failed to break the track. Three No. 75 detonated simultaneously completely severed the track, and a single Mk V. HC mine gave a similar result.

7. Incidents of Fire

(a) Fuel

Two serious fuel fires occurred during the trial. The first was caused by the penetration of a 6-pdr APCBC round (Rd. 43) through the turret nearside at 50 degrees. The whole round passed across the interior of the fighting compartment holding the traverse bulkhead at the offside, and entering the pannier tank behind it. The CO_2 apparatus did not operate automatically and the turret could not be approached, so that manual operation was impossible. A portable CO_2 extinguisher also failed to operate, as did a foam extinguisher attached to a fire hose supplied by trailer pump from a static water tank. The fire was controlled by means of water from to fire hoses and eventually extinguished.

The drain valve from the fuel system was opened in order to run off the remaining fuel, but as none drained out, it was assumed that the remaining onion damage tanks were empty.

The second fire was caused by Round 75 (6-pdr APDS) which missed its intended target and penetrated through the lower armour into a fuel tank below the nearside radiators. Again fire spread throughout the engine and fighting compartments, and was eventually controlled and extinguished.

When the vehicle was stripped after the trial, it was found that the control rod to the petrol tap would not operate the tap. This explained why no fuel had drained out when the drain valve was opened. The fuel tank damaged by Round 75 was cut to ribbons by fragments of the broken core, and fuel had flooded the fuel compartment and gushed through the bulkhead (also torn open by this round) into the engine compartment.

The lower offside tank still had 25 gallons of petrol when stripped out.

Cordite

No ammunition was stowed during the trial, but there was ample evidence from damage caused to racks and bins that cordite fires would be probable as the result of successful attack in the following areas: –

1. Pannier sides; from perforations of any type of AP, and from PIAT
2. Front of turret below mantlet; from AP shot deflected downward through the hull roof, causing damage to bins behind driver and hull machine gunner, or from HE which may drive pieces of the roof plate into the same bins.

SECTION X

Conclusions

1. Vulnerability and quality of Armour.

The results of this trial (Part II) have shown that the estimates of the vulnerability of the Panther, given in the DTD Armour Branch Report M.6815A/3 No. 1 (Armour Quality and Vulnerability of PzKw V Panther), which was prepared after preliminary examination of the vehicle No. 213101, are substantially correct. Where differences between the estimates and the proved results do occur, in each case, the resistance of the vehicle fell short of expectations. Thus, for instance, where was stated that the glacis plate was nominally immune to 17-pdr APCBC Frontal attack, the assumption was made that the quality of German armour would be equal to that of British machineable quality rolled armour; in fact, the trial against this particular vehicle showed that all the plates tended to flake and that all but one of these attacked cracked extensively under AP or APCBC Attack, from 6-pdr or 17-pdr, and that, therefore, the protection given by the armour was less than that expected. The glacis plate was defeated by 17-pdr APCBC at our range of 800 yards and by 17-pdr AP at a range of 900 yards.

Examination of other vehicles damaged in action, and reports of battle damage to Panther tanks indicate that brittleness of the armour is not peculiar to the vehicle used in this trial. (For details of attack on other plates of this vehicle, see Part III of this report.)

Ample confirmation of the weakness of the design of the area between the centre of the mantlet and the hull roof was afforded, both 6-pdr APCBC shot and 75-mm APCBC shell (M.61) caused extensive damage in the driving compartment by breaking through the hull roof after being deflected from the lower half of the mantlet.

The plates forming the roofs of hull and turret were found to be very brittle, and liable to fracture under the effects of HE detonations occurring within 12 inches of the surface. Detonations within 6 inches of the plate will probably cause severe ruptures or even dislodge portions of the fractured plate into the vehicle.

2. Structure

The welds of the main structure revealed extensive junction cracking during the trial, and it was apparent that many of the fractures had existed prior to the trial, as their surfaces were rusted. The presence of the anti-magnetic coating made earlier detection of the cracks almost impossible. As a result of repeated attack, the welds around the glacis plate failed almost completely, but the interlocking joints prevented a general collapse of the front of the vehicle, even when the armour was itself broken into many pieces. It is evident that the interlocking type of joint does give the structure considerable stability, and deficiencies of welding which occur in production would be less likely to lead to serious consequences in battle.

3. Effect of AT Mines

The trial was shown that the Panther track is more easily broken than experience with Churchill tracks had suggested was likely. This trial confirmed a report from Western Europe that a single Mk V (HC) AT mine will in fact sever the track even if not detonated centrally beneath it; and showed that a similar effect may be obtained by combination of three No. 75 AT grenades. Two such grenades will probably fail to achieve the desired effect. Members of the crew are not likely to be affected by either type of mine if detonated by the track.

For details of subsequent mine trials see Part IV of this report.

(G. Guthrie) Major, R.E.M.E.
Officer i/c Armour Trials Section,
Armour Branch.
AY/GP
12.1.45.
M.461 (s)
YC.

SECRET

Appendix A

Trial No. X.794

TARGET	ATTACK	OBSERVATION
Front of turret mantlet	Round 1 6-pdr APCBC at normal. SV 2,321 f.s. Range 280 feet	Code W. Struck 7.5 inches above centre line of mantlet and 17 inches to right of centre line of 75-mm gun. Shot past between top edge of inner mantlet and roof, injuring loader. Struck right side of recoil guard, motor of roof fan unit dislodged. Rear door in turret struck by fragments
Ditto	Round 2 6-pdr APCBC at normal. SV 2,034 f.s. Range 280 feet	Code D. Struck 4.5 inches below centre line of mantlet and 15 inches right centre of 75-mm gun.
Ditto	Round 3 6-pdr APCBC at normal. SV 2,171 f.s. Range 280 feet	Back damage not visible. Nose lodged. Struck 2 inches above centre line and 9.5 inches to right of centre line of 75-mm gun.
Ditto	Round 4 6-pdr APCBC at normal. SV 2,313 f.s. Range 280 feet	Code W. Base lodged. Struck 4 inches above centre line and 28 inches from centre line of 75-mm gun and 4.25 inches from right-hand edge. Base of shot 3.25 inches below face. Five of eight bolts behind offside trunnion holding out casting on to turret front, fractured at reduced section for threads. Shot retained between mantlet and turret front. Elevation free.
Ditto	Round 5 6-pdr APCBC at normal. SV 2,175 f.s. Range 280 feet	Shot shattered. Back damage not visible. Struck 4 inches below centre line of mantlet and 8 inches from edge of mantlet. Shot scooped down breaking hole 8 × 8.25 inches through roof plate behind Hull gunner's hatch. Roof plate fractured for 38 inches from right-hand side, along back edge, from point 8 inches forward of right rear corner of hatch frame. Roof plate brittle, (thickness 17 mm approximately.). Fragments of plate and shot penetrated through top of ammunition bin behind hull gunner and severely distorted all sides of ammunition bin. One bolt securing frame plate of roof hatch assembly dislodged adjacent to point of impact. Hull gunner's roof hatch lifted 2 inches bodily due to displacing of locking clamp below hinges. Fragmentation marks over roof stiffener behind driving compartment, ammunition bin in front right-hand corner of fighting compartment dented by fragments but not penetrated. In all probability, hull machine gunner would receive serious injury and cordite fire would have occurred in bin behind him.

TARGET	ATTACK	OBSERVATION
Ditto	Round 6 6-pdr APDS at normal. SV 2,556 f.s. Range 280 feet	Code W. Plug out 1-inch diameter. Struck 10.75 inches to left of centre line of 75-mm gun and 4 inches above centre line of gun. Shot entered through telescope aperture and passed through dummy gunner's head, and dummy commander's thigh.
Ditto	Round 7 6-pdr APDS at normal. SV 2,238 f.s. Range 280 feet	Back damage not visible. Core broke up. Struck gun jacket 1 inch below centre line of clearance between gun and jacket at left-hand side.
Ditto	Round 8 6-pdr APDS at normal. SV 2,228 f.s. Range 280 feet	Back damage not visible. Nose lodged. Struck 3.25 up above centre line of mantlet and 16.25 inches from centre line of gun.
Ditto	Round 9 6-pdr APDS at normal. SV 2,415 f.s. Range 280 feet	Back damage not visible. Struck 7 inches down below centre line of mantlet and 13 inches left of centre line of 75-mm gun and scooped downwards and shattered on hull roof.
Ditto	Round 10 6-pdr APDS at normal. SV 2,389 f.s. Range 280 feet	Code D. Glanced off left-hand end of mantlet and struck turret front in weld to turret side, and shattered within the armour. Centre portion of interlocking joint fractured 9.5 inches (*i.e.* full length). Weld on turret side cracked from front edge for 4 inches above and below centre section. Turret side forced out 0.1875 inches at point of impact. In a world between front and side broken in junction to side plate from point 1.5 inches above floor for 15.5 inches.
Ditto	Round 11 6-pdr APDS at normal. SV 2,405 f.s. Range 280 feet	Back damage not visible. Nose lodged. Struck 22.5 inches from centre line of 75-mm gun and on centre line of mantlet.
Ditto	Round 12 6-pdr APDS at normal. SV 2,468 f.s. Range 280 feet	Code C. Struck 16 inches from centre line of 75-mm gun and on centre of mantlet 3 inches below point of strike of Round 8.
Ditto	Round 13 6-pdr APDS at normal. SV 2,380 f.s. Range 280 feet	NF struck 3 inches below top edge of glacis plate and 19 inches from edge of nearside of glacis plate.
Ditto	Round 14 6-pdr APDS at normal. SV 2,478 f.s. Range 280 feet	Code B. Struck face of turret below mantlet, 19 inches from nearside bottom corner of turret, 1.5 inches above bottom edge of turret. Bottom edge forced down and together with nose of shot jammed turret. (Nose of core lodged in turret and in hull roof).
Ditto	Round 15 6-pdr APDS at normal. SV 2,485 f.s. Range 280 feet	Code D or E. Whole shot lodged. Bulge 2-inch diameter × 0.5 inches high. Five star cracks 0.75-inch long, maximum opening 0.3125 inches. Struck 5 inches below centre line of mantlet and 16.5 inches to left of centre line of 75-mm gun.
Ditto	Round 16 75-mm APCBC Shell (American M61) Filled and fuzed. Range 280 feet	Struck 7 inches below centre line of mantlet and 16 inches left of centre of 75-mm gun, detonated, scooped downwards and forced portion of roof 15.5 × 8 inches into hull, caused traverse crack in roof plate 48 inches long and linking up to damage caused by Round 5. Driver's hatch removed and deposited clear of vehicle. Clamp of hull gunner's hatch hinge displaced allowing hatch to lift out of roof plate. Main portion of roof between hatches forced down 1 inch. Lid of ammunition bin behind driver torn at corner with probable damage to one round. Considerable damage to fittings on the gearbox, electrical fittings, and light gauge air duct caused by fragments of roof plate and projectile. Probable that vehicle no longer a runner. Existing crack in Weld junction between glacis and top edge of roof plate now visible, extending from nearside to driver's periscope.
Nose plate	Round 17 6-pdr APDS at 53 degrees. SV 3,330 f.s. Range 280 feet	Code C. Scoop. Struck 8.5 inches above bottom edge of nose plate and deflected down. Outer weld, nose to side plate, cracked intermittently. Weld length 31 inches fractured about 50 per cent.

TARGET	ATTACK	OBSERVATION
Ditto	Round 18 6-pdr APDS at 53 degrees. SV 3,599 f.s. Range 280 feet	Code B. Struck glacis plate at 55 degrees 25 inches from front edge and 22 inches from left-hand side.
Ditto	Round 19 6-pdr APDS at 53 degrees. SV 3,628 f.s. Range 280 feet	Code B. Struck 7 inches from front edge of glacis plate at 55 degrees and scooped up. 75-mm barrel has numerous small scoops. Crack in Weld junction to nose plate 7 inches long immediately below scoop.
Ditto	Round 20 6-pdr APDS at 53 degrees. SV 3,635 f.s. Range 280 feet	Code R. Shot shattered. Struck 6.5 inches down from edge of nose plate. Weld fracture between nose and glacis now 10 inches.
Nearside wall of turret.	Round 21 6-pdr APDS at 50 degrees. SV 2,967 f.s. Range 280 feet	Code W. Shot shattered. Struck 7 inches below top edge of turret and 18 inches from front edge. Flake off 3 × 2.5 × 0.375 inches. Left side of recoil guard and compressed air feed torn by fragments. Area 18 × 12 inches on of side wall pitted. Dummy commander wounded in thigh and abdomen. Dummy loader's head and shoulders removed.
Ditto	Round 22 6-pdr APDS at 50-degree compound. SV 2,558 f.s. Range 280 feet	Code W. Struck 19.5 inches down from top edge of turret and 10.5 inches from the front edge.
Ditto	Round 23 6-pdr APDS at 60-degree compound. SV 2,977 f.s. Range 280 feet	Code C. Scoop. Bulge 0.125 inches high. Struck 3.75 inches down from top edge and 25 inches from front edge. Plate cracked across scoop in two places.
Ditto	Round 24 6-pdr APDS at 60-degree compound. SVNO Range 280 feet	Missed target.
Ditto	Round 25 6-pdr APDS at 60-degree compound. SV 3,292 f.s. Range 280 feet	Missed target.
Ditto	Round 26 6-pdr APDS at 60-degree compound. SV 3,539 f.s. Range 280 feet	Code C slight. Struck glacis plate at 55 degrees 7 inches below top edge near centre line.
Ditto	Round 27 6-pdr APDS at 60-degree compound. SV 3,400 f.s. Range 280 feet	Missed target.
Ditto	Round 28 6-pdr APDS at 60-degree compound. SV 3,629 f.s. Range 280 feet	Code C. Bulge 0.25 high high. Struck turret wall 10 inches from front edge and 16 inches down. Weld to front split further 3.25 inches in side plate.

TARGET	ATTACK	OBSERVATION
Glacis plate. Front of tank at normal to gun.	Round 29 17-pdr APDS at 55 degrees. SV 3,226 f.s. Range 280 feet	Code C. Struck 7 inches above bottom edge of glacis plate. Crack in plate below scoop 5 inches long, adjacent to plate edge. Old junction crack to nose plate opened to 0.0625 inches max, 24 inches long (full length between interlocking section at centre).
Ditto	Round 30 17-pdr APDS at 55 degrees. SV 3,501 f.s. Range 280 feet	Code W. Hole 1.75 × 1.5 inches. Struck 17 inches above the bottom and 20 inches from inner edge of offside plate. Crack in glacis plate 6 inches towards top offside corner from shot hole. Internal: casting for final drive housing fractured, fragments probably entered drive housing.
Ditto	Round 31 17-pdr APDS at 55 degrees. SV 3,374 f.s. Range 280 feet	Code C. Shot shattered. Scoop 5.5 × 5.75 × 1.375 inches deep. Struck 10.5 inches above bottom edge of glacis plate and 3.5 inches from offside inner edge of side plate. Crack across scoop 5 inches long. Weld between glacis and side plate fractured full length of the joint, *i.e.* for 2 feet 7 inches. Glacis plate forced down 0.1875 inches adjacent to point of impact. Weld of tenon on offside plate fractured full perimeter (about 2 feet). Crack in glacis from centre of scoop 5.75 inches long running left towards hull nose (at about 45 degrees).
Ditto	Round 32 17-pdr APDS at 55 degrees. SV 3,348 f.s. Range 280 feet	Code C. Scoop 7 × 4.375 × 2 inches deep. Struck 2 feet 4 inches above bottom edge of glacis and 1 foot 10 inches from inner edge of side plate. Crack across scoop 3.5 inches long. Weld attaching machine gun m mounting now cracked for whole circumference. Weld attaching roof to glacis plate cracked from nearside to within 18 inches of offside (approximately 7 feet). Most cracks in this joint are old junction cracks adjacent to the roof plate but around driver's periscope a new crack runs for approximately 8 inches in the junction to the glacis plate. A crack in the glacis plate from point of impact to amateur for ball mounting ran 3.5 inches long.
Ditto	Round 33 17-pdr APDS at 55 degrees. SV 3,449 f.s. Range 280 feet	Code W. Front flake 5.5 × 6.5 × 1 inches dislodged immediately above point of impact. Round struck 1 foot 9 inches from edge of glacis plate. Back damage: flake off in pieces 6 × 5.25 × 0.75 inches, hole 3.25 × 1.75 inches. Switch box fitting removed and badly torn by fragments of shot and plate. Centre portion of the shaft connecting steering controls dented by fragments. Ammunition bin behind driver penetrated in several places. Cover over gearbox severely torn by fragments driver would have been killed, and several fragments caused injury to turret gunner's legs.
Glacis plate.	Round 34 17-pdr APCBC at 55 degrees. SV 2,673 f.s. Range 280 feet	Code R. Shot deflected upwards. Flake off 1 foot 10 inches diameter but retained by internal fittings. Hole 8.75 × 4.5 inches. Struck 14 inches from bottom edge. Cracks from point of impact to Round 19, 12 inches long, to nearside edge 15 inches and two Round 18, 15 inches long. Roof plate lifted 0.1875 inches.
	Round 35 17-pdr APCBC at 55 degrees. SV 2,443 f.s. Range 280 feet	Code D. Bulge 0.375 inches high. Scoop 8 × 3.5 inches. Struck 9 inches below top edge of glacis plate. Extensive cracks in glacis plate. Portion of plate 15 × 16 inches forced down 0.625 inches at bottom edge and hinged about roof joint. Joint between roof and glacis now open 0.5 inches adjacent driver's periscope. Joint between roof and nearside pannier broken 19 inches. Joint glacis to nearside pannier cracked in junction to side plate 16 inches. Three radial cracks in glacis plate 15 inches long from broken piece. Circumference crack on inside face 18 inches long, 18 inches from top edge.
Ditto	Round 36 17-pdr AP at 55 degrees. SV NO Approximate equivalent Range 900–1,000 yards.	Code W. Hole 3 × 2.75 inches. Struck 8 inches below top edge 12 inches from outside. Three radial cracks in plate, 10, 12, and 8 inches long. Joint between glacis and roof now fractured full length. Joint to offside pannier fractured 12 inches from front edge. Flake off in pieces 13 × 11 × 2 inches.
Nearside wall of turret will stop	Round 37 6-pdr APCBC at 50-degree compound. SV 2,227 f.s. Range 280 feet	Code R. Flake off 4.75 × 4.25 × 0.75 inches. Hole 2 × 1.25 inches. Struck 13 inches up and 1 foot 11 inches from front of turret.
Ditto	Round 38 6-pdr APCBC at 50-degree compound. SV 2,041 f.s. Range 280 feet	Code C. Bulge 0.3125 inches high, 6 × 4.5 inches. Scoop 5 × 2.5 × 0.75 inches. Struck 13 inches above turret bottom edge.

TARGET	ATTACK	OBSERVATION
Ditto	Round 39 6-pdr APCBC at 50-degree compound. SV 2,140 f.s. Range 280 feet	Code C. Scoop 6.5 × 2.75 × 1.125 inches. Struck 4 inches down below top edge of turret. Bulge 6.5 × 4 × 0.375 inches.
Ditto	Round 40 6-pdr APCBC at 50-degree compound. SV 2,183 f.s. Range 280 feet	Code C. Struck 1 foot 5 inches from top edge of turret. Bulge 6.5 × 4.25 × 0.375 inches.
Ditto	Round 41 6-pdr APCBC at 50-degree compound. SV 2,221 f.s. Range 280 feet	Not fair hit. Bulge now 0.675 inches high stop double hit on Round 39. Struck 5.5 inches down stop.
Ditto	Round 42 6-pdr APCBC at 50-degree compound. SV 2,230 f.s. Range 280 feet	Code E. Scoop 7 × 2.5 × 2 inches. Struck 11.5 inches up above bottom edge of turret. Flake 5.5 × 4.25 inches lifted 0.875 inches.
Ditto	Round 43 6-pdr APCBC at 50-degree compound. SV 2,259 f.s. Range 280 feet	Code W. Struck on nearside turret 11.5 inches below top ends and 22 inches from front edge of nearside of turret. Vehicle caught fire. Round passed downwards across turret and penetrated engine compartment, bulkhead and front of offside pannier fuel tank. Round recovered whole from offside fuel tank. Flake off 5.25 × 4 × 0.625 inches.
Nearside pannier.	Round 44 6-pdr APCBC at 50-degree compound. SV 2,353 f.s. Range 280 feet	Code D. Shatter scoop 4.125 × 2.375 × 0.875 inches. Horizontal crack in plate 6.5 inches across scoop. Weld joint pannier to floorplate sheared for 43 inches in junction to pannier. Pannier side dished 0.28125 inches at point of impact. Rear. Crack extending from points 25 inches apart on joint to pannier floor through an arc reaching at its centre a point 6 inches from the joint.
Ditto	Round 45 6-pdr APCBC at 50-degree compound. SV 2,341 f.s. Range 280 feet	Code W. NFH Struck 6 inches from Round 44. External weld between pannier side and pannier floor now fractured 7 feet 10 inches. Plate cracks extended forming three star cracks: Two 20 inches long and one 10 inches long.
Ditto	Round 46 6-pdr APCBC at 50-degree compound. SV 2,373 f.s. Range 280 feet	Code W. Struck 13 inches above bottom edge of pannier. Flake off 6 × 4.5 inches in pieces. Rear supports four ammunition racks torn away and distributed about turret. Rim of gun elevating handwheel broken.
Ditto	Round 46 6-pdr APCBC at 50-degree compound. SV 2,297 f.s. Range 280 feet	Code C. Scoop. Struck 7 inches above bottom edge of pannier. Short irregular cracks now apparent in weld hull roof plate to pannier side.
Ditto	Round 48 6-pdr APCBC at 50-degree compound. S.V. 2,335 f.s. Range 280 feet	Code D. Shatter scoop. Struck 7 inches below top edge of pannier. Flake 8 × 5.5 inches lifted 1.25 inches for three quarters of circumference. Weld pannier side to floor now fractured full length except 12 inches at rear and 19 inches at front end

TARGET	ATTACK	OBSERVATION
Pannier side. Nearside of hull at normal to projector.	Round 49 3-lb PIAT at 30 degrees Range 60 feet	Struck 6 inches below top edge of pannier and detonated. Slight pitting on strip weld to pannier for external stowage
Ditto	Round 50 3-lb PIAT at 30 degrees Range 60 feet	Pannier holed. Struck 5.5 inches below top edge of pannier. Numerous strikes on the pannier at 7-inch radius. Hole 0.5-inch diameter with flake off 1.75-inch diameter on inside face. In a face of offside armour marked and pitted. Driver probably killed. Strikes on some of roof fittings from fragments.
Front of tank at normal to projector.	Round 51 3-lb PIAT at 55 degrees Range 30 feet	Struck on glacis plate at front of nearside pannier. Blind.
Ditto	Round 52 3-lb PIAT at 55 degrees Range 30 feet	Blind on glacis plate. Scooped upwards and detonated on overhanging plate laid on hull roof. Glacis plate slightly pitted by fragments of bomb casings
Ditto	Round 53 3-lb PIAT at 55 degrees Range 30 feet	Struck glacis plate and failed to detonate.
Commander's cupola	Round 54 3-lb PIAT at normal Range 30 feet	Struck between periscope protectors and failed to detonate.
Ditto	Round 55 3-lb PIAT at normal Range 30 feet	Struck between periscope protectors and failed to detonate.
Ditto	Round 56 3-lb PIAT at normal Range 30 feet	Struck between periscope protectors and failed to detonate.
Ditto	Round 57 3-lb PIAT at normal Range 30 feet	Detonated on top of periscope protector. Bracket securing machine-gun guide rail dislodged from top of protector. Fragments penetrate inside through periscope aperture and made strikes on recoil guard. Presence of periscope might have kept fragments out.
Ditto	Round 58 3-lb PIAT at normal Range 30 feet	Detonated between periscope and boss for hinge pillar. Hole through boss. Jet would have gone upwards and impinged on cupola hatch hinge arm. No damage caused inside turret.
Ditto	Round 59 75-mm HE shell filled TNT at normal. Instantaneous fuse. Reduced charge.	Missed Cupola. Detonated on mantlet at centre line.
Ditto	Round 60 75-mm HE shell filled TNT at normal. Instantaneous fuse. Reduced charge.	Detonated on the front of cupola 4 inches above roof. Roof plate cracked severely over area 2 feet 9 inches × 2 feet 6 inches and forward down 2.5 inches at a point 4 inches forward of cupola. Guide rail four machine-gun dislodged. Cupola hatch previously screwed down now raised 2 inches. Fittings attached to roof driven off into turret. Bolts securing circular blanking off plate at offside rear of turret roof dislodged.

TARGET	ATTACK	OBSERVATION
Rear wall of turret rear of tank presented to attack	Round 61 75-mm HE shell filled TNT at 20 degrees. Instantaneous fuse. Reduced charge. Range 280 feet	Struck rear wall of turret on centre of escape door and detonated. Offside radiator marked by fragments. Cast grille on nearside has strikes on vertical division bars. Roof plate forward of engine hatch set down 0.75 inches maximum over 2 feet 4 inches. Catch for holding escape door in open position now useless. Door remained shut but welds attaching locking device to door sheared for most of length. Dovetailed tongue forced back slightly. Upper lip of catch bent on rebound of door. Seven bolts, attaching centre plate of engine compartment roof to scallop welded landing edge along back edge of main hull roof plate, dislodged 21 inches of forward portion of landing strip for engine hatch dislodged.
Ditto	Round 62 25-pdr HE at 20 degrees. Filled TNT Fuse 119. Cap off. Charge III.	Struck on rear wall of turret 9 inches from nearside and 12 inches above roof plate. Nearside radiator severely pitted. Nearside vertical weld joint of turret fractured for 19 inches from bottom in weld junction to rear plate. Internal weld fracture 3 inches in junction to rear plate from bottom. Upper lug for hinge boss fractured half through. Upper engaging lip for catch broken off. Door jammed in closed position. Bottom bolt of three securing hinge bracket to turret wall now loose due to fracture and removal of internal castellated nut. Head removed from central bolt. Handle for raised cupola hatch dislodged from crank.
Offside wall of turret	Round 63 25-pdr HE at 25 degrees Filled TNT Fuse 119. Cap off. Charge III.	Struck 12 inches above whole roof and detonated. Crack in forward plate 2 feet 4 inches long parallel to line of turret base. Crack in butt weld between roof plates 4 inches long. Roof plate set down 0.325 inches below point of impact. Outer portion of roof plate set down 0.875 inches on inside at fracture. Crack extends along rear of roof beam. Sheet steel cover of ammunition bins dislodged. Top guide for cover dislodged from hull roof. Welds attaching protector over loader's periscope to turret roof, fractured completely at right side and nearly so at left-hand side.
Offside hull side below pannier.	Round 64 75-mm HE at normal Filled TNT Instantaneous fuse. Reduced charge.	Detonated on hull side 6 inches below pannier floor. Weld pannier floor to hull side fractured 38 inches. Three inner webs of one track link fractured 6 inches below point of impact. Pannier floor bulged up 0.625 inches maximum. Weld pannier side to pannier floor fractured 7 inches in junction to floor. The pannier floor was reinforced internally at this point by a box section stiffener welded to the pannier floor and lower side armour and also by two bulkheads attached to this member between the ammunition racks in the pannier. Stiffener fractured halfway across (about 1.5 inches) at bend opposite junction of pannier floor and lower side armour.
Ditto	Round 65 25-pdr HE at normal. Filled TNT Fuse 119. Cap off. Charge III.	Detonated on hull side 14 inches below pannier floor. Shell passed between trade bars of track. In a third of track fractured. Portion of track 9 × 6 inches forced down crack in pannier side to floor 7 × 7 inches long. Pannier floor lifted 2 inches maximum over 6 feet. In weld between pannier floor and side of hull fractured from glacis plate to roof stiffener below turret. Tyre of road-wheel below point of impact severed. Out a flanged of this road-wheel distorted. Bumper pad for suspension arm forced from side armour half an inch, one nut dislodged
Ditto	Round 66 Two grenades AT No. 75 placed one above the other with detonating plates in contact. Top of upper grenade in contact with track. Both grenades fitted with No. 33 detonators wired in parallel. Longitudinal axes of grenades parallel to hull side, centres 8 inches from outer edge of track under leading offside road-wheel.	Detonation. Track not severed. One pin sheared. Small portion of centre of track broken out. Outer guide lug removed from one link. One tread fractured. Rim of first road-wheel distorted on outer flange. Bumper bracket dislodged due to bolts shearing (previously stressed by detonation of Round 65). Track would probably hold for a time but very liable to snap under heavy strain.
Rear of offside track, beneath outer half of penultimate pair of road-wheels.	Round 67. Three grenades AT No. 75. Lower one set transversely with centre 8 inches from outer edge of track. Upper pair set end to end longitudinally. All three detonated in parallel.	Detonation. Track severed due to fracture of link and not pin. One link broken and fourth one away from this fractured half way across. Five links would be required to repair track. Rim of road-wheel above point of detonation distorted. Vehicle immobilised.

TARGET	ATTACK	OBSERVATION
Front end of nearside track. Centre of mine beneath outer edge of first road-wheel.	Round 68. One Mk V HC AT mine.	Detonation. Track severed. Bumper bracket dislodged. Portion of flanges of road-wheel at point of detonation dislodged for 14 inches. One rubber tyre removed from this road-wheel. Link above mine was destroyed and pin behind this point was sheared. Centre portion of adjacent link cracked to rear of this damage. Land of lower bumper under hull side due to arm of road-wheel having been forced against it.
Nearside pannier	Round 69. 6-pdr APDS at 50-degree compound. SV 3,432 f.s. Range 280 feet	Struck edge of track and shattered. Slight pitting of pannier floor. Three track links scooped.
Ditto	Round 70. 6-pdr APDS at 50-degree compound. SVNO Range 280 feet	Code W. Back damage not visible. Shot shattered. Hole 3.5 × 1.5 inches into fuel compartment. Struck lower side armour, immediately inside end plate and 0.75 inches below floorplate of pannier. (Side armour 41.5 mm thick) Crack from point of impact for 9 inches to centre of tenon from rear plate and cracked for 6 inches to lifting whole. Weld to pannier floor cracked for 13 inches from rear.
Ditto	Round 71. 6-pdr APDS at 50-degree compound. SV 4,127 f.s. Range 280 feet	Missed target.
Ditto	Round 72. 6-pdr APDS at 50-degree compound. SV 3,427 f.s. Range 280 feet	Missed target.
Ditto	Round 73. 6-pdr APDS at 50-degree compound. SVNO Range 280 feet	Code C. Scoop 6.75 × 1.75 × 0.6875 inches. Struck pannier side 5.5 inches above bottom edge
Ditto	Round 74. 6-pdr APDS at 50-degree compound. SVNO Range 280 feet	Struck rim of a second outer road-wheel removing portion of rim and tyre. Penetrated disc immediately above hub of inner wheel braking flange of hub. No other apparent damage.
Ditto	Round 75. 6-pdr APDS at 50-degree compound. SV 4054 f.s. Range 280 feet	Code W. Back damage not visible. Struck 3 inches below pannier floor. Petrol fire in engine compartment spreading to fighting compartment.

After stripping the hull and turret, examination of the engine compartment showed that the shot had broken up and riddled a fuel tank. The nearside longitudinal bulkhead in the engine compartment opposite this fuel tank was burst open for an area of 18 × 12 inches, no metal being dislodged. The dynamo on the engine was also damaged.

APPENDIX B

Trial No. X.794: AT No. 232: Part II: PzKw V Panther

AP Attack

Mantlet after attack by five rounds of 6-pdr APCBC. Round five scooped downwards and shattered the roof plate below. The hull gunner's hatch was dislodged due to the internal locking clamp being displaced. Note: these doors are jettisonable. (*Department of Tank Design*)

Front view of damage caused by round five. (*Department of Tank Design*)

Nearside of mantlet after attack by 6-pdr APDS rounds six to fifteen. Round seven would have interfered with the recoil of the gun. Round fourteen struck the turret below the mantlet, the nose of the shot lodged in the roof plate and turret, thus jamming the turret. (*Department of Tank Design*)

Showing damage to the interlocking joint between the nearside and turret front casting, caused by round ten of 6-pdr APCBC, which scooped off the edge of the mantlet. (*Department of Tank Design*)

General view of mantlet after rounds one to five of 6-pdr APCBC, then rounds six to fifteen of 6-pdr APDS. *Department of Tank Design*)

Showing damage to roof plate caused by round sixteen—75-mm APCBC—after scooping off mantlet and penetrating roof. The damage to the roof plate links up to that caused by round five of 6-pdr APCBC, which also scooped off the mantlet. (*Department of Tank Design*)

View looking into hull gunner's compartment after round five—6-pdr APCBC—and round sixteen—75-mm APCBC—had scooped down off mantlet and penetrated the roof plate. (*Department of Tank Design*)

Showing damage to ammunition being behind the hull gunner's station after round five had scooped down through roof plate. Similar damage was caused by round sixteen to the ammunition bin behind the driver's position. Cordite fires would probably have occurred in both cases. (*Department of Tank Design*)

Glacis and lower hull plates after attack by 6-pdr APDS rounds seventeen to twenty. Arrows near the front edge indicate the extent of the weld failures. (*Department of Tank Design*)

Nearside of turret after attack by 6-pdr APDS rounds twenty-one and twenty-two at 50 degrees and rounds twenty-three and twenty-eight at 60 degrees. (*Department of Tank Design*)

Glacis plate after attack by 17-pdr APDS rounds twenty-nine to thirty-three at 55 degrees. The rounds thirteen, eighteen, nineteen, and twenty-six on the glacis plate, and the rounds seventeen and twenty on the nose plate, were 6-pdr APDS. (*Department of Tank Design*)

Showing point of strike of 17-pdr APCBC round thirty-four. The huge flake off the rear base of the armour was held in position by the final drive support members. The 17-pdr attack caused excessive cracking of the glacis plate. (*Department of Tank Design*)

Showing flake dislodged from rear face of glacis plate by 17-pdr APCBC round thirty-four at 55 degrees. The flake was recovered at the end of the trial after the final drive and its support had been removed. (*Department of Tank Design*)

17-pdr APCBC round thirty-five at 53 degrees was practically a double hit on 6-pdr APDS round thirteen. Note the extent of the cracks in the glacis plate and the failure of the weld to the roof. In many cases, the fractured welds proved to be old junction cracks, which opened up progressively during the trial. (*Department of Tank Design*)

General view of front of vehicle after attack by 6-pdr APDS rounds thirteen, seventeen to twenty, and twenty-six; 17-pdr APDS rounds thirty to thirty-three; and 17-pdr APCBC rounds thirty-four and thirty-five. (*Department of Tank Design*)

Showing extensive cracks (lined in white) that developed on the glacis plate. Some of these cracks appeared at points of impact only after the following round had struck the glacis plate. (*Department of Tank Design*)

Round thirty-six: 17-pdr AP at 55 degrees holed the glacis plate at a velocity equivalent to a range of 900 yards. (*Department of Tank Design*)

Nearside wall of turret after attack by 6-pdr APDS rounds twenty-one and twenty-two at 50 degrees, rounds twenty-three and twenty-eight at 60 degrees, and rounds thirty-seven to forty-three from 6-pdr APCBC at 50 degrees. Round forty-three holed the turret and passed across the fighting compartment through the engine compartment bulkhead, and was held in a fuel tank on the offside. An extensive fire was caused. (*Department of Tank Design*)

View of vehicle at commencement of fire caused by 6-pdr APCBC round forty-three at 50 degrees against nearside wall of turret. (*Department of Tank Design*)

Front view of vehicle towards end of fire. (*Department of Tank Design*)

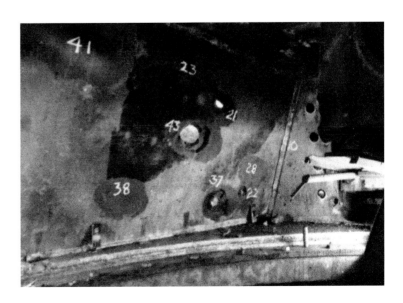

Inner face of nearside wall of turret after attack by 6-pdr APDS rounds twenty-one and twenty-two at 50 degrees, rounds twenty-three and twenty-eight at 60 degrees, and rounds thirty-seven, thirty-eight, forty-one, and forty-three from 6-pdr APCBC at 50 degrees. Round ten was a 6-pdr APDS on the front face of the turret. Note typical flaking where the plate was overmatched. (*Department of Tank Design*)

Nearside pannier after attack by 6-pdr APCBC rounds forty-four and forty-five at 50 degrees. Round forty-five struck 6 inches from round forty-four and is therefore not a fair strike. (*Department of Tank Design*)

View showing extent of fracture in pannier side from rounds forty-four and forty-five. The horizontal crack measured 40 inches and the vertical one 10 inches. (*Department of Tank Design*)

Internal face of nearside pannier after attack by 6-pdr APCBC rounds forty-four and forty-five at 50 degrees. (*Department of Tank Design*)

AP and PIAT Attack

Nearside of tank before attack by 6-pdr APCBC rounds forty-six to forty-eight. (*Department of Tank Design*)

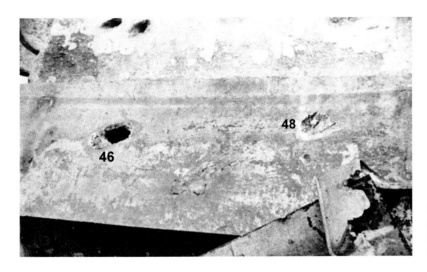

Nearside pannier after attack by 6-pdr APCBC rounds forty-six to forty-eight at 50 degrees. Round forty-six holed the armour at S.V. 2373 f.s. (*Department of Tank Design*)

Forward end of nearside pannier after attack by 3-lb PIAT at 30 degrees. Round forty-nine did not hole the armour. Round fifty made a hole half an inch in diameter and the offside pannier was marked by fragments. (*Department of Tank Design*)

PIAT Attack

Glacis and nearside pannier inside faces: 6-pdr APDS round thirteen; 17-pdr APCBC rounds thirty-four and thirty-five; and 3-lb PIAT round fifty. Three PIAT aimed at the glacier plate failed to detonate (rounds fifty-one to fifty-three). (*Department of Tank Design*)

Commander's cupola after attack by 3-lb PIAT rounds fifty-seven and fifty-eight. Round fifty-seven struck the top edge of the periscope protector. If periscopes had been fitted, it is possible that fragments would not have entered turret, unless periscope was dislodged. Note near the number fifty-eight the lodged tale of that round. (*Department of Tank Design*)

Cupola after removing lodged tale of the 3-lb PIAT round fifty-eight. The boss for the hinge pillar was penetrated; had the hatch been closed, the jet would have struck the hinge arm without causing casualties. (*Department of Tank Design*)

PIAT and HE Attack

Cupola after attack by 3-lb PIAT rounds fifty-seven and fifty-eight. Note bracket dislodged from machine-gun guide rail by round fifty-seven. (*Department of Tank Design*)

Cupola after the detonation of 75-mm HE round sixty. Note expensive cracks in the roof plate. Rail guide for machine-gun is now dislodged. (*Department of Tank Design*)

Inside view of roof plate after the detonation of 75-mm space HE round sixty on the cupola. Note bolts dislodged from segments holding cupola to the roof and the displacement of weld straps. (*Department of Tank Design*)

HE Attack

Rear wall of turret after the detonation of 75-mm HE round sixty-one and 25-pdr HE round sixty-two. Fragments from both rounds cut into the radiator matrix at nearside and offside. The circular escape door was jammed after round sixty-two. (*Department of Tank Design*)

Offside wall of turret after the detonation of 25-pdr HE round sixty-three. The roof plate was set down three-eighths of an inch below the point of impact. The crack extended from the butt joint between the roof plates and ran along the rear of the internal roof stiffener. (*Department of Tank Design*)

Offside lower side armour after the detonation of 75-mm HE round sixty-four 6 inches below the pannier floor. Weld between pannier floor and side armour fractured for 38 inches. Note the floor is stiffened at this point by a box section beam. No skirting plates were fitted. (*Department of Tank Design*)

Showing damage caused to track by 75-mm HE round sixty-four, detonating on the side armour. Three webs of one link were fractured. (*Department of Tank Design*)

Offside lower side armour after the detonation of 25-pdr HE round sixty-five. Weld joints between pannier floor and side armour was fractured for 7 feet 7 inches and open 2 inches top. (*Department of Tank Design*)

Damage to track from 25-pdr HE round sixty-five, which detonated immediately above track. The track was not severed but displaced portion, which was forced downwards, would probably have caused a stoppage by fouling the driving sprocket. (*Department of Tank Design*)

HE and AT Mine Attack

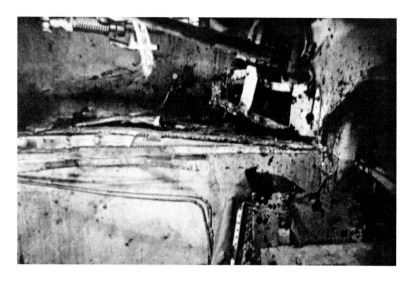

Internal view of offside pannier after 25-pdr HE round sixty-five had detonated against lower armour. (*Department of Tank Design*)

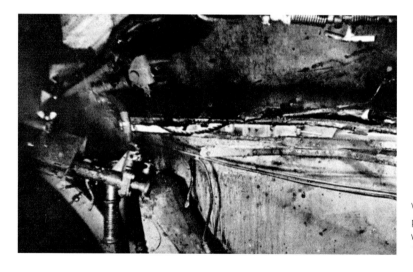

View of forward position of fractured joint between pannier floor and lower side armour after attack with 25-pdr HE round sixty-five. (*Department of Tank Design*)

Forward end of offside track after the detonation of two No. 75 grenades placed one above the other, and 8 inches from the outer edge of the track. The track was not severed. (*Department of Tank Design*)

AT Mine Attack

Rear end of offside track after the detonation of three No. 75 grenades, round sixty-seven. The track was fractured completely across at one point and halfway across at a point four links away. (*Department of Tank Design*)

Front end of nearside track after the detonation of one Mk V H.C. A. T. mine round sixty-eight. Track severed. Note damage to the rim of the first road wheel. (*Department of Tank Design*)

Views obtained after the removal of the engine. Damage to longitudinal bulkhead on nearside of engine compartment for 6-pdr APDS round seventy-five at 50 degrees, which perforated the lower side armour. The shot ripped open a fuel tank before striking this bulkhead. A very severe fuel fire broke out. (*Department of Tank Design*)

Fuel tank that was penetrated by 6-pdr APDS round seventy-five. The core evidently broke up on passing through the armour and the fragments caused this damage to the fuel tank and then to the bulkhead seen above. (*Department of Tank Design*)

APPENDIX C

Trial No. X.794: AT No. 232: Part II

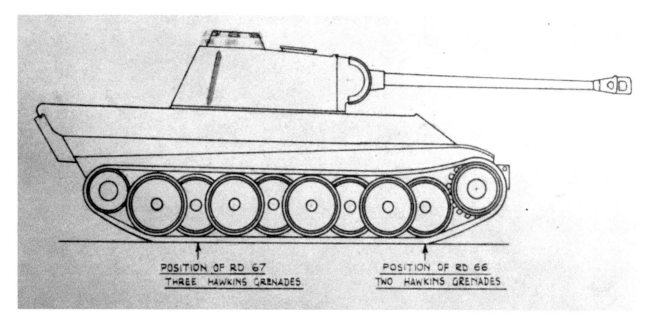

Diagram showing the position of Hawkins Grenade anti-tank mines. (*Department of Tank Design*)

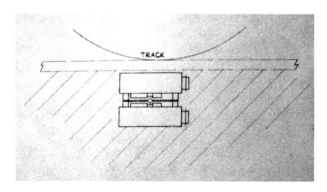

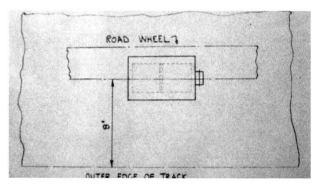

◄ Diagram showing two buried Hawkins Grenade anti-tank mines beneath the track of the Panther tank. (*Department of Tank Design*)

► Diagram showing buried Hawkins Grenade anti-tank mines beneath the road wheel and track of the Panther tank. (*Department of Tank Design*)

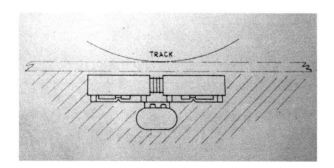

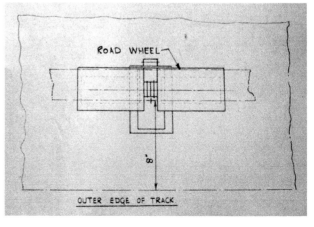

◄ Diagram showing the laying of three Hawkins Grenade anti-tank mines beneath the track of the Panther tank. (*Department of Tank Design*)

► Diagram showing the laying of three Hawkins Grenade anti-tank mines beneath the track and road wheel of the Panther tank. (*Department of Tank Design*)

APPENDIX D

Trial No. X.794: AT No. 232: Part II

Results of Metallurgical Investigation of Sample from Glacis Plate

Hull No. 120404.

DTD No. 3040.

A front flake from the glacis plate, removed by Round 33 (17-pdr APDS) was sent for metallurgical investigation to Messrs. Wm. Beardmore & Co. Ltd. The following extracts are from the report issued by the firm's Research Department.

'The appearance of the flake suggests that the armour might have surface flame hardened. It was therefore cut through its thickness and a section polished and etched, observation then showed that the material was homogeneous and had not been either carburized or flame hardened. This was confirmed by Vickers Pyramid hardness readings which gave values between 286 and 311, with an average of 293 roughly equivalent to a Brinell hardness of 272.'

(N. B. The table in Section II gives a correct Poldi hardness of 270).

A small tensometer test was cut parallel to the face of the plate and gave the following result:

Yield Point	Ult. Stress	Elongation	Reduction in Area
55.0 tons sq. in. (approx.)	62.5 tons sq. in.	24 per cent OMH	58 per cent

These results confirm the hardness readings already taken since the tensometer test can usually be expected to give slightly higher values for the maximum stress than the normal tensile test. The figures for the elongation and reduction are good considering the ultimate stress obtained.

A micro-section was cut through the thickness of the material and examination showed that it was clean, containing only a few small well-distributed inclusions both slag and manganese sulphide. The etched structure was very fine-grained, the rolling structure having been almost completely removed.

Drillings were taken for chemical analysis with the following results:

C	Si	S	P	Mn	Ni	Cr	V	Mo
0.40	0.420	0.019	0.016	0.72	0.09	2.12	0.03	0.01

This material appears to be either Electric Furnace or Basic Open-hearth Steel.'

12.1.45

M.461(S)

SH.

DTD EXPERIMENTAL REPORT: AT NO. 232: PART III

Project No. M.6815A/4 Sheet 3

Trial No: X.795.

File No: 250/14/5.

REPORT OF BALLISTIC TRIAL against PzKw V Model G. (DTD No. 3040) held at Shoeburyness Range on October 24–26, 1944

Present during trial	Representing	Date attended
Lt Tgendinnick	S. of E.	24, 26.10.44
Capt. Gibbs	S. of E.	25.10.44
Major Durrenberger	U.S. Embassy	24.10.44
Capt. Burke	US Embassy	24.10.44
Dr. Harris	Messers. Babcock & Wilcox	24.10.44
Mr. Dunn	Vickers-Armstrongs Ltd	24, 25.10.44
Capt. Harber, R.C.A.C.	DTD EW Lulworth	26.10.44

Major Steane	DTD (General Design Branch)	24.10.44
Major Denaro	DTD (Welding Branch)	24.10.44
Major Gutherie	DTD (Armour Branch)	25, 26.10.44
Mr. Cole	DTD (Armour Branch)	25.10.44
Mr. Young	DTD (Armour Branch)	All dates
Mr. Baker	DTD (Armour Branch)	All dates

Report

Compiled by:-	(Mr. A. Young)	DTD (Armour Branch)
	(Mr. F. Barker)	DTD (Armour Branch)
Checked by:-	Maj. G. Gutherie R.E.M.E.	DTD (Armour Branch)
	Mr. J.B. Sankey	DTD (Armour Branch)

References

Section I.	-	Objects of Trial
Section II.	-	Target Details
Section III.	-	Method of Attack
Section IV.	-	Trial Commentary. (6-pdr AP and APC)
Section V.	-	Trial Commentary. (17-pdr AP)
Section VI.	-	Trial Commentary. (AT Grenades)
Section VII.	-	Summary
Section VIII.	-	Conclusion

Appendices

Appendix A.	-	Details of Damage.
Appendix B.	-	Photographic Record.
Appendix C.	-	Sketch of Armour Disposition.

Note

This report must not be reproduced in full or in part without the written authority if the Director of Tank Design.

SECTION I

Objects of Trial.

(i) To obtain additional ballistic data from the hull and turret of a Model G Panther, when subject to heavy A. P. Attack, and to test the various joints of the structure.

(ii) To determine the effect upon the hull and turret roofs of the detonation of No. 75 grenades placed in contact with these roof plates.

SECTION II

Target Details

The target was a German Panther tank No. 135 (PzKw Mk V Model G) No. 120404, which had been subject to a firing trial reported in A. T. No. 232, Part II. The engine, radiators, fuel tanks, transmission and other internal equipment had been removed to enable the damage to the rear faces of the armour to be inspected. Diagrams giving the plate thickness and angles a presentation, together with the Brinell Hardness figures, will be found in Part II of this report.

SECTION III

Method of Attack

The target was attacked from a range of 40 yards with 17-pdr AP, 6-pdr AP and 6-pdr APC. The plates attacked were as follows:

Nose plate *v*. 17-pdr AP at 55 degrees.

Hull machine-gun *v*. 17-pdr AP at 55 degrees.

Offside pannier *v*. 6-pdr AP at 50 degrees and 6-pdr APC at 50 degrees.

Offside lower side armour *v*. 6-pdr AP at 50 degrees and 6-pdr APC at 50 degrees.

Mantlet nearside edge *v*. 6-pdr AP at 30 degrees.

Front face of turret gun *v*. 17-pdr AP at normal.

Offside walls of turret *v*. 6-pdr AP at 50 degrees and 6-pdr APC at 50 degrees.

Rear wall of turret *v*. 6-pdr AP at 50 degrees.

Turret cupola *v*. 6-pdr AP.

The angles of tilt to the vertical of the various plates were read by means of a clinometer, and the target was turned to present azimuth angles to suit the compound angles of strike required. Azimuth angles were read by means of a sighting protractor. Hawkins Grenades (No. 75) were laid on the hull and turret roofs, and initiated electrically.

SECTION IV

Trial Commentary. (6-pdr AP and APC)

(i) Offside Pannier

With the side of the tank at 42 degrees to the gun, making a compound angle of attack of 50 degrees, six rounds of AP. At velocities lying between 2,760 F.S. and 2,366 F.S. were directed at the pannier side. From these rounds the ballistic limit was found to be 2,458 f.s., Equivalent to a range of 680 yards, and the W/R limit 270 f.s., Indicating that the pannier should behold a range of 370 yards. (Rounds 108-113)

   With similar conditions to those above, 12 rounds of 6-pdr APC shot were fired at the pannier. At velocities of 2,432 f.s. and 2,418 f.s. The damage code was W and C respectively, the other 10 rounds, all at high velocities than these two, showed that at this obtuse angle of attack consistent results could not be obtained; this is shown below:

Round	118	119	117	120	122	121	116	115	123	124
Velocity	2,785	2,735	2,659	2,658	2,603	2,599	2,533	2,474	2,441	2,438
Code	W	W	C	W	C	R	C	D	R	W

All these rounds were fair hits, the shots shattered on impact and either scooped or holed the armour. An estimate of the ballistic limit shows this to be about 2,425 f.s. (Rounds 114–125).

(ii) Offside Lower Side Armour

This plate was attacked at 50 degrees to normal by five rounds of 6-pdr AP shot at velocities between 1,827 f.s., the ballistic limit was found to be 1,843 f. s. and therefore the plate would be immune if attacked at this angle at ranges are greater than 1,520 yards. (Rds. 126–130).

   For the attack by APC shot at 50 degrees, ten rounds were fired. A severe failure occurred at round 132, striking velocity 1928 f.s., when a flake was dislodged, but no confirmatory failures was obtained. A ballistic limit which disregards round 132 was assessed at 2009 f.s., the discrepancy evidently being due to the steep angle and the variable quality of the armour. (Rds. 131–140).

(iii) Turret Mantlet

The nearside edge of the mantlet was attacked by two rounds of 6-pdr, AP at 30 degrees in an attempt either to peg the mantlet to the turret, or to force the mantlet into contact with the turret and so prevent elevation or depression of the mounting. Both rounds scooped off without jamming the mantlet, but it was seen that the two castings were rubbing at certain points, the normal clearance was 0.375 to 0.5 inches. The striking velocity of the rounds was 2,290 f.s. corresponding to a range of 900 yards. (Rds. 106–107).

(iv) Offside Walls of Turret

The side walls of the turret are formed from bent plates, the forward offside wall was attacked with seven rounds of 6-pdr AP one round of 6-pdr APC. Shot at 50 degrees (Rds. 76–82, 105), and the rear offside wall was attacked with one round of 6-pdr. AP and three rounds of 6-pdr APC shot at 50 degrees (Rds. 83–86). The ballistic limit of the forward wall under 6-pdr AP attack was 2,160 f. s. equivalent to a range of 1,070 yards. The rear wall under APC attack at 50 degrees was immune at 2,307 f.s. confirming the Inferiority of the capped shot.

(v) Rear Wall of Turret

Nine rounds of 6-pdr AP shot at 50 degrees were directed against the rear wall of the turret; these gave a ballistic limit of 2,257 f.s. and a W/R limit of 2,579 f.s. These correspond to the ranges of 940 yards and 530 yards respectively. (Rds. 87–89, 98–103).

(vi) Turret Cupola

One round of 6-pdr AP at 50 degrees was aimed at the junction between the cupola and turret roof at a velocity of 2,276 f.s. The interior of the cupola was undamaged, one bolt was dislodged from a retaining segment. (Rd. 104).

SECTION V

Trial Commentary (17-pdr AP)

1. Hull Nose at 53 Degrees (Thickness 51.5 mm)

Reports of vehicles previously examined gave the thickness of the nose plate as 60 mm or 75 mm. The perforations caused by the 17-pdr AP Rounds 90 and 91, made either thickness appear excessive, and the actual thickness of the plate on this whole was measured and found to be 51.5 mm. These rounds at lower velocities indicated that the ballistic limit was approximately 1,800 f.s. and that the flakes were liable to be dislodged by impacts at velocities above this limit. (Equivalent range 2,200 yards.) The plate was also found to be very brittle. (Rds. 90–94).

2. Hull Machine-Gun Mounting (Glacis Plate at 55 Degrees)

One round striking on the joint between the main housing, over the machine-gun mounting, and the Iglesias plate, scooped upwards without causing appreciable damage. Although the weld attaching the housing to the glacis plate had been fractured all-round by previous attack against the glacis plate, the crack was only opened 0.125 inches.

A second round at a similar striking velocity struck directly on the ball, which it broke in pieces and conveyed into the hull, together with the lower part of the housing. Equivalent ranges for these two rounds was approximately 1,940 yards. (Rds. 95–96).

3. Turret Front

One round at a velocity similar to those used against the ball mounting was directed at the turret front adjacent to the joint with the offside plate. The round carried away parts of front and side armour and penetrated into the turret where damage from fragments was widespread. (Rd. 97).

SECTION VI

Trial Commentary (AT Grenades)

1. Hull Roof at Nearside of Turret

A grenade was laid on the roof plate across the butt joint at the nearside of the turret. Its detonation blue in a piece of the plate above the ammunition racks, damage which would have caused a cordite fire had live rounds been stowed. The roof plate was 17 mm thick. (Rd. 141).

2. Engine Compartment Roof

The detonation of a grenade towards the rear edge of the main hatch over the engine, drove a piece of the hatch 9 × 5 inches into the engine compartment, where it would undoubtedly have interfered with the efficiency of the engines, probably by breaking the rear carburettor and causing a fire. (Rd. 142).

3. Turret Roof

The turret roof had been severely cracked by Round 60 (75-mm HE) against the cupola and successive 6-pdr. Attack on the turret walls had extended the cracks. The front portion of the roof plate at the offside was, however, undamaged and it was therefore attacked with a grenade. Again the 17-mm roof plate was holed by the detonation, and considerable internal damage to the machine-gun, offside buffer cylinder of the main piece and to the loader would have resulted.

N.B. 14 mm of I.T. 100 is normally sufficient to keep out a Hawkins No. 75 grenade. The fact that the 17-mm German plate fails so completely is due to its excessive brittleness.

SECTION VII

Summary

1. 6-pdr Attack

The following table summarises the information obtained during the attack on various plates of the hull and turret, with 6-pdr AP and APC ammunition. Ballistic limits and W/R limits are given where possible, and equivalent ranges are based on 6-pdr, 7-cwt Mks IV and V.

| | | | | AP | | | APC | | |
Plate	Thickness	Presentation	Angle of strike	B.L. f.s.	W/R f.s.	Equiv. Range yards	B.L. f.s.	W/R f.s.	Equiv. Range, yards
Turret side	47 mm	Side of turret at 44 degrees	50 degrees	2,160 (2,250)	2,200+	1,070 1,020-	Immune at 2,600		500
Turret rear	47 mm	Rear of turret at 44 degrees	50 degrees	2,257 (2,250)	2,579	940 530			
End of Mantlet	?	Front of turret at 30 degrees	60 degrees	Immune 2,290		900			
Pannier side	52 mm	Side of hull at 42 degrees	50 degrees	2,458 (2,420)	2,700	680 370	2,425 approx.		730
Lower side armour	41.5 mm	Side of Hull at 50 degrees	50 degrees	1,843 (2,070)	1,900+	1,520 1,430	2,000 approx.		1290

(Velocities in brackets are average ballistic limit figures obtained under similar conditions of attack against British machineable quality armour)

It was found in general that AP shot gave more consistent results than APC and, with the exception of the attack on the pannier side, was more successful at given strike velocity.

All the plates attacked showed flaking tendencies, and, with the exception of that forming the turret rear, proved brittle and cracked extensively under attack.

2. 17-pdr AP Attack

This form of attack against the hull nose revealed that on this whole the nose plate was only 51.5 mm thick, and could be penetrated sufficiently to cause lethal damage at ranges up to 2,200 yards. A ballistic limit of 1,800 f.s. was estimated, and the plate proved brittle and flaky.

The hull machine-gun mounting and the turret front plate can both be defeated by 17-pdr AP at a range of 1,940 yards.

3. AT Grenades (No. 75)

Attack from No. 75 grenades on the roofs of hull, turret, and engine compartment, defeated the 17-mm armour in each case by blowing a hole in the plate.

SECTION VIII
Conclusion

1. Armour
All the plates on this vehicle which were attacked with AP shot of either 6-pdr or 17-pdr. Calibre showed pronounced flaking tendencies, and, with the exception of the turret rear plate, cracked extensively.

Where ballistic limits against 6-pdr attack at 50 degrees to normal were assessed on the 40–50-mm plates, they were generally slightly lower than the average of these obtained from machineable quality plates in the United Kingdom. It should be appreciated, however, that they are well within the spread of such results, a spread which is fairly wide at this oblique angle of attack, and is partially due to variations in the quality of the shot used.

Results obtained from a 51.5-mm plate against 17-pdr AP shot at 50 degrees also suggested that the ballistic limit against this form of attack obtained on the Panther hull nose, which was the same thickness, was lower than might have been expected.

Thin plates forming the roofs of hull, turret, and engine compartment, all approximately 17 mm thick, are more brittle than I.T. 100 14-mm plates and fail to withstand the detonation of a No. 75 AT grenade.

2. Welds and Structure
As previously noted in Part II of this report, extensive junction cracking, much of which had existed before the trial, was revealed when various plates were attacked. In general the welds showed little ductility, particularly on the hull. The welds which showed least tendency to fail were those securing the turret roof to the turret sides, and those between the hull roof and pannier sides.

Welds between glacis plate and roof plate, and between glacis plate and nose plate failed completely during the attack on the glacis and hull nose plates.

The structure of the vehicle proved most satisfactory in general, the design of the joints at the front being such that even when welds failed completely no collapse of the hull could occur. The weakest joints were those between lower side armour and pannier floors, but as these are normally protected by skirting plates the weakness is not serious. Another weakness is apparent at the joints between the turret front and sides where frontal attack from AP is likely to force out the side plate by penetrating into the joint at the side of the tenon from the side plate. The target area is, however, small.

3. Hull Machine-Gun Mounting
While direct hits on the mounting from 17-pdr AP at ranges up to 2,000 yards are likely to defeat the protection, it is noticeable that the area around the mounting shows no weakness comparable with that around the ball mountings fitted in British tanks. The vulnerable area is therefore very small, chiefly due to the fact that the aperture required for the machine-gun is so very much smaller than that required for the Besa.

4. Cupola
The method of attaching the cupola to the turret roof proved very effective against HE and AP attack. The heads of bolts in the locking segments may, however, be violently dislodged by either attack, thus providing a potential danger to members of the turret crew.

5. Turret Ring
Impacts from AP shot or shell, of calibre greater than 20 mm, which occur within one calibre of the bottom edge of the turret walls, will almost certainly jam the traversing movement.

G. Guthrie, Major, R.E.M.E.
Officer i/c. Armour Trials Section, Armour Branch.

SECRET

Appendix A: Sheet No. 1

Trial No. X.795

TARGET	ATTACK	OBSERVATION
Offside wall of turret	Round 76 6-pdr AP at 50-degree compound. SV 2,076 f.s. Range 120 feet	Code D. Scoop 5.25 × 2.5 × 1 inch deep. Struck 14 inches below top edge of turret. Bulge 6 × 3.5 × 0.375 inches high. Crack to top edge 13 inches vertically and one diagonal to bottom 28 inches long.
Offside wall of turret	Round 77 6-pdr AP at 50-degree compound. SV 2,154 f.s. Range 120 feet	Code D severe. Shatter scoop 3.75 × 2.5 × 0.75 inches deep. Struck 8 inches above bottom edge of turret. Bulge 3.5 × 2.375 × 0.75 inches high. Two vertical cracks across bulge 2.5 inches and 1.25 inches long. Plate sheared horizontally along edge of weld to floor 2.5 inches. Weld fractured half in throat and half in junction to floor from 3.5 inches
Offside wall of turret	Round 78 6-pdr AP at 50-degree compound. SV 2,159 f.s. Range 120 feet	Code R. Hole 1.875 × 1.25 inches. Struck 10 inches below top edge of turret. Flake off 5.5 × 4 × 0.75 inches
Offside wall of turret	Round 79 6-pdr AP at 50-degree compound. SV 2,127 f.s. Range 120 feet.	Code C. Dent 5.375 × 2.75 × 0.875 inches. Bulge 5.5 × 3.25 × 0.375 inches. Crack extends from Rd. 76 to 77. Turret floor fractured from bend of offside plate for 8.5 inches towards ring. Welded between floor and make up piece at the end of turret fractured for 6 inches in junction to make up piece.
Offside wall of turret	Round 80 6-pdr AP at 50-degree compound. SV 2,174 f.s. Range 120 feet	Code C. Shatter scoop. Dent 1 inch deep. Struck 12 inches below top edge of turret. Bulge 3.5 × 3.5 × 0.75 inches. Floorplate set down 0.1875 inches.
Offside wall of turret	Round 81 6-pdr AP at 50-degree compound. SV 2,190 f.s. Range 120 feet	Code R. Hole 1.75 × 1.5 inches. Struck 9 inches below top edge of turret. Weld to front cracked 9.5 inches from top adjacent to side plate junction 3 inches from front top of interlock. Two cracks in junction to side plates on the front face 5.25 inches and 1 inch. Two cracks in plate 7 inches long from Round 80. One from Rd. 76 across point of impact 41 inches long approx. Flake off 7 × 5 × 1.375 inches. Flake lifted around previous round 1 foot on 4.r inches radius. Crack from Rd. 80 through 81 four 18 inches to junction with front plate. Fragments of shot inside turret.
Offside wall of turret	Round 82 6-pdr APC at 50-degree compound. SV 2,143 f.s. Range 120 feet	Code C. Shatter scoop 3.5 × 2.5 × 0.875 inches. Struck 7 inches below top edge. Bulge 4.5 × 3.5 × 0.5 inches.

TARGET	ATTACK	OBSERVATION
Rear offside wall of turret	Round 83 6-pdr APC at 50-degree compound. SV 2,174 f.s. Range 120 feet	Code C. Shatter scoop 2.375 × 2.75 × 0.875 inches. Bulge 4.5 × 3.5 × 0.5 inches high stop Old junction crack in tenon 2.75 inches long.
Rear offside wall of turret	Round 84 6-pdr APC at 50-degree compound. SV 2,214 f.s. Range 120 feet	Code C. Scoop 5 × 2.5 × 0.875 inches. Triangular portion of turret 12 × 8 inches fell out of bottom corner of turret below point of impact of Rd. 77. Struck 15 inches below top edge of turret and 8 inches to rear of the end of turret wall. Horizontal crack across Rd. 83 14 inches long.
Rear offside wall of turret	Round 85 6-pdr APC at 50-degree compound. SV 2,607 f.s. Range 120 feet	Code D. Scoop 7 × 2.25 × 1.25 inches. Struck 6 inches from top edge and 6 inches from bend. Bulge 7.5 × 4.5 × 0.75 inches.
Rear offside wall of turret	Round 86 6-pdr AP at 50-degree compound. SV 2,181 f.s. Range 120 feet	Code D. Scoop 6.5 × 2.75 × 1 inches. Struck top edge of tenon 4 inches from rear edge of turret. Rear edge of side plate fractured in line with tenon and also at point 6 inches above tenon. Portion 16.5 inches long forced sideways 0.75 inches at point of impact. External fill it between side and rear fractured 19 inches in junction of rear plate and 1.5 inches in throat. Bulge on side plate 2 × 4 × 1.375 inches. Horizontal crack 1.375 inches across bulge. Metal forced back 0.1875 inches. Vertical crack in rear plate 2 inches long.
Rear wall of turret	Round 87 6-pdr AP at 50-degree compound. SV 2,134 f.s. Range 120 feet	Code C. Scoop 5 × 2.25 × 1 inches. External world to nearside wall fractured 19.5 inches in weld metal. Struck 5.5 inches below top edge and 4 inches from nearside edge. Bulge 5.5 × 3.75 × 0.5 inches. Welded to turret side plate broken in junction to side plate 10 inches from top. (Plate 45 mm thick).
Rear wall of turret	Round 88 6-pdr AP at 50-degree compound. SV 2,172 f.s. Range 120 feet	Code C. Shatter scoop 4 × 2.375 × 1.1875 inches. Bulge 4.5 × 4.25 × 0.75 inches. Tenon between rear plate and nearside wall has existing crack down front edge of tenon. New crack opened in rear edge 7 inches long in junction to tenon. Old crack 6 inches long between and on rear of junction to side plate.
Rear wall of turret	Round 89 6-pdr AP at 50-degree compound. SV 2,172 f.s. Range 120 feet	Code C. Shatter scoop 4 × 2.25 × 1.125 inches. Struck 4 inches from nearside edge. Bulge 3.25 × 3.5 × 0.75 inches.
Nose plate. Front of tank at normal to gun	Round 90 17-pdr AP at 53 degrees. SV 2,233 f.s. Range 120 feet	Code R. Hole 3.125 × 2.5 inches. Struck 11 inches below top edge of nose plate. Flake off 7 × 5.25 × 0.75 inches. Offside support for final drive gearbox forced away from hull nose 1.5 inches at top edge and welds to nose plate cracked for 18 inches on offside and 16 inches on nearside.

TARGET	ATTACK	OBSERVATION
Nose plate. Front of tank at normal to gun	Round 91 17-pdr AP at 53 degrees. SV 2,046 f.s. Range 120 feet	Code R. Hole 3 × 2.5 inches. Flake off 6 × 5 × 0.75 inches. (Thickness 51–52 mm) Struck 6 inches below top edge of nose plate. Crack 5 inches long now runs from Rd. 90 to offside
Nose plate. Front of tank at normal to gun	Round 92 17-pdr AP at 53 degrees. SV 1,759 f.s. Range 120 feet	Code C. Scoop 5.5 × 3 × 0.75 inches. Struck 14.5 inches below top edge of nose plate. Crack noted after Rd. 91 now open 0.09375 inches and extended 4 inches on opposite side of Rd. 90. Radial cracks 2 inches and 1.75 inches long at Rd. 91. Bulge 5.5 × 3.5 × 0.375 inches. Fractured world between nose and glacis now open 0.1875 inches at centre.
Nose plate. Front of tank at normal to gun	Round 93 17-pdr AP at 53 degrees. SV 1,915 f.s. Range 120 feet	Code R. Hole 3.5 × 2.625 inches. Struck 17 inches below top edge of nose plate. Flake off 8 × 6.5 inches average thickness 1.25 inches. Nearside support for final drive forced away from armour. Crack 7 inches running radially below hole.
Nose plate. Front of tank at normal to gun	Round 94 17-pdr AP at 53 degrees. SV 1,838 f.s. Range 120 feet	Code E. Scoop 6 × 3 × 1 inches. Plate set back 1 inch at point of impact. Flake off 4 × 6 × 1 inches. Cracks running towards Rd. 93 6 inches. Cracks running towards Rd. 92 8 inches and one running towards bottom 6 inches. Extensive cracking of nose plate from previous rounds. Air ducts to clutch and final drive dislodged.
Hull machine-gun	Round 95 17-pdr AP SV 1,906 f.s. Range 120 feet	Code D. Struck junction of machine-gun housing on glacis plate on offside and scooped upwards removing 4.5 inches of external fillet and portions of adjacent armour. Crack between housing and world now open 0.125 inches below point of impact. Crack running to point of impact of Rd. 36 13 inches long.
Hull machine-gun	Round 96 17-pdr AP SV 1,922 f.s. Range 120 feet	Code W. Struck top in a court of aperture and broke off portion 7 × 11 inches for full thickness. Ball unit dislodged in fragments and floor ribs below turret distorted by impact of these fragments.
Offside front face of turret	Round 97 17-pdr AP at normal SV 1,915 f.s. Range 120 feet	Code W. Struck 2 inches from side at bottom of tongue of side plate. 4 × 1.625 × 4 inches removed from front plate. 9 × 9 inches from side plate for full thickness (47 mm). Crack 24 inches long running to rear to point of impact of Rd. 63. Internal: Hole 3.5 × 4.5 inches. Internal weld to front plate split in the throat for 9 inches. Nose of shot struck edge of turret floor below rear escape door removing 5 × 1 × 1 inches from edge. Teeth of turret traversing rack at bottom side of turret marked by fragments.
Rear wall of turret	Round 98 6-pdr AP at 50-degree compound. SV 2,579 f.s. Range 120 feet	Code W. Hole 2.625 × 2.375 inches. Struck 13 inches below top edge of turret. Flake off 2 × 3 × 0.75 inches. Four teeth of Traverse track damaged by fragments.
Rear wall of turret	Round 99 6-pdr AP at 50-degree compound. SV 2,579 f.s. Range 120 feet	Code R. Hole 2.75 × 2 inches. Struck 12 inches above bottom edge of turret. Metal broke off 2.75 × 2 inches.

TARGET	ATTACK	OBSERVATION
Rear wall of turret	Round 100 6-pdr AP at 50-degree compound. SV 2,306 f.s. Range 120 feet	Code D severe. Shatter scoop 3.75 × 2.75 × 0.875 inches. Bulge 3.5 inches dia. × 0.75 inches high. Struck 10 inches above bottom edge of turret. Three star crack 2 × 1.25 × 1 inches.
Rear wall of turret	Round 101 6-pdr AP at 50-degree compound. SV 2,349 f.s. Range 120 feet	Code R. Shatter scoop 4.25 × 2.5 inches. Hole 2 × 1.75 inches. Part of base lodged. Metal off 2 × 2 inches. Struck 9.75 inches above bottom edge of turret.
Rear wall of turret	Round 102 6-pdr AP at 50-degree compound. SV 2,269 f.s. Range 120 feet	Code R. Shatter scoop 4 × 2.375 inches. Hole 2.125 × 1.125 inches. Struck 11 inches below top edge of turret. Metal of 2.125 × 2.75 inches. Crack in turret floor 10 inches from inner edge near escape door adjacent to damage caused by Rd. 97.
Rear wall of turret	Round 103 6-pdr AP at 50-degree compound. SV 2,255 f.s. Range 120 feet	Code W. Struck 2 inches below top edge and 8 inches from escape door opening. Hole 6 × 3 inches. 2 inches of outer fillet removed. Roof plate cracked 9 inches perpendicular to edge. Flake off 13.5 × 6.125 × 1 inches.
Cupola	Round 104 6-pdr AP at 50-degree compound. SV 2,276 f.s. Range 120 feet	Code D. Scoop 9 × 3 inches in junction of cupola to roof. One bolt dislodged from segment adjacent to impact. Edge of amateur lifted 0.25 inches. Roof plate cracked from edge to cupola opening. 4.5 inches of world metal broken from roof in junction with 0.25 inches of side plate still attached. Roof plate forced down 2 inches at one end. Interior of cupola undamaged.
Offside wall of turret	Round 105 6-pdr AP at 50-degree compound. SV 2,265 f.s. Range 120 feet	Code R (L). Struck 2.75 inches above bottom edge of turret and 3.5 inches from front end of side plate (i.e. centre of joint). Bottom edge of turret plate forced down jamming turret.
Front of turret at 30 degrees to gun.	Round 106 6-pdr AP at 60 degrees SV 2,290 f.s. Range 120 feet	Struck nearside edge of mantlet. Scoop full width of edge 6 × 2 × 0.875 inches. Mantlet not jammed.
Front of turret at 30 degrees to gun.	Round 107 6-pdr AP at 60 degrees SV 2,294 f.s. Range 120 feet	Struck nearside edge of mantlet. Scoop 5.5 × 2.25 × 0.875 inches. Mantlet not jammed. Slight rubbing of mantlet against turret.
Offside pannier	Round 108 6-pdr AP at 50-degree compound. SV 2,366 f.s. Range 120 feet	Code C. Scoop 6 × 2.375 × 1.25 inches. Struck 10 inches below top edge of pannier. Bulge 6 × 4 × 0.5 inches.

TARGET	ATTACK	OBSERVATION
Offside pannier	Round 109 6-pdr AP at 50-degree compound. SV 2,760 f.s. Range 120 feet	Code W. Hole 2.75 × 2.375 inches. Struck 10 inches below top edge of pannier. Flake off 5 × 4.5 × 0.5 inches. Fracture of world to roof plate extended by 3.25 inches.
Offside pannier	Round 110 6-pdr AP at 50-degree compound. SV 2,676 f.s. Range 120 feet	Code R. Base lodged. Struck 12 inches below top edge of pannier. Flake off 6 × 4.125 × 0.625 inches.
Offside pannier	Round 111 6-pdr AP at 50-degree compound. SV 2,476 f.s. Range 120 feet	Code R. Part of base lodged. Struck 6.5 inches below top edge of pannier. Flake off 4.75 × 4.125 × 0.75 inches.
Offside pannier	Round 112 6-pdr AP at 50-degree compound. SV 2,441 f.s. Range 120 feet	Code C. Shatter scoop 4.875 × 2.75 × 1.5 inches. Struck 13 inches below top edge of pannier. Bulge hidden by straps.
Offside pannier	Round 113 6-pdr AP at 50-degree compound. SV 2,419 f.s. Range 120 feet	Code C. Shatter scoop 5 × 2.375 × 1.25 inches. Struck 5.5 inches below top edge of pannier. Bulge 5.5 × 4.5 × 0.75 inches.
Offside pannier	Round 114 6-pdr APC at 50-degree compound. SV 2,418 f.s. Range 120 feet	Code C. Shatter scoop 4.75 × 2.5 × 1.125 inches. Struck 13 inches below top edge of pannier. Bulge 5 × 3.75 × 0.5 inches.
Offside pannier	Round 115 6-pdr APC at 50-degree compound. SV 2,474 f.s. Range 120 feet	Code D. Shatter scoop 5 × 2.625 × 1.25 inches. Struck 5.5 inches below top edge of pannier. Bulge 6 × 4.5 × 0.75 inches. Vertical crack 0.5 × 0.0625 inches open. Horizontal crack to rear 6 inches from point of impact to Rd. 110 on external face. Plate dished inwards 0.5 inches.
Offside pannier	Round 116 6-pdr APC at 50-egree compound. SV 2,533 f.s. Range 120 feet	Code C. Scoop 6.5 × 2.625 × 1.25 inches. Struck 4.5 inches below top edge of pannier. Crack in plate immediately above point of impact 6 inches forward and 9 inches to rear. Inner weld split in throat 17 inches from top edge of glacis plate then from 13 inches in junction to roof plate then from 4 inches in throat total length 34 inches. Bottom weld pannier side to floor cracked 25 inches mostly in junction two floorplate. Crack starts 16 inches from front of pannier bottom. Bulge 7 × 4 × 0.75 inches.
Offside pannier	Round 117 6-pdr APC at 50-degree compound. SV 2,659 f.s. Range 120 feet	Code C. Scoop 6.5 × 2.5 × 1.125 inches. Struck 6.5 inches below top edge of pannier side and floor opposite point of impact – welds fractured. Flange of bulkhead to roof fractured. Bulkhead forced sideways 1 inch and severely buckled.

TARGET	ATTACK	OBSERVATION
Offside pannier	Round 118 6-pdr APC at 50-degree compound. SV 2,785 f.s. Range 120 feet	Code W. Shatter area 6 × 3.375 inches. Hole 2.25 × 2.25 inches. Struck 11 inches below top edge of pannier. Flake off 5.25 × 3.75 × 0.75 inches.
Offside pannier	Round 119 6-pdr APC at 50-degree compound. SV 2,735 f.s. Range 120 feet	Code W. Shatter area 4.75 × 3 inches. Hole 2.75 × 2.25 inches. Struck 13.5 inches below top edge of pannier. Flake off 7 × 5.75 × 1 inches.
Offside pannier	Round 120 6-pdr APC at 50-degree compound. SV 2,658 f.s. Range 120 feet	Code W. Struck 3.25 inches below top edge of pannier. Hole 4 × 2.25 inches. Shatter area 5.25 × 3 inches. Flake off 8.5 × 5.75 × 1 inches.
Offside pannier	Round 121 6-pdr APC at 50-degree compound. SV 2,599 f.s. Range 120 feet	Code R. Struck 10.5 inches below top edge of pannier. Hole 2.375 × 2 inches. Shatter area 4 × 2.75 inches. Flake off 9 × 5.25 × 0.75 inches.
Offside pannier	Round 122 6-pdr APC at 50-degree compound. SV 2,603 f.s. Range 120 feet	Code C. Bulge 6.25 × 4 × 3.75 inches. Struck 7 inches above bottom edge of pannier. Shatter scoop 6 × 2.5 × 1.5 inches.
Offside pannier	Round 123 6-pdr APC at 50-degree compound. SV 2,441 f.s. Range 120 feet	Code R. Struck 5.5 inches above bottom edge of pannier and 3.5 inches behind joint to glacis plate. Shutter scoop 4.25 × 2.5 inches. Metal off 2.5 × 2.25 inches.
Offside pannier	Round 124 6-pdr APC at 50-degree compound. SV 2,438 f.s. Range 120 feet	Code W. Struck 3 inches above bottom edge of pannier. Circum. Crack 15 inches on 6-inch radius from bottom edge of plate. Bottom edge of plate forced down 2.25 inches and cracked into places. Pannier floorplate cracked for 9 inches from edge. Weld, pannier side to floor fractured 10 inches. Bottom corner of roof stiffening bulkhead forced forward 4 inches and torn from welds to pannier side and floor. Flake off 4.5 × 3.75 × 0.75 inches.
Offside pannier	Round 125 6-pdr APC at 50-degree compound. SV 2,432 f.s. Range 120 feet	Code W. Struck 1.75 inches from edge of pannier. 2.75 × 3 inches removed from pannier side. 4.5 × 4 inches removed from roof plate. Roof plate cracked to crack caused by HE Round 63, for distance of 10 inches from hole in roof plate, 14 inches from edge of roof. Top weld split in junction to roof plate 4 inches forward and 2 inches to rear, total 10 inches. Flake off 7 inches × 4.625 × 1 inches.
Offside lower side armour.	Round 126 6-pdr AP at 50 degrees SV NO f.s. Range 120 feet	Code R. Hole 1/32 × 1.625 inches. Struck 11 inches below pannier floor. Metal off 2 × 1.375 inches.

TARGET	ATTACK	OBSERVATION
Offside lower side armour.	Round 127 6-pdr AP at 50 degrees SV 1,834 f.s. Range 120 feet	Code D. Shatter scoop 2.375 × 2 × 0.375 inches. Struck 8.5 inches below pannier floor. Struck opposite web of forward roof gusset and gusset plate removed. Crack in armour 6 inches long diagonally across bulge also radial crack 6 inches long. Flake lifted 0.25 inches about 5 × 4 inches. 2 inches of 10-inch weld remaining intact, now broken away with the gusset plate.
Offside lower side armour.	Round 128 6-pdr AP at 50 degrees SV 1,839 f.s. Range 120 feet	Code D slight. Scoop 2.5 × 2 × 0.5 inches. Struck 12 inches below pannier floor. Bulge 4.5 × 3.5 × 0.375 inches.
Offside lower side armour.	Round 129 6-pdr AP at 50 degrees SV 1,874 f.s. Range 120 feet	Code R. Hole 1.5 × 1.75 inches. Struck 6.5 inches below pannier floor. Metal off 2 × 1.625 inches.
Offside lower side armour.	Round 130 6-pdr AP at 50 degrees SV 1,827 f.s. approx. Range 120 feet	Code R. Hole 1.5 × 1.625 inches. Struck 14 inches below pannier floor. Metal off 1.75 × 1.625 inches.
Offside lower side armour.	Round 131 6-pdr APC at 50 degrees SV 1,851 f.s. Range 120 feet	Code C. Shatter 2.75 × 2 × 0.375 inches. Struck 7 inches below pannier floor. Bulge 2.5 × 2.5 × 0.3125 inches.
Offside lower side armour.	Round 132 6-pdr APC at 50 degrees SV 1,928 f.s. Range 120 feet	Code R. Struck 14 inches below pannier for. Flake off 3.25 × 3.875 × 0.5 inches. Half off flake 2.5 × 3 inches forced back 0.875 inches. Hole 1.75 × 1.625 inches.
Offside lower side armour.	Round 133 6-pdr APC at 50 degrees SV 1,888 f.s. Range 120 feet	Code C. Scoop 2.75 × 2 × 0.375 inches. Struck 13 inches below pannier floor. Bulge 2.5 × 2.5 × 0.375 inches.
Offside lower side armour.	Round 134 6-pdr APC at 50 degrees SV 1,917 f.s. Range 120 feet	Code D. Struck 8.5 inches below pannier floor. Bulge 3.5 inches dia. × 0.375 inches high. Circum. Crack 1.375 inches on 1.125 inches radius.
Offside lower side armour.	Round 135 6-pdr APC at 50 degrees SV 1,935 f.s. Range 120 feet	Code C. Scoop 2.5 × 2 × 0.375 inches. Struck 9.5 inches below pannier floor. Bulge 4 × 4 × 0.375 inches high.
Offside lower side armour.	Round 136 6-pdr APC at 50 degrees SV 1,959 f.s. Range 120 feet	Code C. Shatter 3.75 × 2.5 inches. Struck 8 inches below pannier floor. Struck 5 inches from Rd. 128. Flake off 3 × 3 × 0.625 inches. Hole 2 × 1.25 inches.

TARGET	ATTACK	OBSERVATION
Offside lower side armour.	Round 137 6-pdr APC at 50 degrees SV 1,963 f.s. Range 120 feet	Code C. Scoop 2.5 × 2.25 × 0.625 inches. Struck 8.5 inches below pannier floor. Bulge 3.5 × 3.5 × 0.4375 inches.
Offside lower side armour.	Round 138 6-pdr APC at 50 degrees SV 2,016 f.s. Range 120 feet	Code E severe. Shatter 3.5 × 2.5 × 0.625 inches. Struck 11 inches below pannier floor. Metal off 2.75 × 2 × 0.5 inches.
Offside lower side armour.	Round 139 6-pdr APC at 50 degrees SV 2,003 f.s. Range 120 feet	Code C. Scoop 2.5 × 2 × 0.375 inches. Struck 12.5 inches below pannier floor. Bulge 3.5 × 2.25 × 0.25 inches.
Offside lower side armour.	Round 140 6-pdr APC at 50 degrees SV 2,037 f.s. Range 120 feet	Code R (L). Struck 8.5 inches below pannier floor. Flake off 4.5 × 3.25 inches.
Nearside hull roof at butt weld in plate.	Round 141 No. 75 grenade Filled 704 B. Detonated electrically.	Detonation. Hole 4 × 4 inches. Plate forced in 1.25 inches max. over area 10.5 × 9 inches. Weld to pannier side fracture 3 feet 3 inches mostly in junction to pannier side. Metal off 4.5 × 5 inches. Three radial cracks 6 inches long in roof plate. Pannier floor and remnants of ammunition rack severely dented by fragments of roof plate.
Engine compartment roof. Rear end of central door. (Door 16 mm thick) (Roof plate 17 mm thick).	Round 142 No. 75 grenade Filled 704 B. Detonated electrically.	Detonation. Portion of plate 9 × 5 inches driven into engine compartment. Adjacent area 8 × 5 inches forced down 1.25 inches maximum. Lifting handle removed. External rim of locking spindles fractured. Landing strip around rear end forced down at right and left-hand sides. 8.5 × 7 inches removed from inside of door.
Front of turret roof plate	Round 143 No. 75 grenade Filled 704 B. Detonated electrically.	Detonation. Hole 6 × 5 inches. Area 16 × 7 inches forced downwards max. of 0.5 inches. Lifting eye at offside fractured. Well detaching in an end of eye broken. Cracks in junction adjacent roof plate (weld to turret front) 8 × 1.5 inches long. Weld to protect around ventilator cover fractured 5 inches in junction to protect. Flake off 9 × 6.5 inches. Back edge of turret front forced down 0.375 inches. Weld between turret front and roof cracked 6 inches. Fragments of roof caused damage to offside buffer casing and would have seriously damaged machine-gun mounting if in position.

APPENDIX B

Trial No. X.795: AT No. 232: Part III: PzKw V Panther. 6-pdr Attack

Offside wall of turret after attack by 6-pdr AP rounds seventy-six to eighty-one and eighty-six at 50 degrees and 6-pdr APC rounds eighty-two to eighty-five at 50 degrees. Round sixty-three was a 25-pdr HE round fired during part two of the trial. (*Department of Tank Design*)

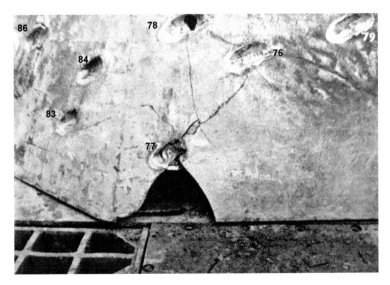

Offside wall of turret at bend after attack by 6-pdr AP rounds seventy-six to seventy-nine and eighty-six at 50 degrees and 6-pdr APC rounds eighty-three and eighty-four at 50 degrees. The triangular portion of the armour was dislodged by round eighty-four. Round seventy-seven struck on the level of the turret floor plate. (*Department of Tank Design*)

Rear offside wall of turret after attack by 6-pdr AP round eighty-six at 50 degrees and 6-pdr APC rounds eighty-three to eighty-five at 50 degrees. Round eighty-six struck on the tenon of the interlocking joint formed by the rear plate. (*Department of Tank Design*)

Inside face of offside wall of turret after 6-pdr AP rounds seventy-six to eighty at 50 degrees and 6-pdr APC rounds eighty-two to eighty-five at 50 degrees. Note extensive cracking. (*Department of Tank Design*)

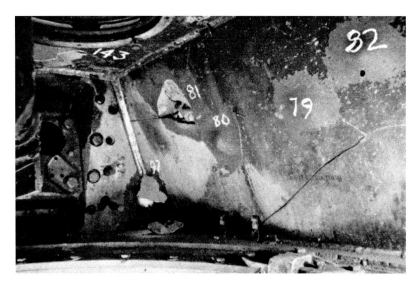

Showing inside face of offside wall of turret after attack by 6-pdr AP rounds seventy-nine to eighty-one at 50 degrees; 6-pdr APC round eighty-two at 50 degrees; and 17-pdr AP round ninety-seven at normal on the front face of the turret. (*Department of Tank Design*)

Inner face of offside turret wall after attack by 6-pdr AP rounds seventy-six to seventy-eight and eighty-six at 50 degrees and 6-pdr APC rounds eighty-two to eighty-five at 50 degrees. (*Department of Tank Design*)

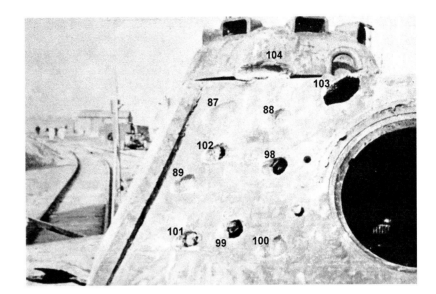

Rear wall of turret after attack by 6-pdr AP rounds eighty-seven to eighty-nine and ninety-eight to 103. The cupola was attacked by one 6-pdr AP round (no. 104) at 50 degrees. (*Department of Tank Design*)

Inner face of rear wall of turret after attack by 6-pdr AP rounds eighty-seven to eighty-nine and ninety-eight to 103 at 50 degrees. This plate had flakes dislodged from the inner face, as had all the other plates of the vehicle, but the extensive cracks that developed in the other plates did not occur in this plate. (*Department of Tank Design*)

Flake off rear wall of turret caused by 6-pdr AP round 103 at 50 degrees. (*Department of Tank Design*)

Trial No. X.795: AT No. 232: Part III: PzKw V Panther, 17-pdr Attack

Nose plate after attack by 17-pdr AP rounds ninety to ninety-four at 53 degrees—note extensive cracking. (*Department of Tank Design*)

Nose plate after attack by 6-pdr APDS round seventeen at 53 degrees and 17-pdr AP rounds ninety to ninety-four at 53 degrees. Glacis plate after attack by 6-pdr APDS rounds eighteen and nineteen at 55 degrees; 17-pdr APDS rounds twenty-nine, thirty, thirty-two, and thirty-three at 55 degrees; and 17-pdr APCBC rounds thirty-four and thirty-five at 55 degrees. The left-hand transmission bracket was flame-cut to permit removal of flake dislodged by round thirty-four. (*Department of Tank Design*)

Nose plate after attack by 17-pdr AP rounds ninety to ninety-two and ninety-four at 53 degrees. Glacis plate after attack by 17-pdr APDS rounds twenty-nine and thirty at 55 degrees. (*Department of Tank Design*)

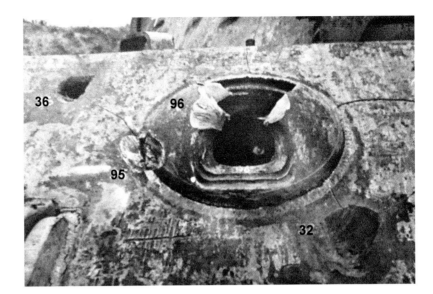

Hull machine-gun after attack by 17-pdr AP round ninety-five—S.V. 1906 f.s. and round ninety-six—S.V. 1922 f.s., which dislodged the ball unit into the hull. (*Department of Tank Design*)

Rear face of hull machine-gun ball-mounting after attack by 17-pdr AP rounds ninety-five and ninety-six. Glacis plate after attack by 17-pdr APDS rounds twenty-nine, thirty, and thirty-two at 55 degrees and 17-pdr AP round thirty-six at 55 degrees. Note extensive cracking of glacis plate. (*Department of Tank Design*)

Fragments of ball-mounting after recovered from inside hull mounting projected into hull by 17-pdr AP round ninety-six. The large proportion, top left, was found outside and is part of the domed upper housing. (*Department of Tank Design*)

Trial No. X.795: AT No. 232: Part III: PzKw V Panther. 6-pdr and 17-pdr Attack

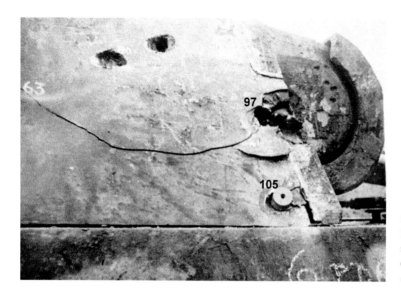

Front face of turret after attack by 17-pdr AP round ninety-seven at normal. Offside turret wall after attack by 6-pdr AP round 105 at 50 degrees. Round ninety-seven holed the turret. Round 105 forced down the edge of the plate and jammed the turret. (*Department of Tank Design*)

Showing nearside edge of turret mantlet after attack by 6-pdr AP rounds 106 and 107 at 60 degrees. The mantlet was not jammed by this attack but rubbing between the mantlet and turret front occurred in places. (*Department of Tank Design*)

Offside pannier after attack by 6-pdr AP rounds 108 to 113 at 50 degrees and 6-pdr APC rounds 114 to 118 and 122 to 125 at 50 degrees. (*Department of Tank Design*)

Trial No. X.795: AT No. 232: Part III: PzKw V Panther, 6-pdr Attack

Offside pannier after attack by 6-pdr AP rounds 110 to 113 at 50 degrees and 6-pdr APC rounds 114, 115, 117 to 122, 124, and 125 at 50 degrees. Note 'edge effect' on the impact of round 124 and 125. (*Department of Tank Design*)

Interior of offside pannier after attack by 6-pdr AP rounds 108 to 110 at 50 degrees and 6-pdr APC rounds 115 and 116 at 50 degrees. The bottom corner of the bulkhead was forced by Round 124. (*Department of Tank Design*)

Offside pannier showing back damage from 6-pdr AP rounds 111 to 113 at 50 degrees and 6-pdr APC rounds 114, 117, 118, 120, 122, 124, and 125 at 50 degrees. (*Department of Tank Design*)

Showing back damage to offside pannier from 6-pdr APC rounds 119 to 122 at 50 degrees. Note excessive flaking and compare damage to round 123, where a similar attack dislodged a plug from the same plate. (*Department of Tank Design*)

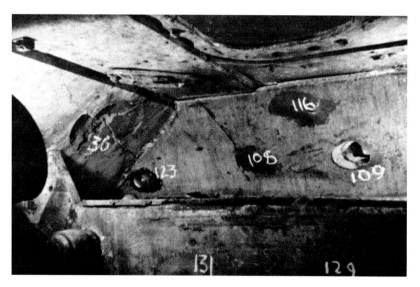

Back damage to front end of offside pannier from attack by 6-pdr AP rounds 108 and 109 at 50 degrees and 6-pdr APC rounds 116 and 123 at 50 degrees. Round thirty-six on the glacis plate was a 17-pdr AP round at 55 degrees. (*Department of Tank Design*)

Offside lower armour after attack by 6-pdr AP rounds 126 and 128 at 50 degrees and 6-pdr APC rounds 134 and 136 at 50 degrees. Round sixty-four was a 75-mm HE round fired during part two of this trial. (*Department of Tank Design*)

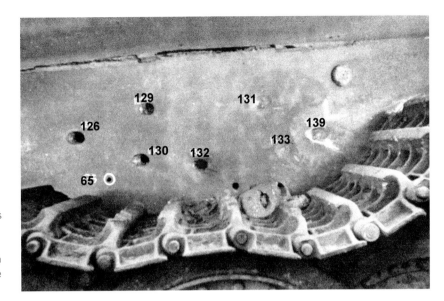

Offside lower armour after attack by 6-pdr AP rounds 126, 129, and 130 at 50 degrees and 6-pdr APC rounds 131 to 133 and 139 at 50 degrees. The weld to the pannier floor was split by the blast from round sixty-five, a 25-pdr HE round fired during part two of the trial. (*Department of Tank Design*)

Offside lower armour after 6-pdr APC rounds 134 to 138 at 50 degrees. Round sixty-four was a 75-mm HE round fired during part two of the trial. (*Department of Tank Design*)

Back damage to lower armour at offside after 6-pdr AP and APC attacks. Note a tendency to form plugs at rounds 126, 129, 130 and flake lifted at Round 127. (*Department of Tank Design*)

Forward end of offside lower armour showing variable back damage. Rounds 129, 126, and 130 forced out plugs, while rounds 127 and 132 lifted or dislodged flakes. (*Department of Tank Design*)

Central portion of offside lower armour showing back damage caused during a 6-pdr attack. The stiffening member was first damaged by round sixty-four (a 75-mm HE round) and weld failures developed during 6-pdr attack. (*Department of Tank Design*)

Another view of a damaged stiffening device below bulkheads in pannier. Note that piston rod of the rear suspension system is fractured, possibly as a result of the detonation of three AT grenades (round sixty-seven) beneath the track. (*Department of Tank Design*)

Right rear corner of fighting compartment, showing hole in bulkhead caused by 6-pdr APCBC round forty-three, which defeated the turret side at 50 degrees and penetrated the fuel tank behind the bulkhead and caused a severe fire. (*Department of Tank Design*)

6-pdr APC round 140 defeated the lower armour at 50 degrees at a velocity equivalent to a range of 2,300 yards. (*Department of Tank Design*)

No. 75 Grenade Attack

Position of No. 75 grenade across butt joint in hull roof at nearside before detonation. (*Department of Tank Design*)

Hole blown in hull roof by No. 75 grenade detonated in contact. Ammunition for 75-mm gun is stowed below this point. Roof plate is 17 mm thick. (*Department of Tank Design*)

Location of No. 75 grenade used to attack the cover over the engine compartment before detonation. (*Department of Tank Design*)

Result of detonation of No. 75 grenade on hatch over the engine compartment. Hatch was 17 mm thick. (*Department of Tank Design*)

Location of AT grenade No. 75 near to joint between turret roof and front casting before detonation. (*Department of Tank Design*)

Result of detonation of No. 75 grenade on turret roof (17 mm thick). (*Department of Tank Design*)

Interior of turret roof after the detonation of round 143. The hole measured 6 inches by 5 inches and the area from which the flake was removed 9 inches by 6.5 inches. (*Department of Tank Design*)

APPENDIX C

Trial No. X.794: AT No. 232: Part III: Panther V model G. Diagrammatic Sketch Showing Armour Disposition

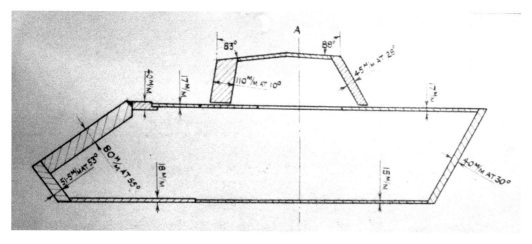

Diagram showing the side view of the Panther tank, its armour thickness and angles. (*Department of Tank Design*)

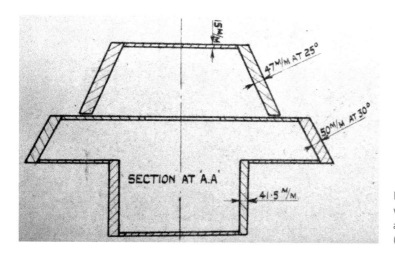

Diagram showing the front view of the Panther tank, its armour thickness and angles. (*Department of Tank Design*)

Report of Mine Trials Against PzKw V (Panthers) Held at S. of E. Range, Shoeburyness on 28, 29, 30 November and 1 December 1944

DTD Experimental Report
AT No. 232: Part IV.
Project No: M.6815A/4
Trial No: X.826
File No: 250/188

Present at Trial

Name	Representing	Date Present Nov.–Dec.
Col. Speechly	C.E.A.D.	30th
Major Edwards	A.2.	29th
Capt. Martin	C.E.A.D.	28th, 30th
Mr. Day	C.S.A.R.	28th, 29th, 30th

Mr. Stout	C.E.A.D.	30th
Lt. Tredinnick	of E. (Range Officer)	28th, 29th, 30th, 1st
Mr. Gray	DTD Armour Branch	28th, 29th, 30th, 1st
Mr. Wild	DTD Armour Branch	30th

Range Personnel

Report
Compiled by: Mr. G.W. Gray   DTD (Armour Branch)

Checked by: Major G. Guthrie   DTD (Armour Branch)
Mr. J.B. Sankey   DTD (Armour Branch)

References
Section I.   -   Objects of Trial.
Section II.   -   Target Details.
Section III.   -   Method of Attack.
Section IV.   -   Trial Commentary
Section V.   -   Summary of Results
Section VI.   -   Conclusion

Appendices
Appendix A.   Detailed Results.
Appendix B.   Photographic Record.
Appendix C.   Sketch

Note
This report must not be reproduced in full or in part without the written authority of the Director of Tank Design.

SECTION I

Object of Trial
To determine the degree of resistance of the tracks, suspensions and hull side to floorplate structure of Panther tanks to attack from various anti-tank mines.

SECTION II

Target Details
These consisted of three PzKw V (Panther) Tanks as follows: –
DTD No. 3,040—Hull and turret with part tracks and suspensions.
DTD No. 3,041—Hull and turret with tracks and suspensions, less certain bogies.
DTD No. 3,031—Hull and turret with one track and suspensions.

SECTION III

Method of Attack
The attack against the tracks and suspensions was carried out by burying the mine in meadowland, with the top of the mine 2 inches below the underside, and central with the track width. In every case spaced flange wheels were selected under which the mines were placed.

When attacking the hull side to floorplate structure, the mines were buried a similar amount but with the centre of the mine under the inner edge of the track. In this case both spaced and closed flange wheels were selected under which the mines were placed.

Throughout the trial every effort was made to maintain the same dimensions, mine to target, for reasons of comparison. Such differences as did occur were due to the waterlogged conditions of the site. These slight differences where they occur were not considered sufficient to influence the result. Confirmation of all types of mines was not possible owing to the limitation of targets.

Reference to Table A following, shows the attack for each item.

Table A: Position of Mines

	ITEM NO.	DETAILS OF MINE	TARGET ATTACKED
Tank No. 3031	1	One 4-lb non-detectable mine Filled TNT (4-lb)	Track and Suspensions
	2	One Mk V reduced depth AT mine. Filled TNT (5-lb)	Track and Suspensions
	3	One 4-lb non-detectable mine Filled TNT (4-lb)	Track and Suspensions
Tank No. 3041	4	One Mk V Standard AT mine. Filled TNT (8-lb)	Hull side to floorplate structure and suspensions.
	5	One Mk V Standard AT mine. Filled TNT (8-lb)	Hull side to floorplate structure and suspensions.
	6	One Mk V Standard AT mine. Filled TNT (8-lb)	Hull side to floorplate structure and suspensions.
	7	One Mk V Standard AT mine. Filled TNT (8-lb)	Hull side to floorplate structure and suspensions.
Tank No. 3040	8	One 5.5-lb Asbestos-cement mine. Filled TNT (5.5-lb)	Track and Suspensions
	9	One 5.5-lb Asbestos-cement mine. Filled TNT (5-5lb)	Hull side to floorplate structure and suspensions.
	10	One 10-lb mine. Filled TNT (10-lb)	Hull side to floorplate structure and suspensions.
Tank No. 3041	11	One 15-lb mine. Filled TNT (15-lb)	Hull side to floorplate structure and suspensions.
	12	One 15-lb mine. Filled TNT (15-lb)	Hull side to floorplate structure and suspensions.

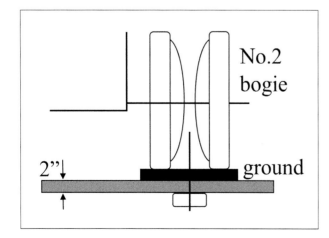

Table A, Item No. 1.

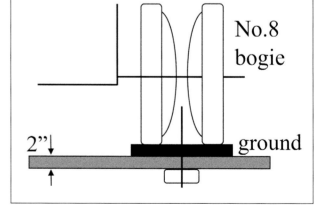

Table A, Item No. 2.

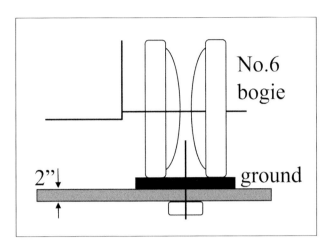

Table A, Item No. 3.

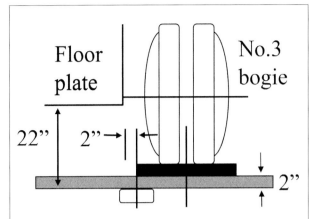

Table A, Item No. 4.

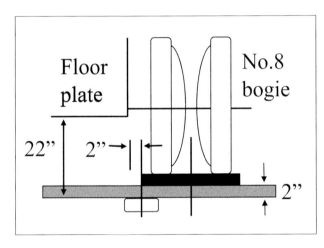

Table A, Item No. 5.

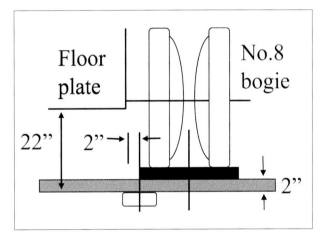

Table A, Item No. 6.

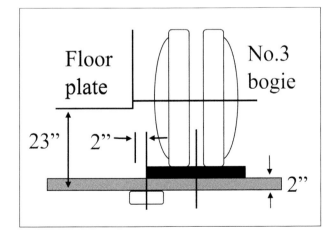

Table A, Item No. 7.

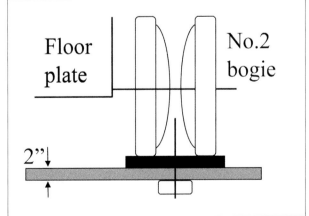

Table A, Item No. 8.

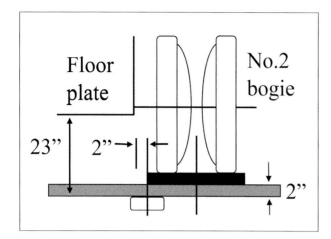

Table A, Item No. 9.

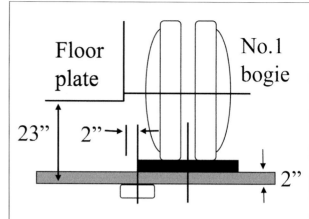

Table A, Item No. 10.

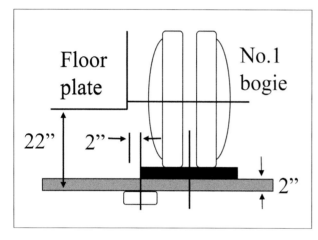

Table A, Item No. 11.

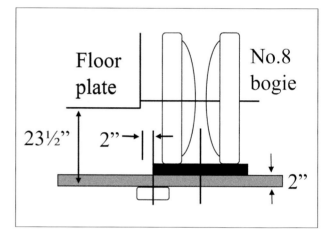

Table A, Item No. 12.

SECTION IV

Trial Commentary

Tank No. 3031—To Test Track and Suspensions

Item 1. Mine Under Centre of Track Detonated in Line with No. 2 Bogie
One 4-lb non-detectable mine (4-lb TNT) failed to detonate an inspection revealed the casing broken and the charge exposed. The mine was therefore destroyed with a 1-lb slab of gun cotton. Only minor damage was caused to the track, due, it is considered, to the loss of power owing to the filling being unconfined. The damage was slight, and the vehicle would still be a runner.

Item 2. Mine Under Centre of Track Detonated in Line with No. 8 Bogie
One Mk V reduced-depth mine (5-lb TNT) broke the track, and No. 8 bogie outer disc was blown away. A field repair to track would be possible.

Item 3. Mine Under Centre of Track Detonated in Line with No. 6 Bogie
One 4-lb non-detectable mine (4-lb TNT) broke the track, confirming the view that a similar mine (Item 1) did not develop its full power. The track in this case could be repaired in the field.

Tank No. 3041—To Test Hull to Floor Plates Structure

The hull to floor plate was constructed on the interlocking joint principle secured by inner and outer fillet welds. The hull side was 40 mm thick, the forward floor 25 mm, and rear floor 15 mm thick. Reference to the sketch Appendix C shows a detail of this joint.

It was intended to test the forward floor by detonating mines under the first road bogies but as the first and second bogies were missing on the right and left-hand sides respectively, it was decided to use the third bogies. Since our object was to compare the behaviour of the hull structure when the forward floor plate was 25 mm, and the rear floor plate was 15 mm, the change of position of mine from the first to third road bogie was considered to be immaterial.

Item 4. Mine Under Inner Edge of the Track Detonated in Line with No. 3 Bogie (Floor plate 25 mm)
One Mk V standard mine (8-lb TNT) broke the track, and split No. 3. bogie in several places. The hull floor to side plate structure was not affected. Field repairs to track would have been possible.

Item 5. Mine Under Inner Edge of the Track Detonated in Line with No. 8 Bogie L. H. side (Floor plate 15 mm)
One Mk V standard mine (8-lb TNT) failed to break the track, but sheared out metal over an area 18 inches long × 6 inches wide from the inner edge, and severely buckled and perforated No. 8. bogie. Apart from some pitting of the floor plate the structure was not affected. The tank would continue to run.

Item 6.
[This] was a repeat of item 5 but on the opposite side of the vehicle. The track inner edge damage was less severe than for item 5 and the hull two-floor plate structure remained intact. The vehicle would continue to run.

Item 7.
[This] was a further test similar to item 4 but with the mine in line with No. 3. bogie R. H. side. The track damage was comparable to item 4. The hull structure was unaffected.

Track No. 3040—To Test Track and Suspensions
The hull two-floor plate structure was not interlocked. The floor plate was secured to the whole side by inner and outer fillet welds. Reference to sketch Appendix C shows a detail of this joint.

Item 8. Mine Under Centre of the Track Denoted in Line with No. 2 R. H. Bogie
One asbestos cement type mine (5.5-lb TNT) broke the track. No. 2. bogie outer disc was completely blown away and the inner disc severely buckled.

Item 9. To Test Hull to Floor Plate Structure. Mine Under Inner Edge of Track Detonated in Line with No. 2 L. H. Bogie
One asbestos cement type mine (5.5-lb TNT) sheared a portion of track away over area 6 inches long × 4 inches wide from inner edge. No damage was caused to the hull to floor plate structure.

Item 10. Mine Under Inner Edge of Track Detonated in Line with No. 1 Bogie
One experimental 10-lb mine (10-lb TNT) broke the track. No. 1. bogie outer disc was blown away, the front sprocket severely buckled and many teeth sheared out. Apart from an area of pitting on the floor plate, this structure remained intact. It is doubtful whether a field repair would have been possible in this case.

Tank No. 3041—To Test Hull to Floor Plate Structure

Item 11. Mine Under Inner Edge of Track Detonated in Line with No. 1 Bogie
One experimental 15-lb mine (15-lb TNT) failed to detonate and was destroyed by a slab of gun cotton. The track was broken, and the leading bogie and shaft forced out of position approximately 9 inches. The final drive sprocket with a length of track, damaged severely in a previous trial was completely off and thrown clear of the vehicle. Slight pitting of the floor plate only was caused and the hull and floor plate structure remained intact. Allowing for the fact that the driving sprocket would probably not have been forced off had it not have been previously damaged, it is considered that a field repair would not have been possible.

Item 12. Mine Under Inner Edge of Track, Detonated in Line with No. 8 Bogie
Owing to failure of the mine, in item 11, to detonate, it was decided to repeat the test. This mine failed to break the track, but sheared out track metal from the inner edge 12 inches long × 6 inches wide. No. 8 bogie inner flange was particularly blown away and the outer flange buckled. The bogie shaft was also forced outwards 4 inches. The whole to floor plate structure remained relatively intact. A field repair in this instance was considered doubtful. This ended the trial.

SECTION V

Summary of Results

The following table gives briefly a summary of the results obtained.

ITEM NO.	POSITION OF MINE	DETAILS OF MINE	SUMMARY OF DAMAGE	EFFECT ON TANK
	Tank No. 3031			
1	Under centre of track	One 4-lb non-detectable mine.	Track dished locally.	Capable of running
2	Under centre of track	One Mk V Reduced depth mine.	Track sheared for full width. Outer flange No. 8 bogie blown away	Temporary immobilised. Field repair to track possible.
3	Under centre of track	One 4-lb non-detectable mine.	Track sheared across the full width. No. 7 bogie out of flanged now completely removed	Temporary immobilised. Field repair to track possible.
	Tank No. 3041			
4	Under inner edge of track.	One Mk V Standard A/T Mine.	Track sheared across the full width. Outer flange No. 3 bogie split. Hull intact.	Temporary immobilised. Field repair to track possible.
5	Under inner edge of track.	One Mk V Standard A/T Mine.	Track partially severed. Hull intact.	Tank would continue to run.
6	Under inner edge of track.	One Mk V Standard A/T Mine.	Track partially severed. Hull intact.	Tank would continue to run.
7	Under inner edge of track.	One Mk V Standard A/T Mine.	Track partially severed. Hull intact.	Tank would continue to run.
	Tank No. 3040			
8	Under centre of track.	One 5.5-lb asbestos cement mine.	Track completely sheared. Out a disc No. 2 bogie blown away.	Temporary immobilised. Field repair to track possible.
9	Under inner edge of track.	One 5.5-lb asbestos cement mine.	Track partially severed. No. 2 bogie disc severely buckled.	Would probably continue to run after freeing jammed bogie
10	Under inner edge of track.	One 10-lb mine	Track completely severed. Front sprocket severely buckled and many teeth broken off. No. 1 bogie out a disc blown off. Hull intact.	Vehicle immobilised. Field repairs improbable.
	Tank No. 3041			
11	Under inner edge of track.	One 15-lb mine.	Mind failed to detonate. Destroyed with 14.5 oz of gun cotton. Track completely severed. Final drive housing damaged in previous trial completely blown off. Hull intact.	(disregarding damage to final drive housing.) Field repairs improbable.
12	Under inner edge of track.	One 15-lb mine.	Track partially severed. No. 8 bogie—in a flange partially blown away. Minor damage to hull floor locally.	Field repairs improbable.

SECTION VI

Conclusions

From the results of this trial it is concluded that: –

(a) Test Against Track and Suspensions

Any of the mines used to test the 'Panther' track and suspensions will break the track if detonated under the centre, which is the most favourable position for the mine.

When mines are detonated somewhat off centre, but within the track width, the higher charge contained in the standard Mk V, it is considered, would be necessary to ensure breaking the track.

Damage to the suspensions and bogies only cause temporary mobilisation and field repairs would have been possible.

(b) Test Against Hull to Floor Plate Structure

None of the mines use for this test, i.e. against the heavy floor plates, succeeded in causing any measurable damage to the structure.

The mines also gave conflicting results in their effect on the tracks, the same type of mime producing complete breakage, and also only partial breakage. It should be noted that for this test the mine was placed under the track inner edge.

Mines containing up to 8-lb TNT only temporarily immobilised the vehicle and in some instances the vehicle would continue to run.

It would appear, however, that suspension is, driving sprockets, and bogie damage was sufficient in the case of the 10-lb and 15-lb mines to preclude the possibility of field repairs.

It is emphasised that owing to the soft nature of the ground throughout this trial, the ground was completely water-logged, it is thought that less damage was done to tracks etc. than would normally be the case.

Finally, it is considered that the standard Mk V mine produced results which would indicate this as being the best general-purpose A/T mine.

G. Guthrie, Major, R.E.M.E.
Officer i/c. Armour Trials Section (Armour Branch)

SECRET

Appendix A

Trial No. X.826: Mine Trials Detailed Results

TARGET	ATTACK	OBSERVATIONS
Tank No. 3031 Item No. 1. Under centre of L. H. track in line with No. 2 bogie. (Spaced flange wheels).	One 4-lb non-detectable mine placed with top of mine 2 inches below lower edge of track. Mine filled TNT (4 lb) with CE exploder pellet and No. 33 electric detonator inserted into a side orifice.	Mine failed to detonate. On inspection the casing was found to be broken open and filling exposed. One lb gun cotton was placed alongside to detonate the mine. This caused the mine to explode. Crater area 4 feet dia × 18 inches deep. The outer bogie disc No. 2 was severely buckled and tyre thrown off. To track guide lugs immediately behind the outer disc were fractured and the track bulged inwards approx. 2 inches over an area 6 × 4 inches, centrally across the width of the track. One link broken. Owing to the splitting of the mine casing the filling was unconfined and therefore unlikely to develop its full power. It is considered that the vehicle would still be capable of running.
Item No. 2. Under centre of LH track in line with No. 8 bogie (Spaced flange wheels).	One Mk V reduced depth mine placed with top of mine 2 inches below lower edge of track. Mine filled TNT (5-lb). Fitted with CE one oz. field primer and No. 33 electric detonator. CE field primer was wedged against one side of exploder cavity.	Mine detonated. Crater area 5 feet dia. × 2 feet 6 inches deep. No. 8 out of bogie disc was blown away together with tyre. The track immediately above detonation was sheared across for its full width. No. 7 tyre partially blown away and the outer flange of outer bogie was split.

TARGET	ATTACK	OBSERVATIONS
Item No. 3. Under centre of LH track in line with No. 6 bogie (Spaced flange wheels).	One 4-lb non-detectable mine placed with top of mine 2 inches below lower edge of track. Mine filled TNT (4-lb) with CE exploder pellet and No. 33 electric detonator and one CE 1 oz field primer, placed near the centre and in contact with mine base, to ensure detonation after removal of detector cover.	Mine detonated. Crater area 4 feet dia. × 2 feet 6 inches deep. Inner and outer wheel discs slightly buckled. Track severed for full width. No. 7 out of flange previously fractured now completely removed together with tyre. Field repairs to track would be possible.
Tank No. 3041 Item No. 4. Under inner edge of LH track in line with No. 3 bogie (closed flange wheels). Distance from top of mine to underside belly plate 22 inches. Hull side wall 2 inches away from inner edge track.	One Mk V Standard AT Mine placed with centre of mine 2 inches below and in line with inner edge of track. Mine filled TNT (8-lb) with No. 33 electric detonator and two CE (1-oz) field primer.	Crater 3 feet dia. × 2 feet deep. Track sheared across the full width. Out of flange of No. 3 bogie split in several places. Field repairs to track would be possible. Hull floor and side plate intact.
Tank No. 3041 Item No. 5. Under inner edge of L.H. track in line with No. 8 bogie (spaced flanged wheels). Distance from top of mine to underside belly plate 22 inches. Hull side wall 2 inches away from inner edge track	One Mk V Standrd AT Mine placed with centre of mine 2 inches below and in line with inner edge of track. Mine filled with 8-lb TNT and initiated by a No. 33 electric detonator and to 1-oz standard CE primers.	Inner edge of track sheared over an area 18 inches long by 6 inches (wide). Crater 3 feet 6 inches dia. × 2 feet deep. No. 8 bogie severely buckled and tyre split. Several perforations in bogie disc, largest 1 × 0.75 inches. Some slight pitting on the outer edge of belly plate. Max. depth approx. 0.125 inches. Tank would continue to run.
Tank No. 3041 Item No. 6. Under inner edge of RH track in line with No. 8 bogie (spaced flanged wheels). Distance from top of mine to underside belly plate 22 inches. Hull side wall 2 inches away from inner edge track	One Mk V Standard AT mine placed with centre of mine 2 inches below and in line with inner edge of track. Mine filled with 8-lb TNT and initiated by a No. 33 electric detonator and to 1-oz standard CE primers.	Crater 5 × 4 × 2 feet deep with main area towards centre of vehicle. Track link sheared over area 6 × 3 inches wide. In a disc of No. 8 bogie severely buckled. Further inspection of vehicle after Item 6 indicated no appreciable damage or pitting to belly plate or hull sides.
Tank No. 3041 Item No. 7. Under inner edge of RH track in line with No. 3 bogie (spaced flanged wheels). Distance from top of mine to underside belly plate 23 inches. Hull side wall 2 inches away from inner edge track	One Mk V Standard AT Mine placed with centre of mine 2 inches below and in line with inner edge of track. Mine filled with 8-lb TNT and initiated by a No. 33 electric detonator and two 1-oz standard CE primers.	Crater 4 feet × 3 feet 6 inches × 18 inches deep with main area towards centre of vehicle. Track link sheared over area 12 × 6 inches wide. Filled repairs to track would be possible. Hull floor and side plate intact.
Tank No. 3040 Item No. 8. Under centre of RH Track in line with No. 2 bogie (Spaced flanged wheels).	One 5.5-lb asbestos cement mine 2 inches below the lower edge of track. Filled TNT with No. 33 electric detonator and two CE 1-oz field primers.	Crater size 5 feet 6 inches dia. × 2 feet 6 inches deep. No. 2 bogie out of disc completely blown away. Inner disc severely buckled. Out of disc of No. 1 bogie buckled. Track sheared across the full width.
Item No. 9. Under inner edge of LH track in line with No. 2 bogie (Spaced flanged wheels). Distance from top of mine to underside belly plate 23 inches. Hull side wall 2 inches away from inner edge track	One 5.5-lb asbestos cement mine 2 inches below and in line with inner edge of track. Filled TNT with No. 33 electric detonator and two CE 1-oz field primers.	Crater size 4 feet 6 inches × 5 feet × 2 feet deep. Portion of the track link 6 × 4 inches removed from inner edge under No. 2 bogie. No. 2 bogie inner disc severely buckled. Tyre partially stripped off. No. 1 bogie forced up and jammed by sprocket teeth. Hull belly and side wall intact.
Item No. 10. Under inner edge of RH track in line with leading bogie. (Closed flange wheels). Distance from top of mine to underside of belly plate 23 inches. Hull side wall 2 inches away from inner edge of track.	One 10-lb mine filled TNT with one CE exploder pellet cast in. Initiated with No. 33 electric detonator and 2 drams of plastic explosive around detonator. Mine 2 inches below and in line with inner edge of track.	Dimensions of mine 10 inches dia. × 2.5 inches deep, in a thin tinned iron casting. Crater size 8 feet × 6 feet × 3 feet 6 inches deep. Track sheared across full width. Front sprocket severely buckled and many teeth broken away. No. 1 bogie out of disc blown off. In a disc still in position, severely buckled. Hull floor and plate intact. Area of pitting approx. 12 × 10 inches max. depth 0.125 inches approx.

TARGET	ATTACK	OBSERVATIONS
Tank No. 3041 Item No. 11. Under inner edge of RH track in line with bleeding bogie. (Closed flange wheels). Distance from top of mine to underside of Benny plate 22 inches. Hull side wall 2 inches away from inner edge of track.	One 15-lb mine filled TNT with one CE exploder pellet cast in. Initiated with No. 33 electric detonator and 2 drams of plastic explosive around detonator. Mine 2 inches below and in line with inner edge of track.	Dimensions of mine 12 inches dia. × 2.5 inches deep in a thin tinned iron casting. Failed to detonate. 14.5-oz gun cotton placed on mine to destroy same. Crater size 9 feet × 7 feet × 3 feet 6 inches deep. Leading bogie and shaft forced out of position sideways approx. 9 inches. Inner tire flange and inner and outer flanges severely buckled. Final drive sprocket complete with length of track, previously damaged, forced away and thrown 20 feet clear of vehicle to right flank. Track sheared for the full width. Area of pitting approx. 12 × 12 inches max. Depth 0.125 inches approx. Hull floor and side plate intact.
Item No. 12. Under inner edge of RH track in line with No. 8 bogie (Spaced flange wheels). Distance from top of mine to underside of belly plate 22.5 inches. Hull side wall 2 inches away from inner edge of track.	One 15-lb mine filled TNT with one CE exploder pellet cast in. Initiated with No. 33 electric detonator and 2 drams of plastic explosive around detonator. Mine 2 inches below and in line with inner edge of track.	Crater 8 × 6 × 3 feet deep. No. 8 bogie inner flange particularly blown away. Tired destroyed. Out of flange severely buckled. No. 7 bogie in a flange buckled. Track link inner edge sheared out over area 12 × 6 inches under bogie. Floor plate split in one place parallel with side 3 inches long, split runs into fabricated hole in base plate. No. 8 bogie shaft forced outwards approx. 4 inches. Pitting over area approx. 24 × 9 inches max. depth 0.125 inches. Hull floor and side plate generally intact.

APPENDIX B

Trial No. X.826: AT No. 232: Part IV: Mine Trials: PzKw V Panther

Item No. 1: Result from 1 × 4-lb non-detectable mine plus 1 lb of gun cotton under centre of left-hand track and beneath No. 2 bogie. Track dished locally. (*Department of Tank Design*)

Item No. 3: Result from 1 × Mk V reduced depth AT mine under centre of left-handed track and in line with No. 8 bogie. Track completely broken. (*Department of Tank Design*)

Item No. 3: Result from 1 × 4-lb non-detectable mine under centre of left-hand track and in line with No. 6 bogie. Track completely broken. (*Department of Tank Design*)

Item No. 4: Result from 1 × Mk V standard AT mine under inner age of left-hand track in line with No. 3 bogie. Track completely broken but hull intact. (*Department of Tank Design*)

Item No. 5: Showing 1 × Mk V standard AT mine under inner age of left-hand track in line with No. 8 bogie. (*Department of Tank Design*)

Item No. 5: Result from 1 × Mk V standard A.T. mine shown in Item No. 5. Track metal sheared out but hull intact. (*Department of Tank Design*)

Item No. 6: Result from 1 × Mk V standard AT mine under inner edge of right-hand track and in line with No. 8 bogie. Small area of track removed but hull intact. (*Department of Tank Design*)

Item No. 7: Result from 1 × Mk V standard A.T. mine under inner edge of right-hand track and in line with No. 3 bogie. Track metal sheared out but hull intact. (*Department of Tank Design*)

Item No. 8: Result from 1 × 5.5-lb asbestos cement mine under centre of left-hand track and in line with No. 2 bogie. Broken track and other debris lying in crater. (*Department of Tank Design*)

Further view of item No. 8; picture taken after tank was placed on the fresh site. (*Department of Tank Design*)

Item No. 9: Result from 1 × 5.5-lb asbestos cement mine under inner edge of left-hand track and in line with No. 2 bogie. Small area of track removed but hull intact. (*Department of Tank Design*)

Item No. 10: Result from 1 × 10-lb mine under inner edge of right-hand track and in line with No. 1 bogie. Track completely broken but hull intact. (*Department of Tank Design*)

Item No. 11: Result from 1 × 15-lb mine under inner edge of right-hand track and in line with No. 1 bogie. Track completely broken but hull intact. (*Department of Tank Design*)

Showing right-hand sprocket and spindle, together with length of track, removed by 15-lb mine (item 11). The final drive casting had been very severely cracked during a previous trial. (*Department of Tank Design*)

Item No. 12: Result from 1–15 lb mine under inner edge of right-hand track and in line with No. 8 bogie. Only partial shearing of track but hull intact. (*Department of Tank Design*)

APPENDIX C

Trial No. X.826: AT No. 232 Part IV: Panther PzKw V: Details of 'Side Wall to Floor' Weld Joint

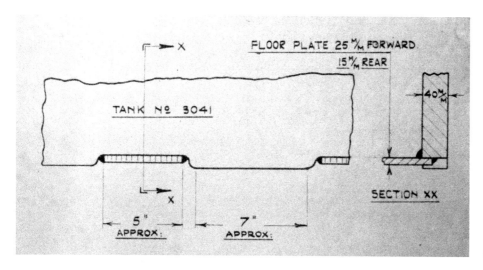

Diagram No. 1.
(*Department of Tank Design*)

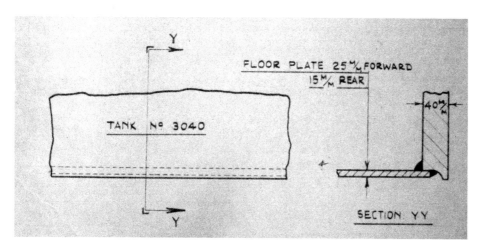

Diagram No. 2.
(*Department of Tank Design*)

13

AUTHORISED BATTLEFIELD MODIFICATIONS

German tank crews and maintenance personnel made several minor modifications to their Panther tanks at the front. Some of these battlefield modifications were authorised by the *Waffenamt* (German Army Weapons Agency). German High Command was aware of the Panther's air intake and exhaust louvres on the rear engine deck, and vulnerability to attack from above as highlighted in the results of the firing trials at Shoeburyness in England.

The *Waffenamt* authorised modifications to the rear engine deck to increase the ballistic protection to the air intake and exhaust louvres. The mechanical engineers at the tank maintenance depots and the tank crews were sent a pamphlet showing them what to do. Protective covers were to be fitted over lovers fabricated from spare side-skirt armour plate. A sufficient air gap was to be retained to enable air to be drawn into the engine and the exhaust gasses to escape.

This diagram was in a German Army pamphlet. It was intended to show the army mechanical engineers how to fabricate the authorised modifications designed to protect the Panther's air-intake and exhaust louvres on the rear engine deck. (*gem. Anweisung OKH (Ch H. Rüst u BdE) vom 18. Dezember 1944; Az.76 g/4 Nr. 234559/44, AHA/In 6(Z/In) WaA/Wa Prüf 6*)

If you look at the back of the tank on the engine deck, you can see this Panzer V Ausf. A Panther tank has been fitted with the authorised air-intake covers. Also, on the top of the turret, the crew used armour plates to add additional protection to the turret roof.

14

AIR ATTACK TRIALS

As part of scientific trials, a Panther tank was driven into the middle of a field to be used as a 'hard target' for rocket-firing RAF Typhon ground-attack fighters. It was painted white and had a large black cross on the turret. (*Department of Tank Design*)

Ground attack aircraft like the rocket-firing Typhoon were feared by German tank crews. During the Second World War, great claims were made about their effectiveness. As you will see from these British test results, those wartime claims must be looked at again. These trials were completed in Britain in controlled conditions. The Panther tank target was painted white with a big black cross on the turret to help the pilots see it. No one was firing back at the pilots. Hit rates were very poor. This was a concentrated attack on a target that was not moving. The lack of accuracy of this weapon system was disappointing. A few did hit the target on each attack, but many missed.

In the first diagram, showing an attack on the rear of the tank, only rocket number thirteen hit the target tank. The second diagram recorded the typhoon attack at the front of the tank. Only three rockets hit the Panther—numbers thirty-seven, twenty-one, and fifty-one. In the third diagram, where the line of attack had changed to assault the side of the tank, only four rockets hit the target—numbers fourteen, sixty, thirty, and fifty-seven. The colourised image on the front cover of this book was taken from this trial.

The aircraft fired 60-lb RP-3 (27-kg, 3-inch rocket projectile) HE/SAP (high-explosive/semi-armour-piercing) with 12-lb (5.4-kg) TNT filling. The '3-inch' designation referred to the diameter of the rocket motor tube. A 25-lb (11.3-kg) solid-shot armour-piercing variant was also used.

In August 1944, rocket-firing ground attack Hawker Typhoons belonging to RAF Second Tactical Air Force (2TAF) attacked German troops, soft-skinned vehicles, and armoured vehicles in the Falaise pocket. They claimed hundreds of tanks and vehicles hit. The 2TAF Operational Research Section was sent to study the vehicle wrecks still littering the battlefield immediately after the fighting in that area had stopped. They concluded that there was only evidence that seventeen vehicles had been destroyed by rocket fire alone. In battle conditions, accurate assessment of the damage caused is problematic for pilots. Smoke and dust clouds are caused by explosions. The pilots are being fired at from the ground and also have to look out for enemy fighters.

A secret report dated 1 March 1951, called *Technical Memorandum ORO-T-117, A survey of Allied Tank Casualties in World War II* by the US ORO (Operation Research Office) concluded that in the sample of 522 knocked out German tanks the team viewed between 1944 and 1945 ninety-one had been destroyed outright by air attack, thirty-five of these by rocket fire. The team concluded that only 7.5 per cent of the total 522 immobilised tanks they sampled had been knocked out by air attack.

Interrogation of captured German infantry and tank crews reviled that the prospect of rocket attack was extremely unnerving for them. Rocket attacks devastated the morale of enemy troops. It caused some vehicles to be abandoned as the crews felt they were in a big target. They felt safer walking. In Normandy in 1944, the fear of air attack and being spotted from the air by artillery observation aircraft resulted in many tanks having to hide in orchards and woods during the day to avoid detection.

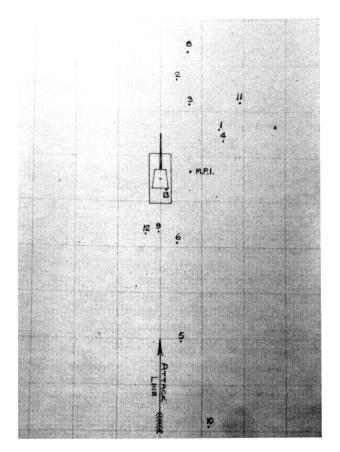 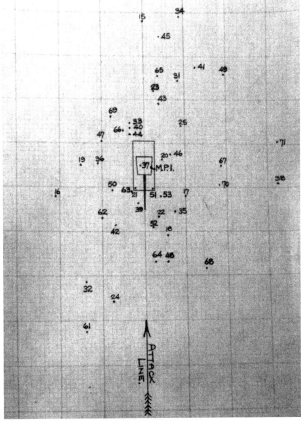

◀ Diagram showing position of strikes in relation to target: Target No. 7 Astern Attack. The letters 'MPI' are an abbreviation for main point of impact. The scale is 1 inch equals 20 feet. Each large square is 1 inch. Impact No. 7 was 30 feet above impact No. 8 and not shown on the sheet (Appendix C to Report A.T. No. 280 Part II O.B.Proc U2679). (*Department of Tank Design*)

▶ Diagram showing position of strikes in relation to target: Target No. 9 Ahead Attack. The scale is 1 inch equals 20 feet. Each large square is 1 inch. The letters 'MPI' are an abbreviation for main point of impact (Appendix C to Report A.T. No. 280 Part II O.B.Proc U2679). (*Department of Tank Design*)

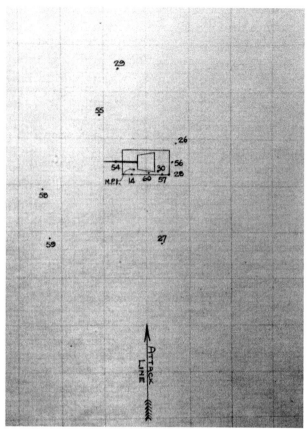

◄ Diagram showing position of strikes in relation to target: Target No. 8 Flank Attack. The letters 'MPI' are an abbreviation for main point of impact. The scale is 1 inch equals 20 feet. Each large square is 1 inch (Appendix C to Report A.T. No. 280 Part II O.B.Proc U2679). (*Department of Tank Design*)

❯ These three photographs show near misses around the white-painted target Panther tank. (*Department of Tank Design*)

◄ A hit on the rear engine deck started a fire. (*Department of Tank Design*)

❯ The fire from the engine compartment spread to the road wheels. (*Department of Tank Design*)

15

BRITISH ANTI-TANK WEAPONS

THE ORDNANCE QF 17 POUNDER ANTI-TANK GUN

The 17-pdr gun's full name was 'Ordnance QF 17 pounder'. It was a British tradition to name their guns after the weight of the shot. The letters 'QF' stand for 'quick firing'. It had a calibre of 3 inches (76.2 mm) and a muzzle velocity that ranged from 2,900 ft/s (884 m/s) to 3,950 ft/s (1,204 m/s) depending on the type of ammunition used.

A towed version was produced, and it was also modified to fit into tank turrets and onto tank hulls to be used as an anti-tank self-propelled gun.

The first 17-pdr prototype was produced in the spring of 1942. With news of the arrival of the heavily armoured Tiger tank in the deserts of North Africa, it was rushed into production. The first 100 were sent without their correct gun carriage. They were fitted onto 25-pdr gun carriages and called the 17/25-pdr. They were given the communications codename 'Pheasants'. If the Germans intercepted any radio traffic about the gun's arrival, it was hoped they would believe an officer had ordered a delivery of game birds for his dinner table. They first saw action in February 1943.

The next delivery of guns was fitted with their bespoke new gun carriage. They saw service in Sicily and on the Italian mainland. They were very effective. Anti-tank regiment units deployed them in north-west Europe from D-Day until the end of the war.

The Mk I was the first production version of the 17-pdr anti-tank gun. The Mk II was used on the Archer self-propelled gun and the A30 Cruiser Mark VIII Challenger tank. The gun carriage mountings were modified so that it would fit in these vehicles. Initially, the muzzle brake was removed and replaced with a counterweight, but with the introduction of the more powerful APCBC rounds, the muzzle brake was refitted. The Mk III was used by the Royal Navy on landing craft. The Mk IV was adapted to fit in the Sherman Firefly turret. The breech block slid to the side rather than down, to take up less room. The Mk V version used different gun mounts to enable it to fit into the US-built 3-inch gun motor carriage M10 (TD Wolverine) and replace its 3-inch 76.2-mm M7 gun.

An Ordnance QF 17-pdr anti-tank gun without its gun shield and sights being restored at Adrian Barrell's workshops in Suffolk, England.

A 17-pdr A30 Cruiser Mark VIII Challenger tank at the Overloon Museum, Holland.

The QF 17-pdr Mk II was fitted into the A30 Cruiser Mark VIII Challenger tank. They were issued to tank regiments equipped with 75-mm armed Cromwell tanks. The A30 Challenger used an adapted Cromwell tank hull so this helped in logistics: the engineers only had to carry Cromwell hull spare parts. Where possible, one Challenger tank was assigned to three Cromwell tanks. It provided a more powerful anti-tank over-watch capability.

The turret had to be totally redesigned to enable the 17-pdr gun to be mounted on the tank hull. It was of a vertical slab armour plate design. To keep the weight of the tank low, the front of the turret armour was only 63 mm thick. The sides were 40 mm thick. The Cromwell tank's turret had 75-mm armour on the front and 60 mm on the side. The hull machine gun was removed to provide extra space for the larger 17-pdr shells. Only 200 were built as priority was given to building more Sherman Firefly tanks and the new A34 Comet tank. They saw action in north-west Europe following D-Day.

Over 2,000 17-pdr Sherman Firefly tanks were built. They were normally issued to tank regiments equipped with 75-mm Sherman tanks. Where possible, one firefly tank fought alongside three 75-mm Sherman tanks as a 'troop'. They provided over-watch as they could knock out enemy tanks at a longer distance.

The front half of the longer 17-pdr barrels were often painted a lighter colour to make it appear the tank was only armed with the shorter barrelled 75-mm gun. The Germans quickly realised that the Firefly was a big threat and was the first tank to be targeted if it could be identified.

The 40-inch (1-m) recoil of the towed Mk 1 was too long to work in a tank turret. The recoil system was redesigned. The cylinders were shortened and placed on either side of the gun. The gun breech now loaded from the left side after it was rotated 90 degrees.

The hull machine gun was removed to enable the larger 17-pdr ammunition to be stored. It still had a coaxial Browning 0.30-calibre (7.62-mm) machine gun in the turret. Although the turret size was increased with a bustle at the back to house the radio, the armour thickness was not increased apart from an extra 13 mm added to the new gun mantlet. They saw action in north-west Europe following D-Day.

The British 17-pdr self-propelled anti-tank gun, Archer entered production in mid-1943 and 655 were built. They entered service in October 1944 and saw action in north-west Europe. In 1942, the British High Command knew they quickly needed a long-range anti-tank gun fitted to a tracked hull that could take on the Tiger tank. It was too big to fit into any of the current British tank turrets then in service. The Valentine tank hull had proven itself to be reliable. Vickers engineers decided to remove the Valentine tank's turret and place the gun behind the driver with the long barrel pointing backwards over the engine deck. The gun crew were protected from small arms fire and shrapnel by a raised open-topped superstructure.

It was designed as a low-profile ambush weapon. The rearward firing capability was seen as an advantage. It did not have to turn around to retreat. The Archer would back into a position, fire at the target, then drive off at full speed to avoid enemy return fire. This tactic was known as 'shoot and scoot'.

The British Army in the Second World War did not use the American Army term 'Tank Destroyer'. Vehicles like the Archer were called self-propelled anti-tank guns.

A 17-pdr Sherman Firefly tank at Bastogne Barracks, Belgium.

A 17-pdr self-propelled anti-tank gun, Archer, at the Overloon Museum, Holland.

A 17-pdr self-propelled anti-tank gun M10c, Achilles, at Bastogne Barracks, Belgium.

The British Army converted 1,100 US-built 3-inch gun motor carriage M10s (TD Wolverine) by replacing its 3-inch 76.2-mm M7 gun with the more powerful QF 17-pdr gun. This also helped with logistics as ammunition could be sourced from Britain rather than relying on US Army supplies.

They were given the designation 17-pdr self-propelled anti-tank gun M10c, Achilles. The letter 'c' indicated that the vehicle was armed with a 17-pdr gun. They saw action with the Royal Artillery and the Royal Canadian Artillery in north-west Europe and took part in the Battle of the Bulge Ardennes offensive. The gun was enclosed in an open-topped turret.

It was powered by a General Motors 6046 conjoined twin 6-71s diesel engine that produced 375 hp. It has a top road speed of 32 mph (52 km/h) with an operational range of around 186 miles (300 km). It had a five-man crew: commander, driver, gunner, loader, and loader's assistant. Its armour was thin but sloped. It ranged from 9 mm to 57.2 mm in thickness.

A number of other vehicles were fitted with the 17-pdr gun, but these were only prototype versions and did not enter into mass production: Centurion Mk1, Black Prince, Avenger, AC4 Sentinel, Terrapin 2, Tortoise, Grizzly Firefly, and the TOG.

The 17-pdr tank APCBC (armour-piercing capped ballistic cap) round projectile weighed 17 lb (7.71 kg). The complete APCBC round weighed 37.5 lb (17 kg). The 17-pdr tank-mounted gun fired the APCBC round at a muzzle velocity of 2,900 ft/s (884 m/s). Firing range penetration performance trials data show that the 17-pdr APCBC round, when fired at homogeneous armour set at a 30-degree angle, could penetrate 140 mm of armour at 500 yards (457 m), 130 mm at 1,000 yards (914 m), 120 mm at 1,500 yards (1.37 km), and 111 mm at 2,000 yards (1.83 km).

The 17-pdr tank APDS (armour-piercing discarding sabot) round projectile weighed 7.9 lb (3.58 kg). The complete APDS round weighed 28.4 lb (12.88 kg). The 17-pdr tank-mounted gun fired the APDS round at a muzzle velocity of 3,950 ft/s (1,204 m/s). Firing range penetration performance trials data show that the 17-pdr APDS round, when fired at homogeneous armour set at a 30-degree angle, could penetrate 208 mm of armour at 500 yards (457 m), 192 mm at 1,000 yards (914 m), 176 mm at 1,500 yards (1.37 km), and 161 mm at 2,000 yards (1.83 km).

THE ORDNANCE QF 6-POUNDER ANTI-TANK GUN

The British 2-pdr tank gun could penetrate the thin 15-mm frontal armour of the German Panzer III tanks that were used during the Battle of France in 1940 and all Italian tanks encountered in the deserts of North Africa. This situation changed when the Germans upgraded their tank's frontal armour to 50 or 60 mm. The armour-piercing rounds were no longer able to penetrate that thickness of armour. The British needed a bigger more powerful anti-tank gun.

A new anti-tank gun was already in development at the Woolwich Arsenal in London. It was called the Ordnance QF 6-pounder (6-pdr) after the British tradition of naming their guns after the weight of the shot. 'QF' is an abbreviation for 'quick firing'. It had a calibre of 57 mm and a muzzle velocity that ranged from 2,700 ft/s (820 m/s) to 4,000 ft/s (1,219 m/s) depending on the type of ammunition used.

The gun was completed in 1940 but work on the gun carriage design was not finished until 1941. Production started in November 1941, and the first towed version of the 6-pdr entered service in May 1942.

A modified 6-pdr gun was fitted into the Crusader Mk III tank turret. It was also mounted in the turrets of the Valentine Mk IX and Churchill Mk III and IV tanks. The AEC Armoured car Mk II was also armed with the 6-pdr anti-tank gun.

An Ordnance QF 67-pdr towed anti-tank gun at Adrian Barrell's workshops in Suffolk, England. (*Adrian Barrell*)

The Centaur, Cavalier, and Cromwell tanks were designed to be armed with the 6-pdr gun. The Cromwell was upgraded and armed with the Ordnance QF 75-mm gun when it was deployed to the beaches of Normandy in June 1944.

One of the advantages of the 6-pdr was that it could fire a variety of ammunition including high explosive (HE) shells. This was one of the tank crew criticisms of the 2-pdr gun: it could only fire armour-piercing rounds.

The introduction of the towed 6-pdr anti-tank gun in the deserts of North Africa meant that with the exception of the Tiger tank crews could once again knock out German tanks. They could not penetrate the Tiger's frontal armour, but lucky shots on the turret ring and tracks could disable it and force the crew to abandon their vehicle.

In 1943, the 6-pdr gun crews could choose to load AP (armour-piercing), APC (armour-piercing capped), APCBC (armour-piercing capped ballistic cap), and HE (high explosive) shells.

In 1944, the introduction of more sophisticated anti-tank ammunition in the form of the APCR (armour-piercing composite rigid) shot and the APDS (armour-piercing discarding sabot) shot helped increase the potency of the gun.

The first mass-produced version was called the Mk 2. It had the shorter L/43 barrel. The 6-pdr Mk 3 was the tank gun version of the Mk 2. The Mk 4 had a longer L/50 barrel and had a single baffle muzzle brake fitted. The Mk 5 was the tank gun version of the Mk 4.

The 6-pdr tank AP (armour-piercing) round projectile weighed 6.28 lb (2.84 kg). The complete AP round weighed 12.92 lb (5.86 kg). The 6-pdr Mk 3 tank gun fired the AP round at a muzzle velocity of 2,830 ft/s (862.58 m/s). The 6-pdr Mk 5 tank gun fired it at 2,920 ft/s (890 m/s).

The 6-pdr tank APCBC (armour-piercing capped ballistic cap) round projectile weighed 7.27 lb (3.30 kg). The complete APCBC round weighed 13.88 lb (6.29 kg). The 6-pdr Mk 3 tank gun fired the APCBC round at a muzzle velocity of 2,580 ft/s (789 m/s). The 6-pdr Mk 5 tank gun fired it at 2,700 ft/s (823 m/s).

The A15, Cruiser Mk VI, Crusader Mk III tank armed with a 6-pdr gun.

The A15, Cruiser Mk VI, or Crusader Mk III was the first tank to be armed with the Ordnance QF 6-pdr anti-tank gun. It had previously been armed with a QF 2-pdr gun. The tank featured Christie suspension, coupled with a relatively powerful V-12 350-hp engine; this gave the Crusader tank greater speed and manoeuvrability compared to others in 1941, especially on flat terrain, as found in the North African landscape. It was built by Nuffield Mechanizations and Aero Ltd.

The 40-mm frontal armour on the early Crusader tanks was strong enough to prevent the early German 3.7-mm anti-tank gun from penetrating its armour. Most Italian tanks' main gun would also have great difficulty penetrating the Crusader's frontal armour in 1940. The frontal glacis armoured plate was sloped. The sides and rear of the turret were also sloped, but the rear and sides of the hull were vertical and more vulnerable. The arrival of Rommel and his upgraded Panzer III tanks in Africa in January 1941 made the need for a gun more effective than the 2-pdr urgent.

The mounting of the 6-pdr gun into the small Crusader turret led to a complete redesign of the interior. The frontal armour was increased to 2 inches (51 mm) thick. Better protection was fitted for the turret mounting and around the ammunition racks. The ventilation system was improved to deal with the gasses and smoke from the new gun. The loader was removed from the crew. His job was now done by the tank commander. Due to limited space, there was only room for fifty of the larger 6-pdr shells compared to 110 for the previous 2-pdr gun. They saw action in Tunisia, Sicily, and Italy.

This Valentine DD tank is armed with a 6-pdr gun. It is owned and restored by John Pearson.

This Churchill Mk III tank armed with a 6-pdr gun is on display at the Canadian War Museum, Ottawa, Canada.

Valentine Mk VII, IX, and X tanks were initially armed with the 6-pdr gun. In 1941, up-armoured German tanks were used against British and Commonwealth forces in the deserts of North Africa. The Valentine tank's 2-pdr gun was no longer effective. Vickers engineers came up with a modified turret design that would accommodate the long-barrel 6-pdr gun. The coaxial Besa machine gun was removed as part of this process.

The Valentine tank was not as fast as the Crusader tank. It was designed as an infantry tank, not a fast cruiser tank. Not being able to fire high-explosive shells against enemy fortifications, machine gun positions, artillery batteries, and soft-skinned vehicles was a negative feature on an infantry support tank. This inability was corrected with the introduction of the 6-pdr gun that could fire HE shells unlike the 2-pdr gun.

The Valentine Mk VIII tank received the British AEC A190 diesel engine. The Valentine Mk IX, an up-gunned Valentine Mk V tank, retained the US-built GMC 6004 diesel. The Valentine Mk X was virtually identical to the IX, but at the start, it incorporated the new GMC diesel, a redesigned turret that reintroduced the coaxial machine-gun. They saw action in North Africa, the Eastern Front, north-west Europe, Burma, and Italy. Some were later armed with a 75-mm gun.

The first Churchill Mk I tank rolled out of the factory gates in June 1941. It was designed as a slow-moving heavily armed infantry support tank that could cross trenches. Officially, it was named in honour of the memory of Sir Winston Churchill's seventeenth-century ancestor Sir John Churchill, 1st Duke of Marlborough, and not the prime minister. It was intended to replace the Matilda and Valentine infantry tanks.

Churchill Mk III tank was manufactured with a completely new turret and internal configuration to enable the 6-pdr gun to replace the turret 2-pdr gun, which was used in early versions and to be able to stow the larger 6-pdr shells. The Churchill tank now had the capability of going against up-armoured German Panzer III/IV tanks in North Africa and proved instrumental during the second battle of El Alamein.

THE PIAT

Men from 1st Canadian Parachute Battalion with PIAT an anti-tank weapon in Lembeck, Germany, 29 March 1945. (*Canadian National Archives*)

The PIAT was a British infantry shoulder-fired anti-tank weapon that entered service in 1943. The abbreviation 'PIAT' stands for 'projector, infantry, anti-tank'. It is not a bazooka; that was a shoulder-fired recoilless anti-tank rocket launcher. The PIAT uses a spring not a rocket to propel the armour-piercing shaped charge warhead towards its target.

The PIAT used a spigot mortar system to launch a 2.5-lb (1.1-kg) high-explosive armour-piercing shaped charge. The round had a propellant filled cartridge in its tail. It was a short-range weapon. To be effective, the soldier had to wait until the enemy vehicle was within 115 yards (105 m), and if he was firing at a heavily armoured tank like the Panther, he had to aim at a weak spot.

One of the advantages of the PIAT over the rocket-firing bazooka was that there was no dangerous back-blast or smoke trail that gave away the soldier's position to an observant enemy.

The PIAT had problems. It was hard to cock the weapon as the spring in the spigot mortar system was very stiff. It had a heavy kick. If the user was not pushing the shoulder pad hard against his shoulder, he would get a severe bruise. The barrel had to be looked after and handled with care. It was fragile and could easily get damaged. The most serious problem was that the ammunition was sometimes unreliable. Faulty fuses meant that 25 per cent of the rounds failed to detonate when they hit their target. Accuracy was also a problem.

Cocking the weapon and loading the initial round took time. The operator was already very close to the enemy and vulnerable to counterattack if his location was spotted. Although the weapon could be operated by one man, it was usually assigned to two soldiers. The second man carried additional ammunition and loaded the rounds whilst looking out for additional threats.

The PIAT was first used by British and Commonwealth forces in the invasion of Sicily and later Italy in 1943. They were issued to troops boarding ships destined for the D-Day beaches of Normandy as well as the Paratroopers.

It was designed by Lieutenant Colonel Stewart Blacker and enhanced by Major Millis Jefferis. In the factory contract documentation, the PIAT is also described as the 'Jefferis Shoulder Gun' or the 'Jefferis Shoulder Projector'. The weapon was manufactured by Imperial Chemical Industries Ltd and later by various other factories in Britain. The contract record is dated 17 May 1942, and around 115,000 were built during the Second World War. They weighed 32 lb (15 kg) and were 3 feet 3 inches (99 cm) long. The weapon had a muzzle velocity of 250 ft/s (76 m/s).

The PIAT round was a shaped charge. This consisted of a recessed metal cone placed into an explosive warhead, when the round hit the armour plate of a tank, the explosive detonated and turned the cone into an extremely high-speed spike. The speed of the spike and the immense pressure it caused on impact allowed it to create a small hole in armour plating and send a large pressure wave and large amounts of armour plate fragments into the interior of the tank. These sharp jagged hot splinters of metal of different sizes ripped through the flesh of the crew, fuel tanks, radiators, engines, and into ammunition, causing fires and explosions.

The round used in the PIAT had a long name: 'Bomb, HE/AT, Infantry Projector, AT Mk 1'. It was put into a trough at the front of the PIAT barrel. When the trigger was pulled, the spring rammed the metal spigot rod into the tail of the bomb, igniting the propellant charge in the tail cartridge and launching it out of the barrel.

The main criticism of the weapon was how difficult it was to initially cock. The shoulder butt of the PIAT had to be placed on the ground. The soldier then had to put two feet on the butt while he turned the weapon to unlock the body and at the same time, lock the firing pin to the butt. He would then have to bend over and pull the body of the weapon upwards. This had the effect of pulling the spring back until it attached to the trigger and cocked the weapon. Then he had to lower the body of the weapon and turn it to reattach it to the rest of the weapon. You needed strength to operate the PIAT, and you had to be relatively tall.

This procedure did not have to be repeated after firing the weapon. The recoil caused by the explosion of the bomb propellant forced the firing spigot pin backwards onto the spring. This automatically cocked the PIAT and a new round could be placed in the trough at the front of the barrel.

❮ Replica PIAT used for Second World War re-enactments.

❯ The front gunsight is above the firing trigger and the rear one by the canvas barrel cover.

❮ The front trough section of the PIAT with round loaded.

❯ Rear PIAT adjustable gun site.

Front PIAT gun site.

THE BRITISH GRENADE MK 75 ANTI-TANK MINE

BRITISH EXPLOSIVE ORDNANCE   OP 1665

PRESSURE PLATE
FOLD IN PRESSURE PLATE
IGNITER POCKETS
BOOSTER CHARGE
CHEMICAL IGNITER
MAIN CHARGE

Internal diagram of the British grenade No. 75 Mk I anti-tank mine. (*War Department Field Manual, Corps of Engineers, Land Mines and Booby Traps, FM 5-31, 1 November 1943*)

These are the instructions given to troops about how to use the British Grenade No. 75 Mk 1, as found in the War Department Field Manual, Corps of Engineers, Land Mines and Booby Traps, FM 5-31, 1 November 1943—insert the open end of the detonator into the open end of the igniter. Then roll the rubber tube on the igniter to cover the joint. This provides a water-tight seal. Insert a detonator assembly, detonator end first, into each of the pockets of the detonator holder through the hole in the back of the striker-plate bracket. Bend over the metal tabs; this secures the detonator assemblies in the pockets. The red-painted portions of the assemblies should now be visible in the slots of the detonator holders.

The grenade is thrown or placed so that it will be run over. The pressure of the vehicle upon the striker plate will force the strikers through the slots in the detonator holders, crush the igniter tubes, and break the glass capsules containing nitric and sulphuric acid. The action of the acid on the potassium chlorate and charcoal ignition composition produces an immediate flash, which sets off the detonators and explodes the grenade.

In the Grenades No. 75 Mk II and Mk III, the igniters were inserted in their pockets, and the tabs bent into place to secure them. When the grenade was run over, the striker pin crushed the glass ampoule and ground the broken glass and contained igniter composition together, igniting the composition. The resultant flash initiated the detonator, which exploded the grenade.

When the Grenade No. 75 is filled with ammonal, the designation is changed to No. 75 A. ammonal is about 80 per cent as powerful as the regular fillings.

The Grenade No. 75 is employed mainly as a land mine for defence against armoured cars, tanks, and other vehicles. It will disable light tanks and vehicles and is used principally for hasty minefields. It is often referred to as the 'Hawkins' grenade. They were manufactured by the Self-Opening Tin Box Co. Ltd, Westerham, Kent.

Specifications
Overall length: 6.5 inches (16.51 cm)
Width: 3.525 inches (9.19 cm)
Height: 1.875 inches (4.76 cm)
Total weight: 2.25 lb (1.02 kg)
Filling: Nobel's No. 704B, ammonal, Burrowite, or TNT (all with exploders or CE pellets)
Filling weight: 1.75 lb (0.79 kg)
Delay: None
Pressure to fire: 300 lb (136 kg)

◀ Bottom view of a replica British grenade No. 75 Mk II anti-tank mine.

▶ Top view of a replica British grenade No. 75 Mk II anti-tank mine showing the pressure plate which has to be forced down to explode the mine.

◀ View of the side filler cap on a replica British grenade No. 75 Mk II anti-tank mine.

▶ Top view of a replica British grenade No. 75 Mk III anti-tank mine showing the pressure plate that has to be forced down to explode the mine.

THE BRITISH MK V ANTI–TANK MINE

The War Department Field Manual, Corps of Engineers, Land Mines and Booby Traps, FM 5-31, 1 November 1943 provided information to troops about the British Mk V anti-tank mine. It consists of three principal components: the loaded mine body, the exploder mechanism, and the mine cover. The cover is fastened to the mine body by three pins, which engage slots provided in three retaining straps attached to the mine body. The mine body is mushroom-shaped and contains a central well for the insertion of the special exploder.

Exploders function on the shear-wire principle. In effect, the exploder is nothing more than a miniature mine. It consists of a fuse body with a well in the top located off-centre for the insertion of a plunger, which is packed separately in the same box as the rest of the exploder mechanism. This plunger is retained by a shear wire. In the side of the exploder body, near the base, is a channel for the insertion of the ampoule cartridge/detonator combination.

The fuse functions when pressure on the mine cover forces the plunger through the shear wire and down onto the ampoule cartridge. The ampoule is crushed, causing a chemical reaction that fires the detonator. The booster charge, also located in the exploder body, is then detonated, setting off the main charge of the mine.

The mine is used as a defence against armoured cars, tanks, and other vehicles. The mine will break the tracks of light or medium tanks and disable other vehicles. These were the instructions for assembly and arming of the mine:

> Lay the mine in the ground and remove the cover. Place an exploder in the inverted cover (to keep dust *etc.* from the plunger) and insert an ampoule, red end first, into the detonator. Fill the open end of the detonator in the hole in the side of the exploder body. Slide the assembly home and seal in place with more luting (sealant). Grease the exploder before inserting it in the fuse well of the mine. Refit the cover.

To neutralise this mine, remove the mine cover without putting any downward pressure on the cover, then lift the exploder from the exploder well of the mine. Remove the plunger from the exploder. Lift the mine and replace the cover.

Some Mk V anti-tank mines have the letters 'G.S.' after them. This stands for 'general service'. Others have the letters 'HC', which are an abbreviation for 'higher capacity'. The two mines are identical in appearance and size. The only difference is that the HC mine has explosives on both sides of the inner wall of the case.

Specifications

Diameter: 8 inches (20.32 cm)
Height: 2.5 inches (6.35 cm)
Weight: 8 lb (3.62 kg)
Explosive weight: 4.5 lb (2 kg)
Explosive: TNT
Material: Sheet metal
Fuse: Exploder E.P. No. 1 or No. 2
Pressure required: 250–350 lb (113–159 kg)

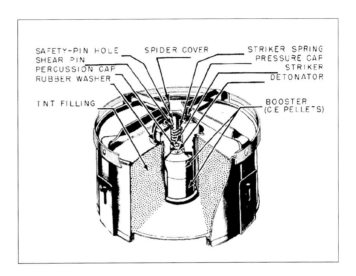

> A diagram showing the inside of a British Mk 5 anti-tank. (*War Department Field Manual, Corps of Engineers, Land Mines and Booby Traps, FM 5-31, 1 November 1943*)

< A Mk 5 high-capacity anti-tank mine next to a matchbox to give an indication of size. (*War Department Field Manual, Corps of Engineers, Land Mines and Booby Traps, FM 5-31, 1 November 1943*)

> A Mk 5 high-capacity anti-tank mine about to be buried in sand. (*War Department Field Manual, Corps of Engineers, Land Mines and Booby Traps, FM 5-31, 1 November 1943*)

Mk 5 anti-tank mines were sometimes called 'pressure cookers' because of the way they looked.

16

BRITISH BATTLE REPORTS

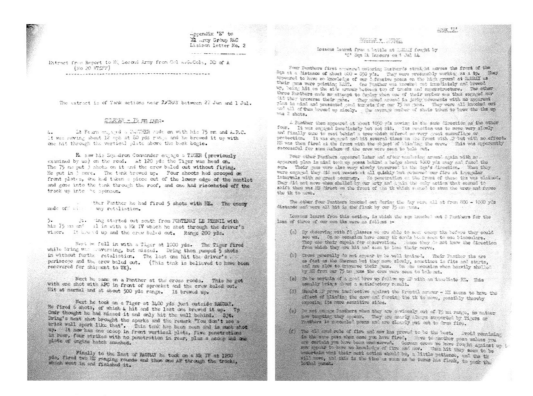

Note: Some of the information in this chapter has been transcribed from original wartime documents. The report format and brief notation style of writing has been kept.

SECRET—CURRENT REPORTS FROM OVERSEAS NO. 5

The War Office, 3 July 1943

Artillery Equipment

The 6-pdr anti-tank gun has been a great success, and has destroyed Pz Mk VI Tigers on many occasions. In one action in Tunisia in early February the gunners held their fire until the tanks were 680 yards away. The first two rounds merely nicked the plates, the next to gouge out scallops of armour, the fifth round went almost through, while the next three penetrated completely and stopped the tank. The first complete penetration was at 600 yards at an angle of impact of 30 degrees from normal, and penetrated through 82 mm of homogeneous armour: the ammunition used was a semi-armour-piercing solid shot. In the desert, 6-pdr shooting often had to be observed from the flank because the gunners were temporarily blinded by the dust kicked up when the gun was fired.

Operational experience of the 17-pdr is still slight. The reasons are that generally these guns have been cited in depth, and the tank attacks had been broken up by concentrations of HE from 25-pdr field guns, or have been destroyed by the 6-pdrs sited forward. Moreover, little use was made of the 17-pdrs (one round from each of three guns) knocked out three tanks. A little later one gun of the same unit destroyed six tanks, including two Mk VI Tigers, before it was itself knocked out.

Criticisms that have been made of the 17-pdr are:

(a) it is a heavy gun for manhandling,
(b) the ammunition is bulky for getting forward,
(c) the gun is heavy to tow,
(d) the flash is enormous, and
(e) the dust kicked up is a severe hindrance to observation.

Nevertheless, long-range anti-tank fire has undoubtedly come to stay. Tiger tanks appear to prefer to stand-off at about 2,000 yards, and all agree that the 17-pdr is an absolute first-class tank-killing weapon.

Our concentrations in the latest breakthrough to Tunis were truly formidable. A highly coordinated, yet simple fire plan enabled infantry commanders to bring down concentrated fire of a very large number of guns onto nominated areas. After the battle 700 German dead were found in one area onto which a concentration had been put down. In this operation, the field guns in First Army fired an average of 384 rounds per gun in the first 24 hours after zero—or four rounds more than was fired in the El Alamein battle.

No. 75 Grenades

Experiments Recently carried out in the Middle East show that No. 75 grenades cannot be relied on to cut the track of a PZ Mk VI Tiger tank unless for grenades can be detonated under one track. When a lesser number them for was detonated, the track links were damaged and the pins bent but the tracks remained serviceable. The conclusions reached were that, to make sure of cutting the track, the grenade should be laid either:
(a) in clumps of four into layers, the top layer overlapping the lower, as a bonded brickwork, or
(b) in one layer of four, each grenade being not more than seven inches from the next.

The former method is suitable in open minefields, while the latter is suitable for roadblocks or defiles. In either case, the grenade should be laid with the long axis parallel to the expected direction of approach of the tank. A single Mk V anti-tank mine is fully effective, and in these trials cut to track pins and shattered three links.

Infantry Weapons and Equipment

PIAT has not been used extensively so far, but is known to have destroyed at least one Pz Mk IV tank.

Tank Gunnery

Up to the time of the battle of El Alamein the 75-mm tank gun was almost invariably fired from hull-down positions over open sites. The intense and prolonged firefight of the October battle, however, suggested the possibility of indirect fire from tanks in turret down positions, only the tank commander's head showing above the forward crest. This practice met with immediate success, for the tanks obtained good results both with shot and shell, while at the same time attracting far less fire to themselves.

The next step was to try out a simple form of indirect HE shooting by the troop. A straightforward procedure was worked out under which one tank was forward observing, and degrees scare was marked on the inside of the other tanks to enable the crews to lay their guns parallel by aiming either at a distant object or onto the controlling tank.

Since the battle of El Alamein, this type of shooting has been used with much success, and has now become the normal procedure in the Eighth Army. It has proved of particular value in the advance, in attacks against weak enemy rear-guards, for it has been found that a concentration of HE from a trooper Sherman tanks, moving near the head of the Vanguard, will often dispose of located enemy anti-tank guns in less time than would be needed for deployment of a proportion of field artillery.

In this type are shooting it is essential that the observing tank should be in a direct, on nearly direct, lying between the troop and the target, and that such shooting should be restricted to a troop basis. Any attempt to introduce observation from the flank of to fire a squadron as a battery, inevitably leads to complications of procedure, and so of training, and would entail the use of artillery instruments which could be carried on a tank only with difficulty.

33rd Armoured Brigade War Diaries, National Archives at Kew WO 171/640

On the 25 June 1944, the war diaries of the British 33 Armoured Division recorded that some of their officers attended a 'shooting trial' of 75 mm and 17-pounder tank guns at a captured enemy Panther tank in Normandy. These trials were shown as occurring at map reference 675687. The following results were recorded and kept in the war diaries.

Three armour-piercing capped (APC) shells were fired at a range of 300 yards, by a 17-pdr Sherman at the Panther's 50 mm thick lower front hull armour plate. They all penetrated into the steering gear. The next shell was fired at the 80 mm glacis plate. The tip of the shell penetrated through the plate. Metal splinters flew around the fighting compartment. The glacis plate cracked in three places. The next 17-pdr APC shell hit the knife-edge formed by the joint between the lower hull plate and the upper glacis plate. It penetrated both plates and caused considerable internal flaking of the amour.

The next 17-pdr APC shell was fired at a longer range of 600 yards and hit the glacis plate one foot below the hull machine gun. It pierced the armour and caused splinters of metal to fly around the driving compartment and bent the machine gun. The armour plate cracked in three places. The next 17-pdr APC shell was also fired at a range of 600 yards and hit the glacis plate 4 inches above the hull machine gun. It pierced the armour and left a hole that was 6 inches by 5 inches. One of the 17-pdr APC shell fired at a range of 600 yards hit the right-hand corner of the turret 4 inches above the hull caused a 1 ½ inch gouge but did not penetrate the armour. A 17-pdr APC shell fired at a range of 600 yards, hit the gun mantlet to the right of the 75 mm main gun. The shell penetrated through the mantlet and shattered on the rear turret hatch.

A 75 mm Sherman tank hit the Panther's glacis plate in the centre, at a range of 150 yards with an APC shell. It did not penetrate the armour. It gouged the armour to a depth of 1 inch. The plate cracked, but the shell ricocheted up towards the Panther's 75 mm gun damaged it putting a 0.625-inch gouge into the barrel.

Extract from Report to HQ Second Army from Col. A. G. Cole, DD of A (No. 20 WTSFF): Appendix 'E' to 21 Army Group RAC, Liaison Letter No. 2

This extract is of tank action near Rauray between 27 June and 1 July 1944 (Operation Epsom)

SHERMAN—78-mm Guns

4. Lt Fern engaged a Panther side on with his 75 mm and APC It was moving about 12 mph at 80 yards range and he brewed it up with one hit through the vertical plate above the back bogie.

He saw his squadron commander engage a Tiger (previously examined by us) on the road. At 120 yards the Tiger was head-on. The 75-mm put three shots on it and the crew bailed out without firing. He put in three more. The tank brewed up. Four shots had scooped on front plates, one had taken a piece out of the lower edge of the mantlet and gone into the tank through the roof. And one had ricocheted off the track up into the sponson. At another Panther he had fired five shots with HE. The enemy made off without retaliation.

5. Sgt Dring started out south from Fontenay-le-Pesnel with his 75-mm and fell in with a Panzer Mk IV tank which he shot through the driver's visor. It brewed up and the crew bailed out. Range 200 yards.

Next he fell in with a Tiger at 1,000 yards. The Tiger fired while Dring was reversing, but missed. Dring then pumped five shots in without further retaliation. The last one hit the driver's periscope and the crew bailed out. (This tank is believed to have been recovered for shipment to UK).

Next he came on a Panther at the crossroads. This he got with one shot with APC in front of sprocket and the crew bailed out. Hit at normal and at about 500 yards range. It brewed up.

Next he took on Tiger at 1,400 yards just outside Rauray. He fired six shots, of which four hit and the last one brewed up. The troop Commander thought he had missed it and only hit the wall behind. Sgt Dring's next shot brought the sparks and the remark, 'You don't see a brick wall spark like that'. This tank has been seen and is much shot up. It now has one scoop in front of vertical plate, five penetrations in rear, for strikes with no penetration in rear, plus a scoop and one plate of engine hatch smashed.

Finally to the east of Rauray he took on a Panzer Mk IV at 1,200 yards, fired two HE ranging rounds and then one AP through the tracks which went in and finished it.

Sherman *v.* Panther (Operation Epsom) Appendix 'D': Lessons Learnt from a Battle at Rauray Fought by 'C' Sqn 24 Lancers on 1 July 1944

Four Panthers first appeared motoring eastwards straight across the front of the squadron at a distance of about 800–850 yards. They were presumably working as a troop. They appear to have no knowledge of our defensive positions on the high ground at Rauray as their guns were pointing east. One Panther was knocked out immediately and brewed up, being hit on the side armour between top of tracks and superstructure. The other three Panthers made no attempt to deploy when one of their numbers was thus engaged nor did they traverse their guns. They moved in jerky movements with no apparent plan in mind and presented good targets for our 75-mm guns. They were all knocked out and all of them brewed up nicely. Average number of shots taken to brew the tanks up was two shots.

A Panther then appeared at about 1,050 yards moving in the same direction as the other four. It was engage immediately but not hit. Its reaction was to move very slowly and finally come to arrest behind a tree which offered no very great camouflage or protection. It was engaged and hit several times on the front with AP but with no effect. HE was then fired at the front with the object of blinding the crew. This was apparently successful for some members of the crew were seen to bail out.

Four other Panthers appeared later and after wandering around again with no apparent plan in mind took up positions behind a hedge about 1,000 yards away and faced the squadron. Their guns were also very slowly traversed in the squadron's direction. When they were engaged they did not react at all quickly but returned our fire at irregular intervals with no great accuracy. No penetration on the front of these tanks was claimed. They did not move when shelled by our artillery and again the only action that seemed to shift them was HE direct on the front of the tank which seemed to stun the crew and forced the tank to move.

The other for Panthers knocked out during the day were all at from 800–1,000 yards distance and were all hit in the flank by our 75-mm guns.

Lessons learnt from this action in which the squadron knocked out eight Panthers for the loss of three of our own tanks were as follows:

(a) By observing with field glasses we are able to see enemy tanks before they could see us. On no occasion have enemy tank commanders been seen to use binoculars. They use their cupola for observation. Hence they did not know the direction from which they are hit and seem to lose their nerve.

(b) Crews generally do not appear to be well trained. Their Panther tanks are as fast as the Sherman but they move slowly, sometimes in fits and starts and are slow to traverse their guns. On the occasion when heavily shelled by HE from our 75-mm guns the crew were seen to bail out.

(c) To be certain of a good brew up follow up AP with an immediate HE. This usually brings about a satisfactory result.

(d) Should AP prove ineffective against the frontal armour—HE seems to have the effect of blinding the crew and forcing the tank to move, possibly thereby exposing its more sensitive sides.

(e) Do not engage Panthers when they are obviously out of 75-mm range, no matter how tempting they appear. They are nearly always supported by Tigers or Panthers in concealed positions and are clearly put out to draw fire.

(f) The old rule of fire and move has proved to be the best. Avoid remaining in the same position when once you have fired. Moved to another position unless you are certain you have been unobserved. German crews we have fought against up to now appear to have no knowledge of fire and move. When hit they seem to be uncertain what their next action should be, with a little patience, the tank will move, and this is the time as soon as he turns his flank, to pack the lethal punch.

PHOSPHOROUS SHELLS STOP A PANTHER

I hit a Panther tank one day at least three times with a shell and never touched him. He just kept on coming. Then my loader accidentally threw a white phosphorous smoke shell in. I hit that tank right in the front end and he stopped. They thought they were hit and penetrated and they thought they were on fire. We used the white phosphorous shell for markers. It burns and a puff of white smoke explodes. They were good for hunting range. We had the old type sights where you guessed the range and we used to use what we called bracketing shots. Some gunners would use high explosive to get their bracket. The first shell, you could see it hitting. Now if it would hit, say, 200 yards short, the gunner would raise his elevation 400 yards, and if he shot over the target, then he would drop down 200 yards. That's bracketing. And if you didn't get him the third shot, you'd better find a hole to get into because he was then going to be shooting at you.

17

THE ARMOUR REPORT

Restricted
Armour Section, School of Tank Technology.
Prepared for Students of the School of Tank Technology. March 1945.
The subject matter of this pamphlet has been arranged in a manner suitable for its ultimate direct inclusion in a new edition of 'Armour for Fighting Vehicles'. The numbering of sections and illustrations conforms to the plan agreed upon for this type of publication. Definitions considered necessary for present use are included at the end of the pamphlet.

THE ARMOUR CODE

2.1

It is first necessary to learn certain terms relating to the perforation of armour, and it is proposed to define these in the present chapter.

Fig. 2.1a illustrates the processes which take place when an armour-piercing AP shot strikes a plate of machineable quality (M.Q.) armour at zero impact angle (normal) and with different values of strike velocity (S.V.)

At (i) the shot has had insufficient remaining velocity (R.V.) to strike the plate with any appreciable S.V.

At (ii) the S.V. has been sufficient to produce only a small dent in the surface.

Conditions (i) and (ii) are defined in Ordnance Board Proceeding (O.B.Proc.) No. 24, 782, dated 20 September 1943, by the code letter A, and by the symbol ⊙ for the purpose of a graphical representation.

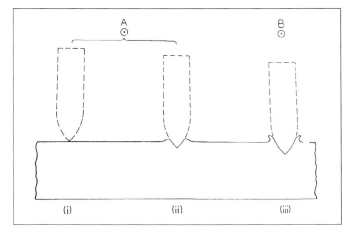

Fig. 2.1a. (*Armour Section, School of Tank Technology*)

At (iii) the S.V. has been sufficient to produce a deep impression, defined as B damage, and symbolised as ⊙.

In the above instances no damage has occurred at the back of the plate. In (ii) and (iii) the shot would rebound, leaving the front damage available for inspection and coding as A or B. In practice code A is confined to damage caused by small arms SA ball ammunition where little more than lead splash has occurred.

2.2

In the discussion which follows in Paras 2.2-2.5 it should be assumed that the shot remains undamaged and does not lodge in the plate.

When the S.V. is raised the damage becomes greater and can be observed at the back of the plate. Examples are shown in Fig. 2.2a (i), (ii) and (iii) and Fig. 2.3a, with equivalent codes as defined as follows:

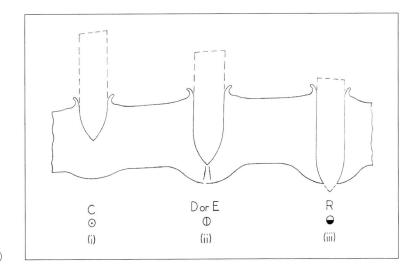

Fig. 2.2a.
(*Armour Section, School of Tank Technology*)

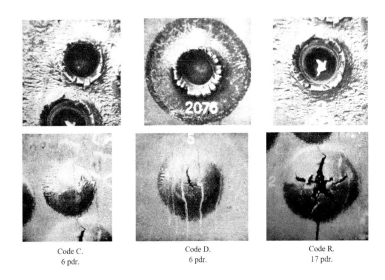

| Code C. | Code D. | Code R. |
| 6 pdr. | 6 pdr. | 17 pdr. |

Fig. 2.3a.
(*Armour Section, School of Tank Technology*)

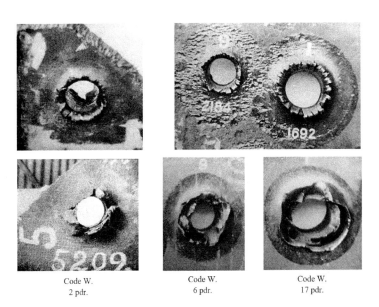

| Code W. | Code W. | Code W. |
| 2 pdr. | 6 pdr. | 17 pdr. |

Fig. 2.3b.
(*Armour Section, School of Tank Technology*)

Code C: Back bulge which has not cracked.

Code D: Back bulge which has cracked, but insufficiently to allow the passage of daylight.

Code E: As for D, except that cracking is sufficient to allow the passage of daylight.

Code R: Is best explained by reference to Fig. 2.3a. The hole at the back of the plate is too small to allow the shot to pass through, but its geometry has been determined chiefly by the nose of the shot.

With the proviso that the shot remains undamaged no missile will have passed through the armour in the cases so far considered. Let the S.V. be raised until a hole is made through the plate and the shot passes through undamaged.

Code W: represents the above condition, and is illustrated in Fig.2.3b.

2.3

It is now opportune to discuss the examples of Figs 2.3a and 2.3b in more detail. During examination of the photographs, care should be taken to differentiate between lacquer applied for anti-erosive purposes and other plate surface effects.

(a) Front Damage

All examples show that some metal has been forced towards the gun in the form of 'front petals'. Surrounding them is zone which has bulged slightly above the main plate surface. The ultimate boundary of the mechanically disturbed zone is the approximate circle where the oxide scale of the plate surface has not been dislodged. In the U.S.A. front petals are sometimes called spurs.

(b) Impression, Penetration, Perforation

The term 'impression implies that the shot knows has not succeeded in pushing its way through the back of a plate, and applies up to E damage. 'Penetration' means that a hole has been made but that it is too small to have allowed the shot to pass through. 'Perforation' means that the whole is of sufficient size to allow the passage of the complete shot. The equivalent American term is 'complete penetration'.

(c) Back Damage

Codes D, E: Sometimes daylight illumination is insufficient to distinguish between D and E. This can then be done by placing a lighted candle or torch behind the bulge and viewing from immediately in front. When the cracks radiate from a centre of origin, the damage may be annotated as 4- or 5-star according to their number.

Code R: In the example of Fig 2.3a the bulge has divided into five 'segments', also called 'back petals'.

Code W: In the 2-pdr example of Fig. 2.3b the segments have bent back to allow the passage of the shot, but remain firmly attached to the plate. In the 6-pdr and 17-pdr examples the segments became detached during the perforation and acted as missiles. Such damage would be annotated as 'segments broken off'. The mechanically disturbed zones can be seen again as areas of oxide scale removal.

2.4

In the examples discussed so far, the shot has defeated the plate only at W damage, and has passed through, with or without the accompaniment of segments as missiles. The letter code W may be remembered easily as being a WIN for the shot. Similarly, the letter code R might be a REBOUND or REJECT, implying a failure on the part of the shot. Figs. 2.3a and 2.3b are characteristic of good M.Q. armour.

2.5

Other types of damage which may occur are flaking and plugging.

Flaking

Fig 2.5a shows the method by which flaking may take place, the photographic examples are given in Fig 2.5b. DTD's description is: 'Severe Flaking—Poor bulging takes place with the appearance of a circumferential crack on a large diameter before any radial cracks are developed.

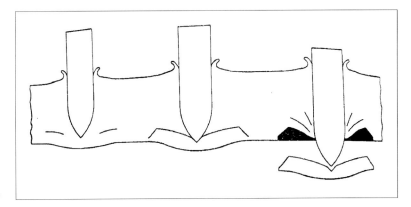

Fig. 2.5a.
(*Armour Section, School of Tank Technology*)

Code R -
flake off

Code W -
flake off shot through

Fig. 2.5b.
(*Armour Section, School of Tank Technology*)

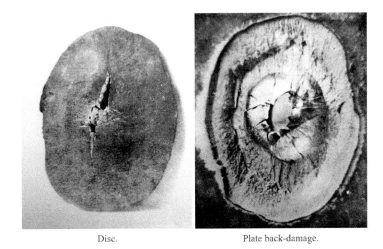

Disc.

Plate back-damage.

Fig. 2.5c.
(*Armour Section, School of Tank Technology*)

In the worst cases, the bulged metal or flake is completely detached before any radial cracks appear, in other cases radial cracks of comparatively small dimensions may be formed before the flake is separated from the plate. (Damage should be described as "flake off in one piece", giving maximum dimensions. In summarising back damage the term "flaking" should be used and the lowest S.V, at which the flake started, quoted).' When a flake is of approximately circular shape it is often called a 'disc' the and further examples are shown in figs. 2.5c and 2.5d. The armour code suffix is (F).

In the photograph of back damage note the central convex burnished area, followed by two zones in which failure has taken place in tension and shear respectively.

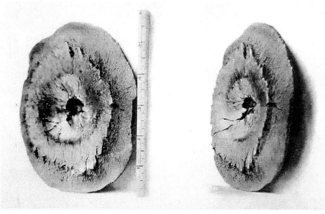

Further views of disc shown in Fig. 2.5c.

Fig. 2.5d.
(*Armour Section, School of Tank Technology*)

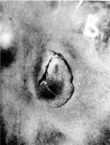

Code D.
Moderate bulge
with circumferential
fracture.

Code E.
Extension of
previous damage.

Code W.
Metal off in two
pieces. Shot through.

Fig. 2.5e.
(*Armour Section, School of Tank Technology*)

Code D.
Plugging started.

Code R.
Plug out & shot not through.

Code W.
Plug out & shot through

Fig. 2.5f.
(*Armour Section, School of Tank Technology*)

Tendency to Flake

Is intermediate between severe flaking and normal damage and is illustrated in Fig. 2.5e. DTD's description is: 'Tendency to Fake—Moderate bulging takes place with the development of radial cracks but accompanied by the appearance of a circumferential crack around the bulge, on a diameter usually about twice the calibre of the shot. As penetration proceeds the separation of the bulged metal into normal segments goes on, but almost simultaneously the increased tension causes complete fracture around the circumference of the bulge. Under these circumstances the displaced metal is usually broken into two or more segments. (Damage should be described as "Normal, segments broken off", giving maximum dimensions of metal off. In summarising the back damage on armour of this type the description, 'Tendency to Flake' should be added).'

Plugging

It is quite different from the types of damage so far considered, and is illustrated in Fig. 2.5f. DTD's description is: 'Severe Plugging—Pressure of shot causes separation by pure shear of an approximately cylindrical plug. The plug usually bears a deep impression of the shot nose and maybe, in length, from 0.3 to 0.75 inches of the plate thickness. Its maximum diameter is usually from 1.25 to 1.5 inches times the shot calibre. Only slight bulging of the plate is apparent before separation, with small cracks in the centre of the bulge. The plug is usually projected rearwards at angles to the plate. (Damage should be described as "Plug out", giving maximum dimensions of hole and depth of shear. - In summarising back damage the term 'Severe plugging' should be used, and the lowest S.V. At which plugging occurs, quoted).' When comparing R and W (Fig. 2.5f) it should be noted that irrespective of apparent hole size, the conditions at R were such that the shot rebounded while at W it passed through.

Code D.	Code R.	Code W.
Plugging started.	Plug out in pieces.	Plug out in three pieces.

Fig. 2.5g.
(*Armour Section, School of Tank Technology*)

Tendency to Plug

Is intermediate between severe plugging and normal damage, and is illustrated in Fig. 2.5g. DTD's description is: 'Tendency to Plug—Separation by pure shear, but commencing after deeper penetration than in severe plugging. Taper of plug more acute with corresponding increase in bulging and consistent crack development. Maximum diameter may be from 1.5 times to nearly twice the calibre of the shot and it is usual for the plug to break into two or more segments on separating from the plate. Such segments may be projected to the rear at angles of from 35 to 45 degrees to the line of fire. (Damage should be described as "Plug out, in pieces", giving maximum dimensions of hole. In summarising back damage the term 'Tendency to Plug' should be used).'

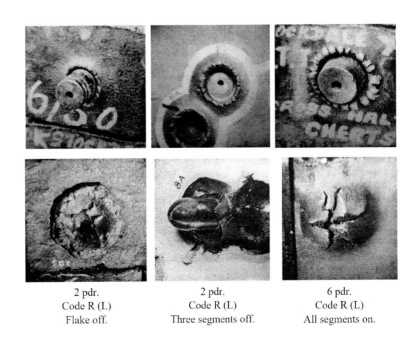

2 pdr.	2 pdr.	6 pdr.
Code R (L)	Code R (L)	Code R (L)
Flake off.	Three segments off.	All segments on.

Fig. 2.6a.
(*Armour Section, School of Tank Technology*)

2.6. Lodging of Shot

When an undamaged shot is held in the plate after penetration it is said to be 'lodged', and the condition is denoted by the suffix (L). The suffix does not necessarily indicate how far the shot has penetrated, and if accurate information is required in this respect, it is usually added as a separate note. The condition is illustrated in Fig. 2.6a.

2.7. Code E—Lodged

The definition of code E stipulates that light must be able to pass through the cracked bulge. When the penetration is filled with a lodged shot however, it becomes obvious that this condition cannot be complied with. In this case, a careful examination of the rear cracking is made, and the damage is reported as code E(L) if any portion of the shot can be seen through the interstices of the cracked bulge, as in Fig. 2.8a.

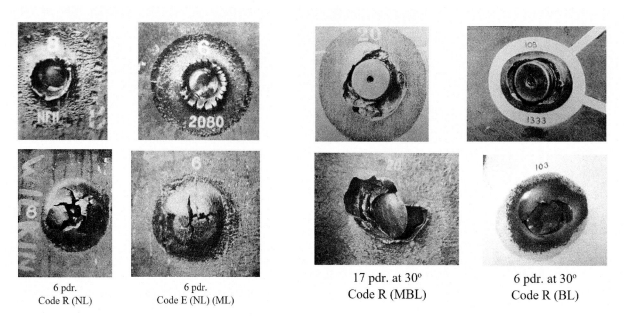

6 pdr. Code R (NL)	6 pdr. Code E (NL) (ML)	17 pdr. at 30° Code R (MBL)	6 pdr. at 30° Code R (BL)

Fig. 2.8a. (*Armour Section, School of Tank Technology*)   Fig. 2.8b. (*Armour Section, School of Tank Technology*)

2.8. Shot Which Break Up

In the previous discussion care was taken to stipulate that the shot remained undamaged. However, it sometimes happens that the shot breaks up into a number of pieces, which might be fitted together again to resemble the original projectile. This phenomenon is important in the assessment of R and W damage, and will be discussed by an examination of the examples shown in Figs. 2.8a and 2.8b.

Nose Lodged (NL)

The pieces which is lodged in the plate is the nose only, a term which covers the portions up to the complete head of the shot. The definition implies that the middle and base have rebounded. In the example shown the head is broken into a number of pieces which can be checked on the actual plate from the fact that the nose can be moved about, while the lower proportion of the head is fixed firmly in the penetration.

Nose Lodged, Middle Lodged (NL) (ML)

Implies that the base only has rebounded. In the example shown, the damage is assessed as code E since on actual examination, the shot nose can be seen through the interstices of the cracked bulge. When (NL) is included in the suffix it may usually be assumed that no proportion of the shot has succeeded in passing through the plate as a missile

The examples shown in Fig. 2.8b. Illustrating (MBL), (BL) described below, are strikes of 30 degrees impact angle. The angle of impact may be neglected for present purposes of definition.

Middle and Base Lodged (MBL)
Usually indicates that the nose has succeeded in passing through the plate as a missile or missiles.

Base Lodged (BL)
Usually indicates that the nose and part of the body have succeeded in passing through the plate as a missile or missiles.

Middle Lodged (ML)
(No example shown) the middle proportion only lodged.

2.9. Influence of Breakup on Assessment at R and W
The definitions of R and W apply to conditions other than those considered for undamaged shot. At present, it suffices to say that examples (MBL) and (BL) of Fig. 2.8b would be defined as W for specific purposes.

2.10. Other Designations in the Armour Code
Other conditions, including a bleak attack and shot shattering, which will be considered later, are included in the armour code.

2.11. Definitions
AP shot: A solid armour-piercing shot without additional modifications such as piercing and ballistic caps.

Machineable quality armour: Armour which is still sufficiently soft to be machined when assembled in the vehicle.

Impact angle: The angle between the plate and the line of flight of the projectile on impact. In British service the angle is measured from the normal to the plate surface.

Striking velocity: The velocity with which the projectile strikes the armour.

Remaining velocity: The velocity of the projectile at any specified point on its trajectory.

Ordnance Board Proceeding: The Ordnance Board is an advisory board consisting of representatives of the three services, and scientific associations. The board publishes certain of its transactions in the form of Ordnance Board Proceedings (secret).

Missile: Is used here in a special sense. The definition includes any object which is projected freely through or from the back of the armour was sufficient velocity to be capable of inflicting wounds or damage. The term 'freely' has been included to imply that any proportion of a projectile which remains lodged, irrespective of its distance of protrusion, is not counted as a missile. In a fighting vehicle the term 'object' is very wide in definition and may include various materials from shot and armour debris to the interior paint substance, which latter may be capable of producing eye wounds.

18

PANZERKETTEN: GERMAN TANK TRACK CLASSIFICATION SYSTEM

Panther Tank tracks Kgs 64/660/150 (Fast running track for motor vehicles, steel castings of all alloys, with rotating bolts, type 64, width 660 mm, spacing 150 mm).

German tank and armoured tracked vehicle's metal tracks were given different designations. This helped identify the type of track link required when ordering spare parts. These abbreviated codenames were designated in the following order:

construction type
material used
connection between links

For example, the Panther Tank's tracks were called Kgs 64/660/150 (Fast running track for motor vehicles, steel castings of all alloys, with rotating bolts, type 64, width 660 mm, spacing 150 mm)

Construction Type Code Letters
K: fast running track for motor vehicles (unlike agricultural tractors)
S: Six-wheeled track for multi-axle driven vehicles
Z: tracks for half-track vehicles
L: tracks for agricultural tractors
P: test tracks (roadway)

Material Used Code Letters

g: steel castings of all alloys

p: forged steel, drop-forged steel

b: sheet steel

t: malleable cast iron

d: duraluminium

ge: cloth fabric

s: silumin

Connection type code letter

no letter: normal bearing. (Bolt and bush without lubrication)

s: rotating bolts

w: roller bearings (with lubrication and sealing)

gu: rubber seals

b: rotating bushing

The Numbering Codes

Type

Width

Spacing

The exception to rule is track Gg 24/660/300: this is thought to be a designation indicating a test version.

Panther Tank tracks Kgs 64/660/150 (Fast running track for motor vehicles, steel castings of all alloys, with rotating bolts, type 64, width 660 mm, spacing 150 mm).

19

THE BUCKET

For years, people have been asking what the bucket that hangs from the back of German tanks, including the Panther tank, was used for. This wartime instructional pamphlet shows that it was intended to be a fluid receptacle when the crew were maintaining the vehicle. A bucket is a very useful piece of equipment and can be used to carry water, wood, coal, eggs, and sand. It is a multi-purpose tool. It is ideal for thinning camouflage paste and holding whitewash when a spray-gun is not available. If it was clean, the crew could also use it to wash their underclothes and socks. They could also use it to hold water to throw over their heads to get the soap and shampoo out of their hair.

◀ The rear of a Panther tank showing the bucket handle secured to the towing bracket.

▶ Second World War German tank crew instructional leaflet.

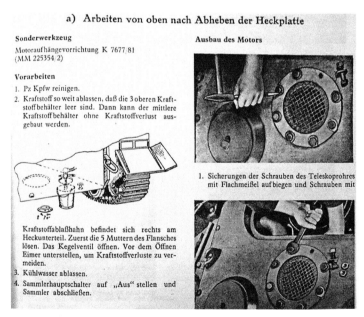

a) Arbeiten von oben nach Abheben der Heckplatte

Sonderwerkzeug

Motoraufhängevorrichtung K 7677/81 (MM 225354/2)

Vorarbeiten

1. Pz Kpfw reinigen.
2. Kraftstoff so weit ablassen, daß die 3 oberen Kraftstoffbehälter leer sind. Dann kann der mittlere Kraftstoffbehälter ohne Kraftstoffverlust ausgebaut werden.

Kraftstoffablaßhahn befindet sich rechts am Heckunterteil. Zuerst die 5 Muttern des Flansches lösen. Das Kegelventil öffnen. Vor dem Öffnen Eimer unterstellen, um Kraftstoffverluste zu vermeiden.
3. Kühlwasser ablassen.
4. Sammlerhauptschalter auf „Aus" stellen und Sammler abschließen.

Ausbau des Motors

1. Sicherungen der Schrauben des Teleskoprohres mit Flachmeißel aufbiegen und Schrauben mit

VORARBEITEN—PREPARATION

1. Clean the tank.
2. Drain enough fuel so that the three upper fuel tanks are empty. Then it is possible to remove the middle fuel tank without fuel loss. The fuel drain cock is on the right lower hull. First loosen the five nuts of the flange. Open conical valve. Before opening put a bucket below to avoid fuel spill.
3. Drain the coolant.
4. Turn the battery's main switch to off and disconnect battery.

20

SURVIVING PANTHER TANKS

Always phone the museum or local town hall to see if the tank is still there before driving to the location as tanks move. That may seem a silly statement, but tanks change locations. Some are sold or temporarily transferred to other museums. Some are withdrawn from public view to enable them to be restored or undergo maintenance. Some tanks are on military bases (Thun in Switzerland, Fort Benning in the USA) and may not be open to the public. A number of the tanks in this list are in private collections and again are not open to the general public.

Panther Ausf. D (No. 534) Breda, Holland (The Netherlands)

This is the only surviving Panther Ausf. D. It can be seen at the junction of Wilhelminapark and Paule Windhausenweg in Breda, Holland (The Netherlands). It was donated by troops of the Polish 1st Armoured Division to serve as a memorial to their fallen comrades and to their part in the liberation of Breda in 1944. It was restored in 2004–2005 for static display by Kevin Wheatcroft in exchange for the engine and gearbox to be used on a working Panther restoration. Tank enthusiast Richard Langdon can be seen at the front of the tank. He is 6 feet (1.83 m) tall, so you can see how large the Panther tank was.

Panzer V Ausf. D Panther tank (No. 534) Breda, Holland (The Netherlands).

Panther Ausf. D, The Hoebig Private Collection, Germany

A second surviving Panther Ausf. D tank is believed to be part of the Hoebig Private Collection. This information has not been verified. No photographs have been published.

Panther Ausf. A, Panzermuseum, Thun, Switzerland

This Panther Ausf. A tank can be seen at the Panzermuseum in Thun, Switzerland. Its hull number is *Fahrgestell* 210530. It was assembled in December 1943 but still has the 16-mm belly plate. This is a mid-production Ausf. A hull with a mid-production or late Ausf. A turret. The mantlet is a replica.

Rear view of the Panzer V Ausf. A Panther tank at the Panzermuseum, Thun, Switzerland. (*Massimo Foti*)

Panzer V Ausf. A Panther tank at the Panzermuseum, Thun, Switzerland. (*Massimo Foti*)

Panther Ausf. A, Kevin Wheatcroft Collection, England (and Two Wrecks)

 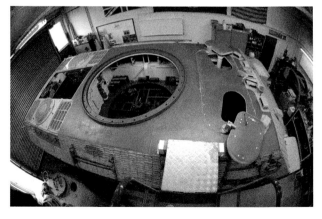

◄ Panzer V Ausf. A Panther tank, Kevin Wheatcroft Collection, England. (*Alex Wheatcroft*)
► Panzer V Ausf. A Panther tank, Kevin Wheatcroft Collection, England. (*Alex Wheatcroft*)

Panther Ausf. A Befehlspanzer, Deutsches Panzermuseum, German Tank Museum, Münster, Germany

Panther Ausf. A Befehlspanzer (Command tank) can be found at the *Deutsches Panzermuseum* (German Tank Museum) Münster (Ortze), Lower Saxony, Germany. It is in running condition. This tank was bought by Sweden in 1948 for trial purposes. It was given back to the *Panzerlehrbrigade* at Münster in 1960. Some years later, it was handed over to the *Panzertruppenschule*. In the 1980s, the commander of the *Panzertruppenschule* initiated a total restoration. Also, the original Maybach HL 230 engine was overhauled by MTU at Friedrichshafen. After some problems with the HL 230 engine and the lack of spare parts, the engine was replaced by a modern MTU Diesel. The sound of this Panther tank, while being driven, is not original.

Panzer V Ausf. A Panther *Befehlspanzer* (Command tank) at the Deutsches Panzermuseum. (*Massimo Foti*)

Panther Ausf. A (No. 224) and (No. 243), Auto and Technik Museum, Sinsheim, Germany

This Panther Ausf. A No. 224 is on display at the Auto and Technik Museum in Sinsheim, Germany. This tank was originally given by the Musée des Blindés, (Museum of Armour) in Saumur, France, to the WTS Koblenz. When the WTS received their Panther Ausf. G from the British Army Defence Academy in Shrivenham, this one was handed over to the Auto and Technik Museum, Sinsheim (Rudi Ehninger, Brigadier General (rtd) German *Panzertruppe*.

This Panther Ausf. A No. 243 wreck is on display at the Auto and Technik Museum in Sinsheim, Germany. It was found in a bog near the town of Spola in Ukraine. It still has its original paint and markings.

◀ The Panzer V Ausf. A Panther tank (No. 224) is on display at the Auto and Technik Museum, Sinsheim, Germany. (*Massimo Foti*)

▶ The Panzer V Ausf. A Panther tank (No. 243) is on display at the Auto and Technik Museum, Sinsheim, Germany. (*Massimo Foti*)

Panther Ausf. A (No. 413), The Hoebig Private Collection, Germany

This Panther Ausf. A (No. 413) is part of the Hoebig Private Collection in Germany. It was part of the 116th Panzer Division *Windhund* and was lost near Falaise. It has been restored. The tank consists of 90 per cent of original parts, some of which have come from other Panthers.

The Panzer V Ausf. A Panther tank (No. 413) is part of the Hoebig private collection in Germany.

Panther Ausf. A (No. 211) and (No. 256), Musée des Blindés, French Tank Museum, Saumur, France

The Panther Ausf. A (No. 211) tank is on display at the Musée des Blindés, (Museum of Armour) in Saumur, France. The turret comes from another Panther hull (*Fahrgestell* number 152451), which is currently preserved in the Omaha Overlord Museum in Colleville-sur-Mer, France.

The Panther Ausf. A (No. 256) tank is an exhibit at the Musée des Blindés, (Museum of Armour) in Saumur, France. It left the factory gate on 2 June 1944 and was recovered by AMX. It was obtained from the French Etablissement d'Expérimentation Technique de Bourges (Tank Proving Ground in Bourges, France) after they had finished conducting tests. It has been restored to a running condition.

The Panzer V Ausf. A Panther tank (No. 211) can be seen at the Musée des Blindés, French Tank Museum, Saumur. (*Massimo Foti*)

The Panzer V Ausf. A Panther tank (No. 256) can be seen at the Musée des Blindés, French Tank Museum, Saumur. (*Massimo Foti*)

Panther Ausf. A, Omaha Overlord Museum, Colleville-sur-Mer, France

This Panther Ausf. A tank can be seen at the Omaha Overlord Museum in Colleville-sur-Mer, France. It is displayed in a mock-up of a German Army field maintenance and repair yard. It was constructed by Daimler-Benz and has the hull number 152451. It was built in April and May 1944. In January 1945, French Army Captain Besnier of 1 GMR went to Ranes, Normandy, looking for abandoned functional German tanks. On 23 January 1945, he returned to Arthon with some German vehicles, including two Panzer IV tanks and this Panther tank, plus an artillery gun. By April 1945, this Panther was restored to running condition and served in the French Army after the Second World War. It was part of the French *6ème Cuirs, 2ème Escadron*.

It spent some time during the 1950s in the city of Baumholder, Germany. In 1955, it returned to Satory, France, where it was then transferred to ETBS for test (Lot 44 in the inventory). In 1980, it was moved from Bourges to Saumur on order of Colonel Aubry. In 1988, it was swapped for a German Sdkfz 251 half-track belonging to the now-closed Falaise Museum.

The damage on the front was done during testing at the French Etablissement d'Expérimentation Technique de Bourges ETBS (Tank Proving Ground in Bourges, France). The barrel comes from Southern France (Perpignan area), the turret is not original to the hull. The original turret from this hull was used to restore Saumur Panther No. 254. The tank has been transferred from Falaise to the new museum in January 2013.

This Panzer V Ausf. A Panther tank can be seen at the Omaha Overlord Museum, Colleville-sur-Mer, France.

Panther Ausf. A, 501/503e Mourmelon-le-Grand, France

This Panther Ausf. A is on display at the French Army barracks of the 501/503e regiment in Mourmelon-le-Grand, France. It has the chassis number *Fahrgestell* 155597 and was built in the MNH factory between July and August 1944. It was abandoned in the Jardin du Senat in Paris, after the battle of Paris in August 1944. After the battle, it was displayed with a Panther Ausf. G in front of the Hôtel National des Invalides, Paris. In 1976, both tanks were transferred to Saumur. The Panther Ausf. G was captured during the Battle of Dompaire in September 1944 and is still preserved in Saumur. The French Army used Panther tanks from 1945 to 1952, in the 503rd RCC and the 6e Cuir.

Panther Ausf. A, Royal Jordanian Tank Museum, Jordan

This Panther Ausf. A tank was previously part of the Saumur Tank Museum collection. In 2010, it was part of an exchange of vehicles between the French President and King Abdullah II of Jordan. It is now on display in the Royal Tank Museum in Amman, Jordan. It is not in running condition as it does not have an engine or gearbox.

Panther Ausf. A, Australian Armour and Artillery Museum, Cairns, Queensland, Australia

This Panther Ausf. A was shipped to the Australian Armour and Artillery Museum in Cairns, Queensland in August 2020. The hull and turret were built by the Hermann Goring Steel Works in Linz, Austria, but the final assembler is unknown due to the loss of its original hull number. The original German hull number was obliterated when it was given a new French AMX hull number, following its post-war refurbishment by the AMX factory. It is believed that this tank served with the French Army 501–503rd RCC, then it went to the Saumur Museum. It was purchased by the Cadman collection and later sold to the Australian Armour and Artillery Museum in 2017. This photograph was taken in 2009 at the War and Peace event in Kent, England, before its restoration. Bruce Crompton's team at axistrackservices.com restored this Panther back to working condition.

This Panzer V Ausf. A Panther tank is on display at the French Army barracks of the 501/503e regiment in Mourmelon-le-Grand, France. (*Pierre-Olivier Buan*)

This Panzer V Ausf. A Panther tank is on display in the Royal Tank Museum, Amman, Jordan. (*Tammam Khasawneh Abu Ahmad, Royal Tank Museum, Jordan*)

This Panzer V Ausf. A Panther tank will be on display at the Australian Armour and Artillery Museum, Cairns, Queensland, Australia.

Panther Ausf. A. (No. 501) American Heritage Museum, Hudson, MA, USA

This Panther Ausf. A (No. 501) tank can be seen at the American Heritage Museum in Hudson, MA, USA. It is in a running condition. On 16 November 1990, it was recovered from the river Czarna Nida in Poland. It was part of the Jacques Littlefield Collection in California. Upon his death, the tank moved to its new home.

This Panzer V Ausf. A Panther tank (No. 501) can be seen at the American Heritage Museum, Hudson, MA, USA.

Panther Ausf. A, Canadian War Museum, Ottawa, Canada

This Panther Ausf. A is on display in the Canadian War Museum in Ottawa, Canada. After its capture, it was shipped to Canada to Canadian Forces Base Borden and had been on outdoor display until the Department of National Defence's Directorate of History and Heritage, CFB Borden, and the Base Borden Military Museum donated it to the Museum in 2005.

The Panther took part in the VE Day (Victory in Europe) celebrations on Sparks Street in Ottawa on 8 May 1945. Therefore, it had to have been transported from Europe before the end of the war, but whether as a war trophy or for testing and experimentation by the military remains unknown. Its restoration was completed in January 2008 and went on public display.

This Panzer V Ausf. A Panther tank is on display in the Canadian War Museum, Ottawa, Canada.

Panther Ausf. G, The Tank Museum, Bovington, Dorset, England

This Panzer Ausf. G Panther is on display at the Tank Museum in Bovington, Dorset, England. Notice it does not have the later gun mantlet with the 'chin guard'. The construction process was finished at the end of the war, in Germany, under the direction of the British Army REME. They completed five Panthers and five Jagdpanthers for testing. These vehicles were already off the production line and in the finishing hall at MNH factory when activities ceased due to power loss and bombing. Those that did not go to museums and private collections were used as hard targets on the Lulworth live firing range.

This Panzer V Ausf. G Panther tank is on display at the Tank Museum, Bovington, Dorset, England.

Panther Ausf. G (No. 801), Wehrtechnische Dienststelle Trier, Germany

This Panther Ausf. G (No. 801), is on display at the *Wehrtechnische Dienststelle* (Military Technology Museum) in Trier, Germany. It is fitted with a reproduction of the FG 1250 *Nachtsichtgerät* infrared system. The construction process was finished at the end of the war, in Germany, under the direction of the British Army REME. This one was previously used as a training exhibit at the British Army Defence Academy in Shrivenham, England, before being transferred to the *Wehrtechnische Dienststelle* Museum in Trier, Germany. It is in a running condition.

This Panzer V Ausf. G Panther tank (No. 801), is on display at the *Wehrtechnische Dienststelle* Museum in Trier, Germany.

Panther Ausf. G, the Flick Private Collection, Northern Germany

This Panther Ausf. G is in the Flick private collection in Heikendorf, Northern Germany. In July 2015, the German Government seized it from the seventy-eight-year-old owner's basement as they believed he did not have the correct German licenses to keep such a vehicle. The construction process was finished at the end of the war, in Germany, under the direction of the British Army REME.

It was purchased by Hardwicks Scrap Metal following a sale by the British War Department in the 1950s. It was kept at their scrap metal yard in Cox Lane, Chessington, Surrey, England. In 1977, it was sold to *Herr* Flick and transported to Germany, where it was restored to a working condition.

This Panzer V Ausf. G Panther tank is in the Flick Private collection, in Heikendorf, Northern Germany.

Panther Ausf. G, (No. 222) Oorlogsmuseum, Overloon, Netherlands (Overloon War Museum, Overloon, Holland)

This Panther Ausf. G is on display in the Oorlogsmuseum, Overloon, Netherlands (Overloon War Museum, Holland). Its hull number is *Fahrgestell Nummer* 128427 and was the 327th-produced Panther *Ausführung* G tank assembled by the MNH factory in Hannover in early August 1944.

The tank has been externally restored and painted in *dunkelgelb*. It was issued to the Panzer Brigade 107 and served on the Eastern Front. The tank was later sent west after the Allies landed in Normandy. It saw action in the Battle of Eindhoven.

It was hit by a British PIAT during the battles around Overloon, which lasted from September till October 1944. Two pairs of road-wheels were knocked off, leaving the vehicle immobile. The crew abandoned the tank as they could not repair it. It was moved to a new location within the Oorlogsmuseum in Overloon. Initial attempts by the museum to arrange for the tank to be restored to a running condition ceased. The engine was sold to the Weald Foundation in England to use in their Jagdpanther.

The Panzer V Ausf. G Panther tank (No. 222) is on display in the Oorlogsmuseum, Overloon, the Netherlands. Here you can see it painted in an 'Ambush' camouflage pattern without its tracks fitted before its recent restoration. (*Massimo Foti*)

The Panzer V Ausf. G Panther tank (No. 222) is on display in the Oorlogsmuseum, Overloon, the Netherlands. Panther Ausf. G (No. 222) was later fully restored externally and painted in *dunkelgelb* dark sandy yellow.

Panther Ausf. G, Houffalize, Belgium

This Panzer V Ausf. G Panther Tank took part in the Battle of the Bulge in the Ardennes. It is on display in the village of Houffalize, Belgium. You will find it at the junction of the N30 Rue de Bastogne with the Rue Saint-Roch. The Houffalize Panther Ausf. G tank originally had the turret number 111 and was part of the Pz.Regt I./24; it was with Pz.Regt I./16 when it was knocked out.

According to statements by veterans of and residents, the tank fell over due to detonation pressure by dropped bombs into the River Ourthe and landed on the turret. The crew died because of the impact or drowned.

This Panther was recovered out of the River Ourthe by French engineers on 20 September 1947; the remains of the crew killed in the attack were discovered when the Panther was pulled from the river. It was left on the banks of the river for many years and used as a playground by the local children. Many original parts were taken off the tank as souvenirs. It displayed the late war camouflage scheme of green, dark red, and *dunkelgelb* (dark sandy yellow).

When it was first placed on display in the town at the top of the high street, a large German black and white cross was painted on the side of the turret and the number 111 was painted in small numbers along the bottom edge of the turret towards the rear. It was later repainted with a similar three-tone camouflage scheme, but the turret was given the number 401 and painted with the *Windhund* insignia of the 116 Panzer Division. In 2017, it was removed to the Bastogne Barracks for restoration.

This photograph of the Panzer V Ausf. G Panther Tank on display in the village of Houffalize, Belgium, was taken before it was moved to Bastogne for restoration.

Panther Ausf. G, Grandmenil, Belgium

This Panther Ausf. G is used as a memorial in Grandmenil, Belgium. It is near the roundabout on the N807 at the junction with the Rue Alphonse Poncelet. This Panther took part in the 1944 Battle of the Bulge Ardennes offensive. It is believed that it belonged to the 2nd SS Panzer Division 'Das Reich' and was abandoned because of lack of fuel during the retreat. It was recovered in a field off the Manhay–Érezée road. It still has its engine and gearbox.

This Panzer V Ausf. G Panther tank is on display in Grandmenil, Belgium.

Panther Ausf. G, Celles, Belgium

This damaged Panther Ausf. G is used as a monument in Celles, Belgium. The Celles Panther was part of the German Army *Kampfgruppe* (combat group) von Cochenhausen, 2nd Panzer Division. On 21 December, Panzer Lehr battle group was pulled out of the fight for Bastogne and regrouped with 2nd Panzer Division and the 116th Panzer Division Windhund for an assault on the town of Dinant to secure the crossing over the river Meuse. It fought its way through the town of St Hubert, and the road to Dinant seemed open. Rochefort was taken on 23 December 1944.

On 24 December 1944, the advanced column of Panther tanks approached the junction of the N510 road with the N48. The local story is that the Germans asked at the cafe 'Pavillon des Ardennes' if the road to Dinant was open and whether vehicles had been using it recently. Marthe Monrique, the cafe owner, lied and said that it was mined and dangerous, so the Panzer V commander decided to go through the fields. This Panzer V Ausf. G was the lead tank. It drove over a mine and was put out of action in the field below Chateau Acteau. The Germans stopped their advance for a while. After the war, Marthe Monrique became known as the woman who stopped the tanks.

When Panzer Lehr resumed its advance to Dinant, it ran into the Combat Command 'A' of the US 2nd Armored Division near Buissonville. On Christmas Day, the protective thick cloud cover of winter disappeared, and the full force of the Allied air power was deployed, bringing the Panzer divisions to a virtual standstill. The majority of 2nd Panzer's tanks, under Major Ernst von Cochenhausen, had become surrounded near the town of Celles.

On 26 December, the rest of Panzer Lehr made two attempts to relieve them, but they were turned back by Allied fighter bombers. Cochenhausen and 600 or so of his men managed to escape on foot, having been forced to abandon all of the division's tanks and equipment to the advancing Allies.

The disabled Panther at Celles was left there for some time after the war. It had flipped over and was resting on its turret by the side of the road to Neufchateau. It was during this period that the hatches, tracks, and road-wheels were removed as they were easy to get to.

The Americans tested anti-tank weapons on it. American Army engineers stripped it to try and make it lighter, but they could not get it out of the field. The Panther had ejectable hatches, so the crew would eject them and leave them on the ground. Marthe Monrique rescued the tank from the field in 1948 and put in pride of place next to the café, now renamed as '*Le Tank*', at the crossroads as a monument.

This damaged Panzer V Ausf. G Panther tank is used as a monument in Celles, Belgium. (*Pierre-Olivier Buan*)

◀ This photograph shows the damage caused by an American armour-piercing round bouncing off the turret and lower gun mantlet armour, smashing its way into the roof above the machine gunner's position on the Celles Panther. (*John Osselaer*)

▶ The white circle marks out where the American armour-piercing shell hit just below the gun mantle and then smashed into the chassis roof above the bow machine gunner's position. You can also see the scooping effect of other rounds that failed to penetrate the Panther's upper front glacis plate. (*John Osselaer*)

Panther Ausf. G (No. 332), Musée des Blindés, (Museum of Armour), Saumur, France

This Panther Ausf. G (No. 332), is on display at the Musée des Blindés, (Museum of Armour), in Saumur, France. Its hull number is *Fahrgestell* number 120790, built by MAN factory at the end of July 1944. The French 2e Division Blindée captured several intact Panthers from I./Pz.Rgt.29 of Panzer Brigade 112 during the fighting at Dompaire on 13 September 1944. Two were sent back to Paris as presents to General de Gaulle to commemorate the victory. Panther 332 sat outside *Hôtel National des Invalides* in Paris for some years (along with a Panther Ausf. A abandoned in the Jardin du Sénat, Paris, in August 1944); it was then sent to Saumur in 1976. The other Panther from the Invalides, an Ausf. A, is now on display at Mourmelon-le-Grand.

This Panzer V Ausf. G Panther tank (No. 332), is on display at the Musée des Blindés, French Tank Museum, Saumur, France. (*Massimo Foti*)

Panther Ausf. G, Kubinka Tank Museum, Russia

This Panther Ausf. G tank is on display at the Kubinka Tank Museum in Russia but may be moved to the nearby Patriot Park tank museum. It may be moved to the nearby new Patriot Park in Kubinka. During restoration work on a fuel tank, the serial or production number 887/44 was found. As you can see, original Zimmerit anti-magnetic mine paste is still on the tank. Zimmerit ceased to be applied to Panther tanks in September 1944. Therefore, it is possible to work out that this tank's serial number was 120887 and built by MAN in August 1944.

This Panzer V Ausf. G Panther tank was photographed on display at the Kubinka Tank Museum, Russia.

Two Panther Ausf. Gs, One Ausf. A, and a Panther II Hull, the US Army Armor and Cavalry Collection, Fort Benning, GA, USA

These four Panther tanks are the only ones that remain from the testing and trials that occurred at the US Army Ordnance Proving Ground at Aberdeen in Maryland, USA. Some Panthers that were shipped to America were destroyed during firing trials and scrapped. Records of these vehicles are hard to find. Over the years data plates were removed from the tanks as a precaution against theft and turrets were swapped between vehicles during testing. When the Aberdeen Museum closed, they were moved to the US Army Armor and Cavalry Collection at Fort Benning, where they await restoration.

A Panzer V Ausf. A Panther awaiting restoration at the US Army Armor and Cavalry Collection, Fort Benning, GA, USA. (© *US Army Armor and Cavalry Collection*)

A Panzer V Ausf. G Panther with the rounded gun mantlet awaiting restoration at the US Army Armor and Cavalry Collection, Fort Benning, GA, USA. (© *US Army Armor and Cavalry Collection*)

A Panzer V Ausf. G Panther awaiting restoration at the US Army Armor and Cavalry Collection, Fort Benning, GA, USA. Notice it has a 'chin guard' gun mantlet. (© *US Army Armor and Cavalry Collection*)

The Panther II prototype with Panzer V Ausf. G turret at the US Army Armor and Cavalry Collection, Fort Benning, GA, USA. (© *US Army Armor and Cavalry Collection*)

Panther Ausf. G, the Hoebig Private Collection, Germany

A Panther Ausf. G tank is believed to be part of the Hoebig Private Collection, though this information has not been verified. No photographs have been published.

Surviving German *Bergepanthers* Armoured Recover Vehicles (Sd.Kfz 179)

The *Bergepanther* was an armoured recovery vehicle that was used by the German Army during the Second World War. It was based upon the hull of the Panzer V Panther. The turret was not fitted. For defence, it could be armed with a 20-mm KwK 38 tank gun and a 7.92-mm MG 38 or MG 42 machine gun. It was fitted with a 40,000-kg winch and cable system.

An early *Bergepanther* Ausf. D is awaiting restoration in Cadman Collection in southern England. A *Bergepanther* Ausf. G is stored in the André Becker Collection in Belgium. It is also awaiting restoration.

A restored *Bergepanther* Ausf. A can be seen at the *Wehrtechnische Dienststelle* (Military Technology Museum) in Trier, Germany. It was the last Panther produced at the Daimler-Benz production plant in Berlin. There is a shot through the rear plate. It was taken to France after the war and used for testing land mines at the *Etablissement d'Expérimentation Technique de Bourges* (Tank Proving Ground) in Bourges, France. When it was no longer required for trials, it first went to the *Musée des Blindés* (Museum of Armour), in Saumur, France, with two others and then moved to the *Wehrtechnische Dienststelle*, Trier, Germany, where it was restored. The large spade at the rear was copied and rebuilt at Rheinmetall, Germany.

A restored *Bergepanther* Ausf. G is on display at the *Musée des Blindés* (Museum of Armour), in Saumur, France. In 1972, it was transferred from Camp Satory to the French Tank Museum. The winch is operational. The 20-mm machine gun and mount were added later. It was found in a barn in Normandy by someone from the museum.

This restored *Bergepanther* Ausf. A can be seen at the *Wehrtechnische Dienststelle* Museum in Trier, Germany.

This *Bergepanther* Ausf. G is on display at the Musée des Blindés, French Tank Museum in Saumur.

BIBLIOGRAPHY

Jentz T. L. and Doyle H. L., *Panzer Tracts No. 5-1* (Boyds, Maryland, USA: Panzer Tracts, 2003)
Jentz T. L. and Doyle H. L., *Panzer Tracts No. 5-2* (Boyds, Maryland, USA: Panzer Tracts, 2003)
Jentz T. L. and Doyle H. L., *Panzer Tracts No. 5-3* (Boyds, Maryland, USA: Panzer Tracts, 2004)
Jentz T. L. and Doyle H. L., *Panzer Tracts No. 5-4* (Boyds, Maryland, USA: Panzer Tracts, 2006)
Jentz T. L. and Doyle H. L., *Panzer Tracts No. 23* (Boyds, Maryland, USA: Panzer Tracts, 2001)
Spielberger W. J., *Panther and its Variants* (Atglen, Pennsylvania, USA: Schiffer Publishing Ltd, 1993)

OFFICIAL REPORTS, PAMPHLETS, AND FIELD MANUALS

33 Armoured Brigade War Diaries June 1944, National Archives at Kew WO 171/640
Armour Quality and Vulnerability of PzKw V Panther, DTD Armour Branch Report M.6815A/3 No. 1.
Comprehensive Firing Trials against the German Panther PzKw V, Department of Tank Design, Materials Division, Armour
  Branch Report A.T. No. 232 Parts I-IV, Project Nos.M.6815A/4.
Equipment—German PzKw V (Panther), Central Registry Army 166297
gem. Anweisung OKH (Ch H. Rüst u BdE) vom 18. Dezember 1944, Az.76 g/4 Nr. 234559/44, AHA/In 6(Z/In) WaA/Wa Prüf 6.
German (Pz.Kpfw) Panther, F.V.P.E. Reports No FT.1391 & WS.413
Land Mines and Booby Traps, FM 5-31, 1 November 1943, War Department Field Manual, Corps of Engineers
O.B.Proc U2679 Appendix C to Report A.T. No. 280 Part II. School of Tank Technology
O.G.44/PC(T)32E. Report Number A.T.320
Ordnance Pamphlet No. 1665 10 June 1946, British Explosive Ordnance by Commander, US Naval Ordnance System Command
PzKw V (PANTHER) Preliminary Report on Armour and Vulnerability. Department of Tank Design, Materials Division,
  Armour Branch Report No. M.6815A/3 No. 1.
The Armour Report, Prepared for Students of the School of Tank Technology. March 1945, School of Tank Technology